FRIEDRICH NIETZSCHE

FRIEDRICH NIETZSCHE

H.L. MENCKEN

With a New Introduction
by Richard Flathman

Transaction Publishers
New Brunswick (U.S.A.) and London (U.K.)

Second printing 1997

New material this edition copyright © 1993 by Transaction Publishers, New Brunswick, New Jersey 08903. Originally published in 1913 by Luce and Company.

This book is printed on acid-free paper that meets the American National Standard for Permanence of Paper for Printed Library Materials.

Library of Congress Catalog Number: 92-34210
ISBN: 1-56000-649-8
Printed in the United States of America

Library of Congress Cataloging-in-Publication Data

Mencken, H.L. (Henry Louis), 1880–1956.
  [Philosophy of Friedrich Nietzsche]
  Friedrich Nietzche/H.L. Mencken; with a new introduction by Richard Flathman
    p. cm.
  Originally published: Boston: Luce and Co., 1913.
  Includes index.
  1. Nietzsche, Friedrich Wilhelm, 1844–1900. I. Title.
B3317.M5   1993   92-34210
193–dc20   CIP

CONTENTS

NIETZSCHE THE MAN

NIETZSCHE THE PHILOSOPHER

NIETZSCHE THE PROPHET

v

INTRODUCTION TO THE
TRANSACTION EDITION

A crusty curmudgeon constructively critiquing a cantankerous crank. A sardonic skeptic circulating the atavistic animosities of an irreverent antinomian. An arrogant elitist applauding the pseudo-aristo-cratic snarlings of a soon-to-be psychotic snob.

Not so many years ago, when Nietzsche was widely regarded as a progenitor and Mencken an apologist for the worst evils of this and hence of any other century, the first two of these characterizations of this book might have been thought too generous, the third regarded as the least of the condemnations the book deserves and of the neglect it has for some time been receiving. If anti-Nietzscheans have since promoted their *bête-noire* (or *bête-blond*) from proto-Nazi to nihilist post-modernist, if anti-Menckenians have reduced their charge from racist to reactionary, it is not unlikely that some will prefer that at least this among the attempts to champion Nietzsche's think-ing, at least these among Mencken's hundreds of thousands of published words, would remain in the decent repose of rare book rooms. There are, however, substantial reasons, by no means restricted to the current boom in both Nietzsche and Mencken studies, for rejecting this judgment.

With a high school education, a beginner's knowledge of German, and a few years on the newspaper police detail firmly in hand, in 1906 and 1907 Mencken spent much of his free time immersed in the Enoch Pratt Free Library's copy of Friedrich Nietzsche's *Samtlich Werke*. The result, in 1908, was one of the first comprehensive treatments of Nietzsche's thinking in the English language and easily one of the most thoughtfully sympathetic such books to appear in any language until well into the twentieth century.

Of course numerous better-informed and academically more sophisticated treatments have since appeared and it might be thought that, from the perspective of Nietzsche studies, the present work is of no more than antiquarian interest. Those who hate Nietzsche as a nihilist, protofascist and antichrist may find support and comfort from the enthusiasm for him of the notoriously nay-saying, democracy-debunking and boisterously blasphemous Mencken, but Nietzsche's own now abundantly available books will more than suffice to sustain their animus. Those favorably disposed to Nietzsche may find unexpected pleasure in this early exception to the general Anglo-American hostility to him, but they will hardly prefer it to studies that incorporate the large body of intervening scholarship or that participate in the importantly changed philosophical, literary, and political controversies. True, the book is of recognized importance among students of Mencken. Some Mencken scholars think that the "sage of Baltimore" formed his basic and abiding ideas in his encounter with Nietzsche; virtually none deny that writing this book did much to crystallize and consolidate much of what would remain his lifelong thinking.[1] But these ideas are abundantly and trenchantly expressed, with respect to topics much closer to the continuing concerns of most of his readers, in the vast corpus of Mencken's later writing.

Due weight given to these considerations, students of Nietzsche, of Mencken, and of the philosophical and cultural questions that were their mutual preoccupations, will find matter of much more than historical or biographical interest in this work. Rapidly gaining mastery of the lucid and pungent prose on which much of his reputation rests, Mencken's *Nietzsche* is a singularly accessible and continuously provocative account of Nietzsche's complex and elusive ideas. It is also an engagement with and an appropriation of Nietzsche's thinking, one that is enhanced by a style that often reverberates with a verve and dynamism approaching Nietzsche's own.

Mencken's interest in Nietzsche seems to have been first aroused by George Bernard Shaw whose recognizably if crudely Nietzschean thinking was the subject of Mencken's first prose book.[2] However this may be, it is hard to resist the thought that the spirited encounter that occurs in this book was ar-

ranged by higher forces. Caricatural as they are, the
sentences with which I began this introduction convey respects in which these two thinkers/writers
were made for one another. Although Nietzsche
never embraced antinomianism, anarchism or the
nihilism of which he is still frequently accused, he
had wonderfully sensitive antennae for the impositional, repressive and *ressentiment*-generating
characteristics of modern, Christian and finally of all
established social and cultural arrangements and
institutions. The synchronic and diachronic range of
Mencken's later and most famous unmaskings and
debunkings was of course narrower. His attentions
concentrated on his own American society—a society
of marginal interest to the "good European"
Nietzsche —and within it on the puritanical com-
stockeries and pseudo-democratic (or all-too-demo-
cratic) despotisms and babbitries that were among
but by no means the primary objects of Nietzsche's
scorn. But it is evident from the ease with which
Mencken follows and engages Nietzsche's extraordinary intellectual adventures that these were self-imposed limitations, functions of Mencken's
self-conscious adoption of a primarily journalistic
rather than a more technically philosophical or academic vocation. Having read this book, readers of
Mencken's later and more widely circulated writings—should they, inappropriately, have any doubts
on the point—will better appreciate that his biting
critiques of American society and culture were
grounded in much wider understandings and sensi-

bilities. If the same readers then follow Mencken's trail back to Nietzsche himself, the specificities of Mencken's use of Nietzschian ideas in criticizing America may well help them better to appreciate the depth and force of Nietzsche's thinking.

In short, there is Mencken on Nietzsche as a way of understanding Nietzsche; Mencken on Nietzsche as a way of understanding Mencken; Mencken on Nietzsche and on Mencken himself as a way of grappling with the still salient issues with which both Nietzsche and Mencken were occupied.

I

Mencken clearly felt an intellectual and indeed a spiritual kinship with the man Friedrich Nietzsche. This sense of affinity was no doubt due in part to Mencken's own self-identification with the "high German" culture of which Nietzsche—notwithstanding his protestations—was a product and a part. But Mencken felt and saw more closely personal as well as more specifically intellectual likenesses between himself and the already feared and despised German thinker. Consider his remarks concerning Nietzsche's upbringing by his pious mother (the daughter as well as the wife of a Lutheran minister; Nietzsche's father died when Friedrich was five years old) and his equally devout and attentive maiden aunts. This was, Mencken opines, the "ideal training" for a "sham-smasher and freethinker." "Let a boy of alert, restless intelligence come to early manhood in an atmosphere of strong faith, wherein doubts are blasphemies and inquiry is a crime, and rebellion is certain to appear with his beard. So long as his mind feels itself puny besides the overwhelming pomp and circumstance of parental authority, he will remain docile and even pious. But so soon as he begins to see authority as something ever finite, variable and all-too-human ... he will fly precipitately toward the intellectual wailing places, to think his own thoughts in his own way and to worship his own gods beneath the open sky" (3). If over-generalized as an account of the usual results of an upbringing at once pampering and pervasively controlling, this encomium exhibits Mencken's strong sense of identification with his subject and prefigures the tonalities and predominant themes of his study of Nietzsche's thinking. (Mencken's own father lived until Henry was nineteen, but young "Harry" successfully resisted his father's persistent efforts to conscript him to the family cigar business—albeit (much to his credit) not his addiction to its product!—and soon substituted his own brand of "sham-smashing and freethinking" for his mother's worshipful Lutheran religiosity.)[3]

Rebel against parental, religious, academic, moral and political authority. But not mere or obsessive and therefore self-diminishing rebellion. Mencken sees Nietzsche as much more complex and engaging than those who are merely reactive to the forces surrounding and attempting to shape them. At the same time that he castigated and protested against the crowd of persons and received beliefs and ideas that would otherwise have formed and controlled him, Mencken's Nietzsche shrinks from intimate contact with them, ascends and descends into the intensely personal world of his own thinking and imagining. Mencken's Nietzsche, in this respect undeniably Nietzsche himself, is a fastidious as well as a rebellious man, a man driven by his craving for "cleanliness" always to maintain a "pathos of distance" from the very culture whose values he sought to transvaluate and transform. (By choice a professional journalist and essayist-publicist, Mencken himself was, at once voluntarily and necessarily, more directly involved with the persons and events of his time than the often reclusive Nietzsche. But no one who reads and writes as avidly and continuously as Mencken did can have been untouched by Nietzsche's sentiment that "he who does not have two-thirds of his day to himself is a slave, let him be what he may otherwise."[4] Although not quite a Nietzschean wanderer who at once loves and craves escape from his own shadow, Mencken must have spent the largest part of his adult life in the privacy of his study.)

II

These highly personal appreciations are echoed and amplified in more intellectual registers throughout Mencken's engagement with Nietzsche.[5]

As is evident from his readiness to adjust his own views to new ideas and emergent events, Mencken shared Nietzsche's conviction that "the will to system is a lack of integrity"; he believed that thinking must be alert and responsive rather than confined in the prison of an aridly abstract philosophical schema. As the commentators mentioned above have observed, however, early on Mencken formed a medley of beliefs that remained central to his thinking throughout his life. As he saw it, Nietzsche did the same. And Mencken's intense admiration for Nietzsche was due in no small part to his judgment that the abiding and even controlling element in the latter's work was a commitment that Mencken himself prized, namely to a complex and agonal form of "the gospel of individualism" (39). (Nietzsche, together with his teacher Ralph Waldo Emerson, would say "individuality".)

In its Nietzschean-Menckenian formulation, this "gospel" had a sweeping and powerfully negative side. Nietzsche "applied the acid of critical analysis to a hundred and one specific ideas." He assaulted the "moraline" and life-denying slave moralities that he descried in Plato and Socrates, in Stoicism, in Kant and Hegel, in Judaism, and above all in every established, institutionalized form of Christianity.[6] Along with Schopenhauer, Huxley and Spencer, Ibsen, and above all Darwin, Nietzsche attacked the pale and desiccated but bovinely optimistic rationalism of the enlightenment (33), despised the decadent and parasitic German aristocracy (72-73, 165-66) as well as the pseudoskeptical bourgeoisie (38) and the "grasping buccaneer[s] of finance" (197-98) who were in the way of supplanting it; he hated both monarchy and democracy (192-93), nationalism and militarism (206), socialism (97-99) and "the beery, collarless anarchy preached by Herr Most and his unwashed followers" (196-97).

Arguing that most of these relentlessly critical views were foreshadowed in *The Birth of Tragedy*, Mencken associates them with the Apollonian side of Nietzsche's thinking, with the latter's "own fanatical striving for the truth" (28) and his unrivalled capacity for critical analysis. Contemptuous of the shallow but bombastic pseudo-Apollonianism of the professorial philologists and historians (28), of the caste of degenerates "who stood for formalism and permanence" and whose aim was that human beings "live in strict obedience to certain invariable rules ... which found expression as religion, law and morality" (72), as Mencken saw it the complex ideal for which Nietzsche stood was provided by the "best days" of Greek culture, the days "when Apollo and Dionysus were properly balanced, one against the other" (71).

It is arguable that in Mencken's view the "most general conclusion" of Nietzsche's gospel of individualism was in important part a product of the Apollonian side of his thinking, arrived at by critical analysis of "a hundred and one specific ideas." Having subjected the regnant ideas of his own and earlier days to such analysis, he drew the admirable conclusion that none of them gave any human being the "right, in any way or form, to judge or direct the actions of any other being" (39).

This conclusion, however, was no mere negation and Mencken's Nietzsche is no mere critic and certainly not a passive nihilist. If the conclusion is in part an inference from the manifest inadequacy of all claimed or purported bases for judging and ruling anyone but oneself, it is far more powerfully an affirmation, a yes-saying to life itself. An admirer and follower of the Apollonian dimensions of Nietzsche's thought, Mencken's greatest enthusiasm was for Nietzsche the Dionysian.

Beyond the biographical observations already noted, Mencken's intense appreciation of Nietzsche's Dionysian passion for life and individuality first appear in his account of Nietzsche's discovery and lifelong struggle with and against Arthur Schopenhauer. Liberated from dreary Kantian and Hegelian rationalisms by Schopenhauer's doctrine that "intelligence ... was not the source of the will, but its effect" (19, and see 33), Nietzsche transformed Schopenhauer's will in itself into the will to life or will to power[7] and rejected Schopenhauer's asceticism and pessimism. He agreed "that human life, at best, was often an infliction and a torture, but in his very first book he showed that he admired, not the ascetic who tried to escape from the wear and tear of life altogether, but the proud, stiff-necked hero who held his balance in the face of both seductive pleasure and staggering pain" (29).[8]

Having made himself into a "prophet of defiance not of resignation," Schopenhauer could not remain Nietzsche's "God" (33) (albeit Mencken acknowledges that he remained one of Nietzsche's intellectual heroes until the end of his thinking life). And Nietzsche's defiance soon extended to the whole notion of a, and especially the, God towering above and to be worshipped by humankind. It also carried him forward to the potentially liberating and inspiriting conviction that humankind's gods and heroes are projections of themselves, images they devise for themselves out of their own fears and hopes, hatreds and loves. His studies of pre-Socratic religious cults and especially their representations in Greek tragedy were a powerful impetus to this new conception. Expressing his own views as well as reporting what he takes to be Nietzsche's, Mencken says that the "ancient Greeks were fond of tragedy because it reflected their life in miniature. In the mighty warriors who stalked the boards and defied the gods each Greek recognized himself. In the conflicts on the stage he saw replicas of that titanic conflict which seems to him to be the eternal essence of human existence" (66).

Although tempered in essential ways by its Apollonian elements, the vitality, creativity, and joy in Greek life and thought came primarily from its Dionysian forces; took their origins and their power from the "impulse to exploit and explore," to overthrow "artificial, permanent rules" and especially to vanquish the idea that life should be lived "in strict obedience" to such rules (72). Appropriated into his own (and Mencken's) thinking, this became Nietzsche's ideal of the free spirit, of the person who would "formulate his own morality as he progressed from lower to higher things. He should reject the old conceptions of good and evil and substitute for them the human valuations, good and bad. In a word, he should put behind him the morality invented by some dead race to make its own progress easy and pleasant, and credited to some man-made god to give it authority, and put in the place of this a ... personal morality based upon his own power of distinguishing between the things which benefit him and the things which injure him. ... All notions of sin and virtue should be banished from his mind. He should weigh everything on the scales of individual expedience" (93). (Nietzsche would not use the word expedience, but, purged of its social Darwinist overtones, what Mencken means by the word is not far from what Nietzsche would say.)

How would those who attained to this ideal conduct themselves? What effects would they have on the others around them?

Such a man, were he set down in the world today, would bear an outward resemblance, perhaps, to the most pious and virtuous of his fellow citizens, but it is apparent that his life would have more of truth in it and less of hypocrisy and cant and pretense than theirs. He would obey the laws of the land frankly and solely because he was afraid of incurring their penalties[9] ... and he would not try to delude his neighbors and himself into believing that he saw anything sacred in them. He would have no need of a god to teach him the difference between right and wrong and no need of priests to remind him of this god's teachings. He would look upon the woes and ills of life as inevitable and necessary results of life's conflict, and he would make no effort to read into them the wrath of a peevish and irrational deity at his own or his ancestor's sins. His mind would be absolutely free of thoughts of sin and hell, and in consequence he would be vastly happier than the majority of persons about him. All in all, he would be a powerful influence for truth in his community, and, as such, would occupy himself with the most noble and sublime task possible to mere human beings: the overthrow of superstition and unreasoning faith, with their long train of fears, horrors, doubts, frauds, injustice and suffering. (97-98)

Nietzsche would of course have left out the "mere" and would have spoken of, say, joy and strength not of happiness.

This key passage leads us directly to Mencken's appreciations and appropriations of three of the closely connected but most difficult elements in Nietzsche's thinking: the Eternal Return; his still underappreciated ideas about government, law and politics; and the notion of the Superman.[10]

III

"He would look upon the woes and ills of life as inevitable and necessary results of life's conflict." But what if each and all of us are fated to an endless cycle in which, eternally, *the very same* miseries repeat themselves again and again? In various and changing versions, Nietzsche broaches and seriously addresses this dismal possibility. What did he mean by the strange and haunting notion of an eternal return or recurrence? Why did he brood so interminably over it?

Mencken's first response is to lament the fact that Nietzsche took the idea seriously. It "was not original with ... [him, he took it over from the Pythagoreans] and it would have been better for his philosophy and for his repute as an intelligent thinker had he never sought to elucidate it." Indeed it manifests an "ever-evident strain of mysticism" that was in conflict with the "worship of the actual" for which Mencken admired him (118). But Mencken thinks that Nietzsche's later treatments of the eternal return, particularly in *Zarathustra*, overcame this unfortunate tendency and turned the notion to the advantage of the most estimable aspects of his thinking. On Nietzsche's and more particularly his own behalf, Mencken tries to improve further on Nietzsche's efforts.

Having disabused himself of the metaphysical or pseudoscientific pretensions of the idea, Nietzsche transformed it into a test, the self-imposed, ultimate and ultimately confirming test, of the superman. "The superman is one who realizes that all his struggles will be in vain, and that, in future cycles, he will have to go through them over and over again. Yet he has attained such a superhuman immunity to all emotion —to all ideas of pleasure and pain—that the prospect does not daunt him. Despite its horror, he faces it unafraid. It is all part of life, and in consequence it is good. He has learned to agree to everything that exists—even to the ghastly necessity for living again and again. ... 'Let us not only endure the inevitable,' says Nietzsche, 'and still less hide it from ourselves: *let us love it*'" (119).

Astonishingly given his initial remarks on the topic, Mencken then proceeds to argue that the *Zarathustra* version of the eternal return shows us Nietzsche at his hardheaded materialist and indeed scientific best. Punctuating his exposition with a capsule version of his own empiricist epistemology and (then) highly conventional philosophy of science, he argues that the superman is the supreme scientist. Having abandoned concern with the "why" or the "meaning" of the world and of life he "will devote himself to acquiring knowledge of *how* it exists. This knowledge ... will be within his capacity even more than it is within our capacity today. ... The superman's developed senses will give him absolute knowledge about everything that exists on earth. He will know exactly *how* a tubercle bacillus attacks the lung tissue, he will know exactly *how* the blood fights the bacillus, and he will know exactly *how* to interfere in this battle in such a manner that the blood shall be invariably victorious. In a word, he will be the possessor of exact and complete knowledge regarding the workings of all the benign and malignant forces in the world about him, but he will not bother himself about insoluble problems" (123).

As with Mencken's (closely related) attempts to turn Nietzsche into the remorseless social Darwinist that Mencken prided himself on being, these intrusions are not only foreign but antithetical to Nietzsche's thinking.[11] Happily, the interruption is brief and Mencken ends his discussion of the Eternal Return on the appropriate note of a celebration of Nietzsche's *lebensanschauung*. "'I am a dionysian!,' cries Nietzsche. 'I am an immoralist!' He means simply that his ideal is a being capable of facing the horrors of life unafraid, of meeting great enemies and slaying them, of gazing down upon the earth in pride and scorn, of making his own way and bearing his own burdens." It is Nietzsche's commitment to individuality that matters. "In the profane folk-philosophy of every healthy and vigorous people, we find some trace of this dionysian idea. 'Let us so live day by day,' says a distinguished [but unidentified] American statesman, 'that we can look any man in the eye and tell him to go to hell!' We get a subtle sort of joy out of this saying because it voices our racial advance toward individualism and away from servility and oppression. We believe in freedom, in toleration, in moral anarchy. ... So we phrase it. The

superman, did he stalk the earth, would say the same
thing" (124-25).

IV

Freedom, toleration, and moral anarchy. But at
the same time, "He would obey the laws of the land."
Government, politics, and law were hardly at the
center of Nietzsche's concerns, but trenchant observations concerning them recur in his works and
Mencken gave them more and more sympathetic
attention than have most Nietzsche students.

"Despite the fantastic theory which would found
... [government] upon some general agreement"
(204) and thereby delude its subjects into thinking
that there is something "sacred" about it, in fact it is
invariably created and maintained by violence and
terror, usually of a few over the many. And while
Nietzsche could imagine "a democracy to come" the
"mission" of which would be "the decline and *death
of the state*,"[12] he thought, and Mencken agreed, that
for the forseeable future the alternative was a rapine
anarchy pervaded by "chaos" and "carnage" (200).
Government being impossible without "general obedience," the free spirit will for the most part "obey
the laws of the land."

We should not, however, look to government, law
or politics, no matter how organized and conducted,
for anything more than the constraints necessary to

suppress the worst evils. "Democratic institutions are quarantine arrangements to combat that ancient pestilence, lust for tyranny" (*Human, All Too Human,* vol. 2, pt. 2, par. 289, p. 383). Punishment, the chief means by which laws are enforced, does "nothing more than 'augment fear, intensify prudence and subjugate the passions.' And in so doing it *tames* man, but does not make him better. If he refrains from crime in future, it is because he has become more prudent and not because he has become more moral. If he regrets his crimes of the past, it is because his punishment, and not his so-called conscience, hurts him" (212).

Even our somewhat improved peace and security is due only in small part to government.

> "The most important result of progress in the past is the fact that we no longer live in constant fear of wild beasts, barbarians, gods and our own dreams." It may be argued, in reference to this, that organized government is to be thanked for our deliverance, but a moment's thought will show the error of the notion. Humanity's war upon wild beasts was fought and won by individualists, who had in mind no end but their personal safety and that of their children, and the subsequent war upon barbarians would have been impossible, or at least unsuccessful, had it not been for the weapons invented and employed during the older fight against beasts. Again, it is apparent that our emancipation from the race's old superstitions regarding gods and omens has been achieved, not by communal effort, but by individual effort. (201-2)

As to such higher accomplishments as we have managed, they have been despite rather than because of government:

> Knowledge and not government brought us the truth that made us free. Government, in its very essence, is opposed to all increase

of knowledge. Its tendency is always toward permanence and against change. It is unthinkable without some accepted scheme of law or morality, and such schemes ... stand in direct antithesis to every effort to find the absolute truth. Therefore, it is plain that the progress of humanity, far from being the result of government, has been made entirely without its aid and in the face of its constant and bitter opposition. The code of Hammurabi, the laws of the Medes and Persians, the Code Napoleon and the English common law have retarded the search for the ultimate verities almost as much, indeed, as the Ten Commandments. (202)

Government is indispensable but should be minimal. Free spirits will obey its laws just as they submit to other necessities and necessary restrictions. But their obedience will be "proud," will be accorded out of strength and magananimity not weakness or any sense of the truth or nobility of the laws and rules they obey.

This estimation of government and hence of the most rawly impositional form of the rule of some over others must be borne in mind in considering other respects in which Nietzsche and Mencken himself promote such arrangements. But there are other and substantially less attractive elements in Nietzsche's and especially Mencken's treatment of the most specifically political aspects of the human condition; elements that collect and magnify the least appealing features of their partly overlapping, partly diverging conceptions of the "superman."

Programmatically or officially opposed to all sacralizing or even dignifying theories of government and politics, both Nietzsche and Mencken sometimes indulge themselves in the most repugnant version of such theories, that according to which some few superior human beings are "by nature" and hence properly the rulers of the many inferior human beings. Worse, they indulge themselves in the most obnoxious variant of this view, that according to which the naturally inferior and subordinate parts of the human race are unqualifiedly at the disposal of their natural superiors/rulers.

V

In *The Will to Power* Nietzsche says that his "philosophy aims at an ordering of rank: not at an individualistic morality. The ideas of the herd should rule in the herd—but not reach out beyond it: the leaders of the herd require a fundamentally different valuation for their own actions, as do the independent, or the 'beasts of prey', etc."[13] And he took encouragement from the fact that, in his time, the members of the "herd" had been well "prepared" for their subservient role. "I have as yet found *no* reason for discouragement. Whoever has preserved, and bred in himself, a strong will, together with an ample spirit, has more favorable opportunities than ever. For the trainability of men has become very great in this democratic Europe; men who learn easily and adapt themselves easily are the rule: the herd animal, even highly intelligent, has been prepared. Whoever can command finds those who *must* obey: I am thinking, e.g., of Napoleon and Bismarck. The rivalry with strong and *un*intelligent wills, which is the greatest obstacle, is small" (Ibid., par. 128, p. 79).

Mencken had less confidence in the "herd animals" of his time and place, yet he seems (but see below) to hesitate not at all before the thought that it would be for the best if they cheerfully adapted themselves, willingly submitted themselves, to the few. A properly "dionysian state would see the triumph . . . of the very men whose efforts are making for progress today: those strong, free, self-reliant, resourceful men whose capacities are so much greater than the mobs' that they are often able to force their ideas upon it, despite its theoretical right to rule them and its actual endeavour so to do." Such a state would work the "speedy annihilation" of the "mob" (197-98).

If we take those of "strong will and ample spirit," of "independence," "self-reliance," and "resourcefulness" as the Nietzschian "supermen," the doctrine of the superman emerges, in both Nietzsche and Mencken, as positing superior persons who form a distinct rank, stratum, or class. It also emerges as a doctrine that promotes the rule—political and otherwise—of these superior few over the herd or mob. With Mencken's substitution of the "annihilation" of the mob for Nietzsche's view of the herd as a usefully intelligent resource, it presents itself as a form of social Darwinism in which the rule of the superior few is the chief enforcement agent of the "law of natural selection"—"that invariable natural law which ordains that the fit shall survive and the unfit shall perish" (102-3).

How should we assess Mencken's renderings/appropriations of Nietzsche's most widely discussed and most frequently reviled doctrine? An essential first step in doing so is to note qualifications that Mencken himself enters to the idea that the supermen form, by nature or otherwise, a fixed and closed elite. Of course Mencken thought that the supermen are such "by nature" in one sense of that unstable notion, namely that their superiority emerges and is demonstrated by their triumph in the struggle for survival. But he recognized and warmly applauded Nietzsche's scorn for the idea of an "elect" or "elite," an "aristocracy" that is "by nature" in the sense of an originally given, inherited or otherwise undeniable and unalterable superiority. Those who claim such standing, or who are accorded it by theorists who are their apologists and lackeys, are for the most part parasites who hedge themselves about "with purely artificial barriers" and privileges. "Next only to its desire to maintain itself without actual personal efforts," the "elite" of European and American society is compromized by its "jealous endeavor to prevent accessions to its ranks. Nothing . . . disgusts the traditional belted earl so much as the ennobling of some upstart brewer or ironmaster. This exclusiveness, from Nietzsche's point of view, seemed ridiculous and pernicious, for a true aristocracy must be ever willing and eager to welcome to its ranks—and to enroll in fact, automatically —all who display those qualities which make a man extraordinarily fit and efficient. There should always be, he said, a free and constant interchange of individuals between the . . . castes of men. It should always be possible for an abnormally efficient man of the slave class to enter the master class, and, by the same token, accidental degeneration or incapacity in the master class should be followed by swift and merciless reduction to the ranks of slaves. Thus, those aristocracies which presented the incongruous spectacle of imbeciles being intrusted with the affairs of government seemed to him utterly abhorrent, and those schemes of caste which made a mean birth an offset to high intelligence seemed no less so." (166)

Again following Nietzsche, Mencken used this notion of a "circulation of elites" to refigure and redirect the argument that the slaves or mob should passively submit to the rule of the supermen. In a passage that captures Nietzsche's powerfully affirmative valorization of the agonal character of life Mencken writes:

> It is evident . . . that the feeling of superiority has a complement in the feeling of inferiority. Every man . . . sees himself, in respect to some talent possessed in common by himself and a rival, in one of three ways: he knows that he is superior, he knows that he is inferior, or he is in doubt. In the first case, says Nietzsche, the thing for him to do is to make his superiority still greater by yielding to its stimulation: to make the gap between himself and his rival wider and wider. In the second case, the thing for him to do is to try to make the gap smaller: to lift himself up or to pull his rival down until they are equal or the old disproportion is reversed. In the third case, it is his duty to plunge into a contest and risk his all upon

the cast of the die. "'I do not exhort you to peace,'" says Nietzsche, "'but to victory!'" If victory comes not, let it be defeat, death and annihilation — but, in any event, let there be a fair fight. Without this constant strife—this constant testing—this constant elimination of the unfit—there can be no progress. "'As the smaller surrenders himself to the greater, so the greater must surrender himself to the will to power and stake life upon the issue. It is the mission of the greatest to run risk and danger—to cast dice with death.'" Power, in a word, is never infinite: it is always becoming. (104-5)

VI

Of course this construal, even if it files the fangs or draws some of the sting of the superman doctrine, will itself further affright those who crave the very condition that Nietzsche and Mencken hope it will destroy, the condition of a culture that aims to "rob the strong of . . . their strength" by imposing on them a "system of ethics which brands it with infamy, and so makes the" very will to power, that is "the one all-powerful instinct of every sentient creature[,] loathsome and abominable." (105)

Unfortunately, Mencken's thoroughly anti-Nietzschean version of social Darwinism puts massive and unnecessary obstacles in the path of those prepared to entertain Nietzsche's contest conception of life. If the Nietzschean struggle is over death versus mere life itself, and if before long it is the death of all of us, it is indeed hard to resist Schopenhauer's conclusion that it would be better if each of us would still the will to life/will to power.

That will cannot keep us alive for long and it is the source of our misery for as long we fight off our enemies.

Mencken is aware that Nietzsche specifically rejected the law of natural selection. He cites and partially summarizes the discussion in *Twilight of the Idols* in which Nietzsche argues that, as a matter of regrettable historical fact, the weak are constantly triumphing over the strong and the story of the human race is a tale of decline and degeneration (141-43). But Mencken puts this down as "a moment of sophistry" due partly to Nietzsche's declining powers, partly to his hatred of "everything English;" he insists that "the law itself is unassailable," "that all of Nietzsche's work . . . helps to support it," and even that "without Darwin's work, . . . [Nietzsche's] own philosophy would have been impossible." (142n)

The beliefs that "all things happen in obedience to invariable natural laws" (141), that science is the dogged and unblinkered empiricist pursuit of exact knowledge of those laws, and that Darwinian biology is the highest achievement of such science thus far, were articles of Mencken's faith. He had more than a little appreciation for Nietzsche's skepticism, but in respect to natural science he treated it (as did his empiricist predecessors and positivist contempories) as a rejection of metaphysical speculation and sentimental moralizing concerning plain natural "facts." More than sympathetic to Nietzsche's view that religion, morality, and most of the rest of our thinking about cultural matters consists primarily of fantasies and prejudices, he refused to understand or at least to credit Nietzsche's view that science is not and cannot be different in kind. For Nietzsche, our access to the world, or rather our very conceptions of "the world" and of what counts as access to it, are due not to "it" but to our own diverse and fluctuating conceptions, beliefs, prejudices, imaginings and fantasizings. As with everything else that we come to regard as "true," for Nietzsche the truths of science are and can be nothing more (nor less) than propositions on which, here and now, our thinking and judging have converged. When we treat those truths as something higher or deeper, something objective, invariable, and undeniable, we are doing no more and no other than we do in religion and morality, that is attempting to reassure ourselves concerning them as we seek to impose them on others. Nietzsche's commitment to the contest conception of life is a commitment not to a scientific truth but to an ideal of life. If *per impossibile*, it were established that his ideal is a truth that he must share with everyone because everyone is obliged by evidence or reason to accept it, he would almost certainly have forsaken it.[14]

From a Nietzschean perspective, then, Mencken's Darwinism is simply one of Mencken's most uncritically held beliefs. Epistemically, the same is true of the particular imperatives that Mencken thought were mandated by that belief, in particular his social Darwinist rendering of the agonal conception of life. Nietzsche accepted the view that we ought to think of and conduct life as an incessant struggle, but his conception of the terrain on which and the issues over which that struggle should be fought was importantly different than that which Mencken advances.

Passages concerning his "philosophy of rank" and the weak as resources of the strong are admittedly frequent in Nietzsche's work; Mencken is neither alone in nor without warrant for reading the superman doctrine as promoting the dominance of one small and superior set of human beings over another much larger and inferior set. There is, however, another and much more powerful tendency in this part of Nietzsche's thinking. The struggles of the supermen are less, or less directly, with or against other persons than with elements in themselves, struggles against features of their own believing, thinking, and acting that they abhor and seek to "overcome." Of course those beliefs and hopes have come to them from, were instilled in them by, the culture of which they are part. If only for this reason, in order to struggle against them the supermen must unmask and challenge, denounce and fight against that culture and those who represent and enforce its restrictions and requirements. But their objective is to rid *themselves* of qualities and characteristics that diminish *them*, to envision and struggle to achieve higher, freer, more joyous selves. Their aspiration, rather than to triumph in the war for mere survival, is to remake themselves into "free spirits."

This objective is importantly in conflict with a quest for power and dominance over other human beings. Ruling others requires constant attention to and involvement with them. The free spirits cannot avoid such contact altogether, cannot withdraw from or isolate themselves from their society or culture. But they must cultivate a "pathos of distance" from it and all of its members—or all save those few that they recognize as true friends or genuinely worthy enemies. If they do not achieve and sustain such distance, if they seek to rule over others, they will constantly be drawn back into the very ways of thinking and acting that they are trying to escape.[15]

On this understanding of the superman and the contest conception of life, the "Darwinian" struggle for survival is not only futile but self-defeating. Those who are most "successful" in that struggle, those who keep themselves alive for the longest time, thereby insure that they will remain in the most debilitated of all conditions, the condition of self-contempt.

VI

Mencken, it is pleasing to conclude by noting, was neither oblivious to nor unappreciative of these elements in Nietzsche's thinking. If not quite for the reasons just given, there is a strong tendency for those in the "highest caste" to "drop out of it and seek peace in the castes lower down," to sink back to the condition from which they had struggled to escape. But we must fight against this tendency. "'Let your highest thought be: Man is something to be surpassed.'" "'Propagate yourself upward. Thus live your life. What are many years worth? I do not spare you. . . . Die at the right time!'" (169). "Schopenhauer regards suicide as a means of escape. Nietzsche sees it as a means of good riddance. It is time to die, says Zarathustra, when the purpose of life ceases to be attainable—when the fighter breaks his sword arm or falls into his enemy's hands. And it is time to die, too, when the purpose of life is attained—when the fighter triumphs and sees before him no more worlds to conquer. 'He who hath a goal and an heir wisheth death to come at the right time for goal and heir'" (226-27). "The vulgarian may boast of his bluff honesty, but at heart he looks up to the gentleman, who goes through life serene and imperturable. There is in the latter . . . an unmistakable air of fitness and efficiency, and it is this which makes it possible for him to be gentle and to regard those below him with tolerance. 'The demeanor of high-born persons,' says Nietzsche, 'shows plainly that in their minds the consciousness of power is ever-present. . . . To a provoking speech, they reply with politeness and self-possession—and not as horrified, crushed, abashed, enraged or out of breath, after the manner of plebians. The [true] aristocrat knows how to preserve the appearance of ever-present physical strength, and he knows, too, how to convey the impression that his soul and intellect are a match to all dangers and surprises, by keeping up an unchanging serenity and civility, even under the most trying circumstances'" (240-41).

These and the other major components of the "gospel of individualism" that Mencken found in Nietzsche and refashioned for himself comprise a sensibility—a spirit — without which, if we can do at all, we cannot do well. Flaws and all, this book is a powerful expression of that spirit.

Richard Flathman

Notes

1. See, for example, Carl Bode, *Mencken* (Carbondale: Southern Illinois University Press, 1969) and especially George H. Douglas, *H.L. Mencken: Critic of American Life* (Hamden, CT: Archon Books, 1978).

2. *George Bernard Shaw: His Plays* (Boston: Luce, 1905). "Through the theatre I became interested in George Bernard Shaw, and through Shaw I found my vocation at last. My first real book, begun in 1904, was a volume on his plays and the notions in them, critical in its approach. It was the first book about him ever published, and it led me to begin a longer volume on Nietzsche in 1907...." Quoted in George H. Douglas, *H.L. Mencken* 28. Mencken had previously published a small book of poetry, *Ventures into Verse* (Baltimore: Marshall, Beck and Gordon, 1903).

3. On these points see especially William Manchester, *Disturber of the Peace: The Life of H.L. Mencken* (New York: Harper & Bros. 1950).

4. Friedrich Nietzsche, *Human All Too Human*, vol. one, pt. 5, par. 283. Trans. R.J. Hollingdale (Cambridge: Cambridge University Press, 1966).

5. As regards Nietzsche's life, Mencken was dependent on the largely unreliable accounts provided by Nietzsche's sister Elisabethfor whom, to make matters worse, he had a quite uncritical and excessive enthusiasm. (See especially 59.) Happily, the persona he created for himself out of Elisabeth's skewed and self-serving reports was a figure largely in his own image.

6. Mencken's overwhelming favorite among Nietzsche's books was *The Anti-Christ*. "Beginning *allegro* it proceeds from *forte*, by an uninterrupted *crescendo* to *allegro con moltissimo molto fortissimo*. . . . It is German that one cannot read aloud without roaring and waving one's arms" (133). Mencken later published a translation of *The Anti-Christ* with his own avidly enthusiastic Introduction (New York: Alfred Knopf, 1920, 1923). There are indications, however, that he shared Nietzsche's considerable admiration for the historical Jesus.

7. Mencken's Darwinism, which I discuss below, leads him to conflate will to life and will to power and, mistakenly, to think that Nietzsche as staying closer to Schopenhauer than he in fact did (albeit reversing Schopenhauer's evaluation of the will to life). In other, particularly epistemological respects, he underestimates Nietzsche's continuing debt to Schopenhauer.

8. Mencken goes on to say that Nietzsche's hero "cultivated within himself a sublime indifference, so that happiness and misery, to him, became mere words and no catastrophe, human or superhuman, could affright or daunt him" (Ibid.). This is close to the mark (perhaps on the mark as regards *Birth of Tragedy*) but it tends to confuse indifference and magnanimity and to make Nietzsche into a Stoicwhich he decidedly was notrather than a Dionysian. But see 71, 104, 124, and 255-56 for more perspicuous treatments of this question.

9. This does seem to have been Mencken's own reason for obedience to law but it is mistaken concerning that which Nietzsche urges on free spirits. They are to obey not out of fear but out of strength; out of the conviction that law, while necessary to social life, can neither bring them to nor deflect them from the attainment of their highest ideals.

10. Were I writing (more explicitly!) in my own name, I would render "superman" and "supermen" as "overwo/man" and "overwo/men". This usage would be decidedly unfaithful to Mencken's predominantly masculist thinking, albeit, as with Nietzsche's own for the most part comparable tendencies, his views about women are by no means unqualifiedly or unrelievedly misogynist. See chapter 9, especially 178-79 and 189-91.

11. Quite generally, Mencken's scientistic prejudices, while perhaps help-ing him to see and to appreciate Nietzsche's skepticism (see Chapter Seven), closed his eyes or at least his mind to the equally deep person-alism of Nietzsche's perspectivalist epistemology. This is the single most serious weakness in his account and appropriation of Nietzsche's thinking and the chief source of other difficulties to be discussed by way of concluding this introduction.

12. Friedrich Nietzsche, *Human, All Too Human*, vol. I, sec. 8, par. 472, 172.

13. Friedrich Nietzsche, *The Will to Power*, par. 287, p. 162. Trans. Walter Kaufmann and R.J. Hollingdale. Ed. Walter Kaufmann (New York: Vintage Books, 1967).

14. "This is *my* good; this I love; it pleases me wholly; thus alone do *I* want the good. I do not want it as a divine law; I do not want it as human statute and need: it shall not be a signpost for me to overearths and paradises." *Thus Spoke Zarathustra*, pt. I, sec. 5, p. 36. Trans. Walter Kaufmann (New York: Penguin Books, 1966). "This is what I am; this is what I want: you can go to hell! " *Will to Power*, par. 349, p. 191.

15. For a more extended development and defense of this reading of Nietzsche than is possible here, see my *Willful Liberalism: Voluntarism and Individuality in Political Theory and Practice* (Ithaca: Cornell University Press, 1992).

A Note on the Text

Allison Bulsterbaum, in *H. L. Mencken: A Research Guide* (New York & London: Garland Publishing, Inc., 1988), gives the following account of publication history of this book. First published in 1908 (Boston: Luce). "Issued also in London by Fisher Unwin, 1908, which omitted the section 'Books and Articles about Nietzsche.' [Herein entitled "How to Study Nietzsche."] Second edition [no date given] was only a reprinting. Third edition: Boston: Luce, 1913 [with a new Preface], reprinted: Port Washington, NY: Kennikat Press, 1967. Edition of 1908 reprinted: Folcroft, PA: Folcroft Press, 1973; Norwood, PA: Norwood Editions, 1977; Philadelphia: R. West, 1978. Partially reprinted in *The Young Mencken: The Best of His Work*. Collected by Carl Bode (New York: Dial Press, 1973)." (Pp. 4, 87.)

All of these editions are out of print. The present one is reprinted, with the kind permission of The Enoch Pratt Free Library, Baltimore, MD, from the edition of 1913.

PREFACE TO THE THIRD EDITION

———◆———

WHEN this attempt to summarize and interpret the principal ideas of Friedrich Wilhelm Nietzsche was first published, in the early part of 1908, several of his most important books were yet to be translated into English and the existing commentaries were either fragmentary and confusing or frankly addressed to the specialist in philosophy. It was in an effort to make Nietzsche comprehensible to the general reader, at sea in German and unfamiliar with the technicalities of the seminaries, that the work was undertaken. It soon appeared that a considerable public had awaited that effort, for the first edition was quickly exhausted and there was an immediate demand for a special edition in England. The larger American edition which followed has since gone the way of its predecessor, and so the opportunity offers for a general revision, eliminating certain errors in the first draft and introducing facts and opinions brought forward by the publication of Dr. Oscar Levy's admirable complete edition of Nietzsche in English and by the appearance of several new and informative biographical studies, and a large number of discussions and criticisms. The whole of the section upon Nietzsche's intellectual origins has been rewritten, as has been the section on his critics, and new matter has been added to the biographical chapters. In addition, the middle portion of the book has been carefully revised, and a final chapter upon the study of Nietzsche, far more extensive than the original bibliographical note, has been appended. The effect of these changes, it is believed, has been to increase the usefulness of the book, not only to the reader who will go no further, but also to the reader who plans to proceed to Nietzsche's own writings and to the arguments of his principal critics and defenders.

That Nietzsche has been making progress of late goes without saying. No reader of current literature, nor even of current periodicals, can have failed to notice the increasing pressure of his ideas. When his name was first heard in England and America, toward the end of the nineties, he suffered much by the fact that few of his advocates had been at any pains to understand him. Thus misrepresented, he took on the aspect of an horrific intellectual hobgoblin, half Bakúnin and half Byron, a sacrilegious and sinister fellow, the father of all the wilder ribaldries of the day. In brief, like Ibsen before him, he had to bear many a burden that was not his. But in the course of time the truth about him gradually precipitated itself from this cloud of unordered enthusiasm, and his principal ideas began to show themselves clearly. Then the discovery was made that the report of them had been far more appalling than the substance. Some of them, indeed, had already slipped into respectable society in disguise, as the original inspirations of lesser sages, and others, on examination, turned out to

be quite harmless, and even comforting. The worst
that could be said of most of them was that they stood
in somewhat violent opposition to the common plati-
tudes, that they were a bit vociferous in denying this
planet to be the best of all possible worlds. Heresy, of
course, but falling, fortunately enough, upon ears fast
growing attuned to heretical music. The old order now
had fewer to defend it than in days gone by. The
feeling that it must yield to something better, that contentment must give way to striving and struggle, that
any change was better than no change at all — this
feeling was abroad in the world. And if the program of
change that Nietzsche offered was startling at first
hearing, it was at least no more startling than the programs offered by other reformers. Thus he got his day
in court at last and thus he won the serious attention of
open-minded and reflective folk.

Not, of course, that Nietzsche threatens, today or in
the near future, to make a grand conquest of Christendom, as Paul conquered, or the unknown Father of
Republics. Far from it, indeed. Filtered through the
comic sieve of a Shaw or sentimentalized by a Roosevelt, some of his ideas show a considerable popularity,
but in their original state they are not likely to inflame
millions. Broadly viewed, they stand in direct opposition to every dream that soothes the slumber of mankind in the mass, and therefore mankind in the mass
must needs be suspicious of them, at least for years to
come. They are pre-eminently for the man who is *not*
of the mass, for the man whose head is lifted, however
little, above the common level. They justify the success

of that man, as Christianity justifies the failure of the man below. And so they give no promise of winning the race in general from its old idols, despite the fact that the pull of natural laws and of elemental appetites is on their side. But inasmuch as an idea, to make itself felt in the world, need not convert the many who serve and wait but only the few who rule, it must be manifest that the Nietzschean creed, in the long run, gives promise of exercising a very real influence upon human thought. Reduced to a single phrase, it may be called a counterblast to sentimentality — and it is precisely by breaking down sentimentality, with its fondness for moribund gods, that human progress is made. If Nietzsche had left no other vital message to his time, he would have at least forced and deserved a hearing for his warning that Christianity is a theory for those who distrust and despair of their strength, and not for those who hope and fight on.

To plat his principal ideas for the reader puzzled by conflicting reports of them, to prepare the way for an orderly and profitable reading of his own books — such is the purpose of the present volume. The works of Nietzsche, as they have been done into English, fill eighteen volumes as large as this one, and the best available account of his life would make three or four more. But it is sincerely to be hoped that the student, once he has learned the main paths through this extensive country, will proceed to a diligent and thorough exploration. Of all modern philosophers Nietzsche is the least dull. He was undoubtedly the greatest German prose writer of his generation, and even when one reads him through the English veil it is impossible to escape the charm and color of his phrases and the pyrotechnic brilliance of his thinking.

MENCKEN.

BALTIMORE, November, 1913.

NIETZSCHE THE MAN

FRIEDRICH NIETZSCHE

———◆———

I

BOYHOOD AND YOUTH

FRIEDRICH NIETZSCHE was a preacher's son, brought up in the fear of the Lord. It is the ideal training for sham-smashers and freethinkers. Let a boy of alert, restless intelligence come to early manhood in an atmosphere of strong faith, wherein doubts are blasphemies and inquiry is a crime, and rebellion is certain to appear with his beard. So long as his mind feels itself puny beside the overwhelming pomp and circumstance of parental authority, he will remain docile and even pious. But so soon as he begins to see authority as something ever finite, variable and all-too-human — when he begins to realize that his father and his mother, in the last analysis, are mere human beings, and fallible like himself — then he will fly precipitately toward the intellectual wailing places, to think his own thoughts in his own way and to worship his own gods beneath the open sky.

As a child Nietzsche was holy; as a man he was the

3

symbol and embodiment of all unholiness. At nine he
was already versed in the lore of the reverend doctors,
and the pulpit, to his happy mother — a preacher's
daughter as well as a preacher's wife — seemed his logical
and lofty goal; at thirty he was chief among those who
held that all pulpits should be torn down and fashioned
into bludgeons, to beat out the silly brains of theologians.

The awakening came to him when he made his first
venture away from the maternal apron-string and fire-
side: when, as a boy of ten, he learned that there were
many, many men in the world and that these men were of
many minds. With the clash of authority came the end
of authority. If A. was right, B. was wrong — and B.
had a disquieting habit of standing for one's mother, one's
grandmother or the holy prophets. Here was the beginning
of intelligence in the boy — the beginning of that weighing
and choosing faculty which seems to give man at once
his sense of mastery and his feeling of helplessness. The
old notion that doubt was a crime crept away. There
remained in its place the new notion that the only real
crime in the world — the only unmanly, unspeakable
and unforgivable offense against the race — was unreasoning belief. Thus the orthodoxy of the Nietzsche
home turned upon and devoured itself.

The philosopher of the superman was born on October
15th, 1844, at Röcken, a small town in the Prussian
province of Saxony. His father, Karl Ludwig Nietzsche,
was a country pastor of the Lutheran Church and a man
of eminence in the countryside. But he was more than a
mere rural worthy, with an outlook limited by the fringe
of trees on the horizon, for in his time he had seen some-

thing of the great world and had even played his humble part in it. Years before his son Friedrich was born he had been tutor to the children of the Duke of Altenburg. The duke was fond of him and took him, now and then, on memorable and eventful journeys to Berlin, where that turbulent monarch, King Friedrich Wilhelm IV, kept a tinsel court and made fast progress from imbecility to acute dementia. The king met the young tutor and found him a clever and agreeable person, with excellent opinions regarding all those things whereon monarchs are wont to differ with mobs. When the children of the duke became sufficiently saturated with learning, the work of Pastor Nietzsche at Altenburg was done and he journeyed to Berlin to face weary days in the anterooms of ecclesiastical magnates and jobbers of places. The king, hearing by chance of his presence and remembering him pleasantly, ordered that he be given without delay a vicarage worthy of his talents. So he was sent to Röcken, and there, when a son was born to him, he called the boy Friedrich Wilhelm, as a graceful compliment to his royal patron and admirer.

There were two other children in the house. One was a boy, Josef, who was named after the Duke of Altenburg, and died in infancy in 1850. The other was a girl, Therese Elisabeth Alexandra, who became in after years her brother's housekeeper, guardian angel and biographer. Her three names were those of the three noble children her father had grounded in the humanities. Elisabeth — who married toward middle age and is best known as Frau Förster-Nietzsche — tells us practically all that we know about the Nietzsche family and the private life of its dis-

tinguished son.[1]   The clan came out of Poland, like so
many other families of Eastern Germany, at the time of
the sad, vain wars.   Legend maintains that it was noble
in its day and Nietzsche himself liked to think so.   The
name, says Elisabeth, was originally Nietzschy.   " Germany is a great nation," Nietzsche would say, " only
because its people have so much Polish blood in their veins.
. . . I am proud of my Polish descent.   I remember that
in former times a Polish noble, by his simple veto, could
overturn the resolution of a popular assembly.   There were
giants in Poland in the time of my forefathers."   He
wrote a tract with the French title " *L'Origine de la famille
de Nietzsche*" and presented the manuscript to his sister,
as a document to be treasured and held sacred.   She tells
us that he was fond of maintaining that the Nietzsches
had suffered greatly and fallen from vast grandeur
for their opinions, religious and political.   He had no
proof of this, but it pleased him to think so.

Pastor Nietzsche was thrown from his horse in 1848
and died, after a lingering illness, on July 28th, 1849, when
Friedrich was barely five years old.   Frau Nietzsche then
moved her little family to Naumburg-on-the-Saale — " a
Christian, conservative, loyal city."   The household
consisted of the mother, the two children, their paternal
grandmother and two maiden aunts — the sisters of the
dead pastor.   The grandmother was something of a blue-
stocking and had been, in her day, a member of that queer
circle of intellectuals and amateurs which raged and
roared around Goethe at Weimar.   But that was in the
long ago, before she dreamed of becoming the wife of one

---

[1] " *Das Leben Friedrich Nietzsche's*," 3 vols.   Leipsic, 1895-7-9.

preacher and the mother of another. In the year '50 she was well of all such youthful fancies and there was no doubt of the divine revelations beneath her pious roof. Prayers began the day and ended the day. It was a house of holy women, with something of a convent's placidity and quiet exaltation. Little Friedrich was the idol in the shrine. It was the hope of all that he would grow up into a man illimitably noble and impossibly good.

Pampered thus, the boy shrank from the touch of the world's rough hand. His sister tells us that he disliked the bad little boys of the neighborhood, who robbed bird's nests, raided orchards and played at soldiers. There appeared in him a quaint fastidiousness which went counter to the dearest ideals of the healthy young male. His school fellows, in derision, called him " the little pastor " and took delight in waylaying him and venting upon him their grotesque and barbarous humor. He liked flowers and books and music and when he went abroad it was for solitary walks. He could recite and sing and he knew the Bible so well that he was able to dispute about its mysteries. " As I think of him," said an old school-mate years afterward, " I am forced irresistibly into a thought of the 12-year-old Jesus in the Temple." " The serious introspective child, with his dignified politeness," says his sister, " seemed so strange to other boys that friendly advances from either side were out of the question."

There is a picture of the boy in all the glory of his first long-tailed coat. His trousers stop above his shoe-tops, his hair is long and his legs seem mere airy filaments. As one gazes upon the likeness one can almost smell the soap that scoured that high, shiny brow and those thin, white cheeks. The race of such seraphic boys has died out in the world. Gone are their slick, plastered locks and their translucent ears! Gone are their ruffled cuffs and their spouting of the golden text!

Nietzsche wrote verses before he was ten: pious, plaintive verses that scanned well and showed rhymes and metaphors made respectable by ages of honorable employment. His maiden effort, so far as we know, was an elegy entitled " The Grave of My Father." Later on he became aware of material things and sang the praises of rose and sunset. He played the piano, too, and knew his Beethoven well, from the snares for the left hand in " *Für Elise* " to the raging tumults of the C minor symphony. One Sunday — it was Ascension day — he went to the village church and heard the choir sing the Hallelujah Chorus from " The Messiah." Here was music that benumbed the senses and soothed the soul and, boy as he was, he felt its supreme beauty. That night he covered pages of ruled paper with impossible pot-hooks. He, too, would write music!

Later on the difficulties of thorough-bass, as it was taught in the abyssmal German text-books of the time, somewhat dampened his ardor, but more than once during his youth he thought seriously of becoming a musician. His first really ambitious composition was a piano *pièce* called " *Mondschein auf der Pussta* " — " Moonlight on the Pussta " — the pussta being the flat Bohemian prairie. The family circle was delighted with this maiden *opus*, and we may conjure up a picture of little Friedrich playing it of a quiet evening at home, while mother, grandmother, sister and aunts gathered round and marvelled at his genius. In later life he wrote songs and sonatas, and — if an enemy is to be believed — an opera in the grand manner. His sister, in her biography, prints some samples of his music. Candor compels the admission that it is even worse than it sounds.

Nietzsche, at this time, still seemed like piety on a monument, but as much as he revered his elders and as much as he relied upon their infallibility, there were yet problems which assailed him and gave him disquiet. When he did not walk and think alone, his sister was his companion, and to her he opened his heart, as one might to a sexless, impersonal confessor. In her presence, indeed, he really thought aloud, and this remained his habit until the end of his life. His mind, awakening, wandered beyond the little world hedged about by doting and complacent women. Until he entered the gymnasium — that great weighing place of German brains — he shrank from open revolt, and even from the thought of it, but he could not help dwelling upon the mysteries that rose before him. There were things upon which the scriptures, search them as he might, seemed to throw no light, and of which mothers and grandmothers and maiden aunts did not discourse. "One day," says Elisabeth, "when he was yet very young, he said to me: 'You mustn't expect me to believe those silly stories about storks bringing babies. Man is a mammal and a mammal must get his own children for himself.'" Every child, perhaps, ponders such problems, but in the vast majority knowledge must wait until it may enter fortuitously and from without. Nietzsche did not belong to the majority. To him ideas

were ever things to be sought out eagerly, to be weighed
calmly, to be tried in the fire. For weal or for woe,
the cornerstones of his faith were brought forth, with
sweat and pain, from the quarry of his own mind.

Nietzsche went to various village schools — public and
private — until he was ten, dutifully trudging away each
morning with knapsack and lunch-basket. He kissed his
mother at the gate when he departed and she was waiting
for him, with another kiss, when he returned. As happiness
goes, his was probably a happy childhood. The fierce
joy of boyish combat — of fighting, of robbing, of slaying
— was never his, but to a child so athirst for knowledge,
each fresh discovery — about the sayings of Luther, the
lions of Africa, the properties of an inverted fraction —
must have brought its thrill. But as he came to the last
year of his first decade, unanswerable questions brought
their discontent and disquiet — as they do to all of us.
There is a feeling of oppression and poignant pain in facing
problems that defy solution and facts that refuse to fit
into ordered chains. It is only when mastery follows that
the fine stimulation of conscious efficiency drowns out all
moody vapors.

When Nietzsche went to the gymnasium his whole
world was overturned. Here boys were no longer mute
and hollow vessels, to be stuffed with predigested learning,
but human beings whose approach to separate entity was
recognized. It was possible to ask questions and to argue
moot points, and teaching became less the administration
of a necessary medicine and more the sharing of a delightful meal. Your German school-master is commonly a
martinet, and his birch is never idle, but he has the saving

grace of loving his trade and of readily recognizing true
diligence in his pupils.   History does not record the name
of the pedagogue who taught Nietzsche at the Naumburg
gymnasium, but he must have been one who ill deserved
his oblivion.   He fed the eager, inquiring mind of his little
student and made a new boy of him.   The old unhealthy,
uncanny embodiment of a fond household's impossible
dreams became more likeable and more human.   His
exclusiveness and fastidiousness were native and ineradi-
cable, perhaps, for they remained with him, in some degree,
his whole life long, but his thirst for knowledge and yearning for disputation soon led him to the discovery that there
were other boys worth cultivating: other boys whose
thoughts, like his own, rose above misdemeanor and
horse-play.   With two such he formed a quick friendship,
and they were destined to influence him greatly to the end
of his youth.   They organized a club for mutual culture,
gave it the sonorous name of " *Der litterarischen Vereini-
gung Germania* " (" The German Literary Association ")
and drew up an elaborate scheme of study.   Once a week
there was a meeting, at which each of the three submitted
an essay or a musical composition to the critical scrutiny
of the others.   They waded out into the deep water.   One
week they discussed " The Infancy of Nations," and after
that, " The Dæmonic Element in Music," " Napoleon
III " and " Fatalism in History."   Despite its praiseworthy earnestness, this program causes a smile — and
so does the transformation of the retiring and well-
scrubbed little Nietzsche we have been observing into the
long, gaunt Nietzsche of 14, with a yearning for the com-
panionship of his fellows, and a voice beginning to grow

comically harsh and deep, and a mind awhirl with unutterable things.

Nietzsche was a brilliant and spectacular pupil and soon won a scholarship at Pforta, a famous and ancient preparatory academy not far away. Pforta, in those days, was of a dignity comparable to Eton's or Harrow's. It was a great school, but tradition overpowered it. Violent combats between amateur sages were not encouraged: it was a place for gentlemen to acquire Euclid and the languages in a decent, gentlemanly way, and not an arena for gawky country philosophers to prance about in. But Nietzsche, by this time, had already become a frank rebel and delighted in elaborating and controverting the doctrines of the learned doctors. He drew up a series of epigrams under the head of " *Ideen* " and thought so well of them that he sent them home, to astonish and alarm his mother. Some of them exhibited a quite remarkable faculty for pithy utterance — as, for example, " War begets poverty and poverty begets peace " — while others were merely opaque renderings of thoughts half formed. He began to believe in his own mental cunning, with a sincerity which never left him, and, as a triumphant proof of it, he drew up a series of syllogisms designed to make homesickness wither and die. Thus he wrestled with life's problems as his boy's eyes saw them.

All this was good training for the philosopher, but to the Pforta professors it gave disquiet. Nietzsche became a bit too sure of himself and a bit too arrogant for discipline. It seemed to him a waste of time to wrestle with the studies that every oafish baron's son and future guardsman sought to master. He neglected mathematics and gave himself up to the hair-splitting of the Eleatics and the Pythagoreans, the Sophists and the Skeptics. He pronounced his high curse and anathema upon geography and would have none of it. The result was that when he went up for final examination he writhed and floundered miserably and came within an ace of being set down for further and more diligent labor with his books. Only his remarkable mastery of the German language and his vast knowledge of Christian doctrine — a legacy from his pious childhood — saved him. The old Nietzsche — the shrinking mother's darling of Naumburg — was now but a memory. The Nietzsche that went up to Bonn was a young man with a touch of cynicism and one not a little disposed to pit his sneer against the jurisprudence of the world: a young man with a swagger, a budding moustache and a head full of violently novel ideas about everything under the sun.

Nietzsche entered Bonn in October, 1864, when he was just 20 years old. He was enrolled as a student of philology and theology, but the latter was a mere concession to family faith and tradition, made grudgingly, and after the first semester, the reverend doctors of exegetics knew him no more. At the start he thought the university a delightful place and its people charming. The classrooms and beer gardens were full of young Germans like himself, who debated the doings of Bismarck, composed eulogies of Darwin, sang Rabelaisian songs in bad Latin, kept dogs, wore ribbons on their walking sticks, fought duels, and drank unlimited steins of pale beer. In the youth of every man there comes over him a sudden yearning to be a good fellow: to be " Bill " or " Jim " to multitudes, and to go down into legend with Sir John Falstaff and Tom Jones. This melancholy madness seized upon Nietzsche during his first year at Bonn. He frequented the theatres and posed as a connoisseur of opera *bouffe*, malt liquor and the female form divine. He went upon students' walking tours and carved his name upon the mutilated tables of country inns. He joined a student corps, bought him a little cap and set up shop as a devil of a fellow. His mother was not poor, but she could not afford the outlays that these ambitious enterprises required. Friedrich overdrew his allowance and the good woman, no doubt, wept about it, as mothers will, and wondered that learning came so dear.

But the inevitable reaction followed. Nietzsche was not designed by nature for a hero of pot-houses and duelling sheds. The old fastidiousness asserted itself — that queer, unhealthy fastidiousness which, in his childhood, had set him apart from other boys, and was destined, all his life long, to make him shrink from too intimate contact with his fellow-men. The touch of the crowd disgusted him: he had an almost insane fear of demeaning himself. All of this feeling had been obscured for awhile, by the strange charm of new delights and new companions, but in the end, the gloomy spinner of fancies triumphed over the university buck. Nietzsche resigned from his student corps, burned his walking sticks, foreswore smoking and roistering, and bade farewell to Johann Strauss and Offenbach forever. The days of his youth — of his care-free, merry gamboling — were over. Hereafter he was all solemnity and all seriousness.

" From these early experiences," says his sister, " there

remained with him a life-long aversion to smoking, beer-drinking and the whole *biergemüthlichkeit.* He maintained that people who drank beer and smoked pipes were absolutely incapable of understanding him. Such people, he thought, lacked the delicacy and clearness of perception necessary to grasp profound and subtle problems."

THE BEGINNINGS OF THE PHILOSOPHER

AT Bonn Nietzsche became a student of Ritschl, the famous philologist,[1] and when Ritschl left Bonn for Leipsic, Nietzsche followed him. All traces of the good fellow had disappeared and the student that remained was not unlike those sophomores of medieval Toulouse who " rose from bed at 4 o'clock, and having prayed to God, went at 5 o'clock to their studies, their big books under their arms, their inkhorns and candles in their hands." Between teacher and pupil there grew up a bond of strong friendship. Nietzsche was taken, too, under the wing of motherly old Frau Ritschl, who invited him to her afternoons of coffee and cinnamon cake and to her evening soirées, where he met the great men of the university world and the eminent strangers who came and went. To Ritschl the future philosopher owed many things, indeed, including his sound knowledge of the ancients, his first (and last) university appointment and his meeting with Richard Wagner. Nietzsche always looked back

[1] Friedrich Wilhelm Ritschl (1806-1876), the foremost philologist of modern times. He became a professor of classical literature and rhetoric in 1839 and founded the science of historical literary criticism, as we know it to-day.

upon these days with pleasure and there was ever a warm spot in his heart for the kindly old professor who led him up to grace.

Two years or more were thus spent, and then, in the latter part of 1867, Nietzsche began his term of compulsory military service in the fourth regiment of Prussian field artillery. He had hoped to escape because he was near-sighted and the only son of a widow, but a watchful *oberst-lieutenant* found loopholes in the law and so ensnared him. He seems to have been some sort of officer, for a photograph of the period shows him with epaulets and a sword. But lieutenant or sergeant, soldiering was scarcely his forte, and he cut a sorry figure on a horse. After a few months of unwilling service, in fact, he had a riding accident and came near dying as his father had died before him. As it was he wrenched his breast muscles so badly that he was condemned by a medical survey and discharged from the army.

During his long convalescence he busied himself with philological studies and began his first serious professional work — essays on the Theogony of Hesiod, the sources of Diogenes Laërtius and the eternal strife between Hesiod and Homer. He also made an index to an elaborate collection of German historical fragments and performed odd tasks of like sort for various professors. In October, 1868, he returned to Leipsic — not as an undergraduate, but as a special student. This change was advantageous, for it gave him greater freedom of action and protected him from that student *bonhomie* he had learned to despise. Again old Ritschl was his teacher and friend and again Frau Ritschl welcomed him to her *salon* and gave him of her good counsel and her excellent coffee.

Meanwhile there had occurred something that was destined to direct and color the whole stream of his life. This was his discovery of Arthur Schopenhauer. In the 60's, it would appear, the great pessimist was still scarcely more than a name in the German universities, which, for all their later heterodoxy, clung long to their ancient first causes. Nietzsche knew nothing of him, and in the seminaries of Leipsic not a soul maintained him. Of Kant and of Hegel there was talk unlimited, and of Lotze and Fichte there were riotous disputations that roared and raged about the class-room of Fechner, then the university professor of philosophy. But of Schopenhauer nothing was heard, and so, when Nietzsche, rambling through an old Leipsic bookshop, happened upon a second-hand copy of " *Die Welt als Wille und Vorstellung*," [1] a new world came floating into his view. This was in 1865.

" I took the book to my lodgings," he said years afterward, " and flung myself on a sofa and read and read and read. It seemed as if Schopenhauer were addressing me personally. I felt his enthusiasm and seemed to see him before me. Every line cried aloud for renunciation, denial, resignation ! "

So much for the first flush of the ecstasy of discovery. That Nietzsche entirely agreed with everything in the book, even in his wildest transports of admiration, is rather doubtful. He was but 21 — the age of great passions and

[1] Arthur Schopenhauer (1788-1860) published this book, his *magnum opus*, at Leipsic in 1819. It has been translated into English as " The World as Will and Idea" and has appeared in many editions.

great romance — and he was athirst for some writing that would solve the problems left unanswered by the accepted sages, but it is probable that when he shouted the Schopenhauer manifesto loudest he read into the text wild variations of his own. The premises of the pessimist gave credit and order to thoughts that had been rising up in his own mind; but the conclusions, if he subscribed to them at all, led him far afield. No doubt he was like one of those fantastic messiahs of new cults who search the scriptures for testimony — and find it. Late in life, when he was accused of inconsistency in first deifying Schopenhauer and then damning him, he made this defense, and despite the derisive sneers of his enemies, it seemed a fairly good one.

Schopenhauer's argument, to put it briefly, was that the will to exist — the primary instinct of life — was the eternal first cause of all human actions, motives and ideas. The old philosophers of Christendom had regarded intelligence as the superior of instinct. Some of them thought that an intelligent god ruled the universe and that nothing happened without his knowledge and desire. Others believed that man was a free agent, that whatever he did was the result of his own thought and choice, and that it was right, in consequence, to condemn him to hell for his sins and to exalt him to heaven for any goodness he might chance to show. Schopenhauer turned all this completely about. Intelligence, he said, was not the source of will, but its effect. When life first appeared upon earth, it had but one aim and object: that of perpetuating itself. This instinct, he said, was still at the bottom of every function of all living beings. Intelligence grew out of the fact that mankind, in the course of ages, began to notice that certain manifestations of the will to live were followed by certain invariable results. This capacity of perceiving was followed by a capacity for remembering, which in turn produced a capacity for anticipating. An intelligent man, said Schopenhauer, was merely one who remembered so many facts (the result either of personal experience or of the transmitted experience of others) that he could separate them into groups and observe their relationship, one to the other, and hazard a close guess as to their future effects; *i. e.* could reason about them.

Going further, Schopenhauer pointed out that this will to exist, this instinct to preserve and protect life, this old Adam, was to blame for the unpleasant things of life as well as for the good things — that it produced avarice, hatred and murder just as well as industry, resourcefulness and courage — that it led. men to seek means of killing one another as well as means of tilling the earth and pro- curing food and raiment. He showed, yet further, that its bad effects were a great deal more numerous than its good effects and so accounted for the fact — which many men before him had observed — that life, at best, held more of sorrow than of joy.[1]

The will-to-live, argued Schopenhauer, was responsible for all this. Pain, he believed, would always outweigh pleasure in this sad old world until men ceased to want to live — until no one desired food or drink or house or wife

---

[1] Schopenhauer *("Nächträge zur Lehre vom Leiden der Welt")* puts the argument thus : " Pleasure is never as pleasant as we expect it to be and pain is always more painful. The pain in the world always out· weighs the pleasure. If you don't believe it, compare the respective feel- ings of two animals, one of which is eating the other."

or money. To put it more briefly, he held that true happiness would be impossible until mankind had killed will with will, which is to say, until the will-to-live was willed out of existence. Therefore the happiest man was the one who had come nearest this end — the man who had killed all the more obvious human desires, hopes and aspirations — the solitary ascetic — the monk in his cell — the soaring, starving poet — the cloud-enshrouded philosopher.

Nietzsche very soon diverged from this conclusion. He believed, with Schopenhauer, that human life, at best, was often an infliction and a torture, but in his very first book he showed that he admired, not the ascetic who tried to escape from the wear and tear of life altogether, but the proud, stiff-necked hero who held his balance in the face of both seductive pleasure and staggering pain; who cultivated within himself a sublime indifference, so that happiness and misery, to him, became mere words, and no catastrophe, human or superhuman, could affright or daunt him. [1]

It is obvious that there is a considerable difference between these ideas, for all their similarity in origin and for all Nietzsche's youthful worship of Schopenhauer. Nietzsche, in fact, was so enamoured by the honesty and originality of what may be called the data of Schopenhauer's philosophy that he took the philosophy itself rather on trust and did not begin to inquire into it closely or to

---

[1] Later on, in "*Menschliches allzu Menschliches*," II, Nietzsche argued that the ascetic was either a coward, who feared the temptations of pleasure and the agonies of pain, or an exhausted worldling who had become satiated with life.

compare it carefully with his own ideas until after he had committed himself in a most embarrassing fashion. The same phenomena is no curiosity in religion, science or politics.

Before a realization of these differences quite dawned upon Nietzsche he was busied with other affairs. In 1869, when he was barely 25, he was appointed, upon Ritschl's recommendation, to the chair of classical philology at the University of Basel, in Switzerland, an ancient stronghold of Lutheran theology. He had no degree, but the University of Leipsic promptly made him a doctor of philosophy, without thesis or examination, and on April 13th he left the old home at Naumburg to assume his duties. Thus passed that pious household. The grandmother had died long before — in 1856 — and one of the maiden aunts had preceded her to the grave by a year. The other, long ill, had followed in 1867. But Nietzsche's mother lived until 1897, though gradually estranged from him by his opinions, and his sister, as we know, survived him.

Nietzsche was officially professor of philology, but he also became teacher of Greek in the pedagogium attached to the University. He worked like a Trojan and mixed Schopenhauer and Hesiod in his class-room discourses upon the origin of Greek verbs and other such dull subjects. But it is not recorded that he made a very profound impression, except upon a relatively small circle. His learning was abyssmal, but he was far too impatient and unsympathetic to be a good teacher. His classes, in fact, were never large, except in the pedagogium. This, however, may have been partly due to the fact that in 1869, as in later years, there were comparatively few persons impractical enough to spend their days and nights in the study of philology.

In 1870 came the Franco-Prussian war and Nietzsche decided to go to the front. Despite his hatred of all the cant of cheap patriotism and his pious thankfulness that he was a Pole and not a German, he was at bottom a good citizen and perfectly willing to suffer and bleed for his country. But unluckily he had taken out Swiss naturalization papers in order to be able to accept his appointment at Basel, and so, as the subject of a neutral state, he had to go to the war, not as a warrior, but as a hospital steward.

Even as it was, Nietzsche came near giving his life to Germany. He was not strong physically — he had suffered from severe headaches as far back as 1862 — and his hard work at Basel had further weakened him. On the battle-fields of France he grew ill. Diphtheria and what seems to have been cholera morbus attacked him and when he finally reached home again he was a neurasthenic wreck. Ever thereafter his life was one long struggle against disease. He suffered from migraine, that most terrible disease of the nerves, and chronic catarrh of the stomach made him a dyspeptic. Unable to eat or sleep, he resorted to narcotics, and according to his sister, he continued their use throughout his life. " He wanted to get well quickly," she says, " and so took double doses." Nietzsche, indeed, was a slave to drugs, and more than once in after life, long before insanity finally ended his career, he gave evidence of it.

Despite his illness he insisted upon resuming work, but during the following winter he was obliged to take a vacation in Italy. Meanwhile he had delivered lectures to his classes on the Greek drama and two of these he revised and published, in 1872, as his first book, "*Die Geburt der Tragödie*" ("The Birth of Tragedy"). Engelmann, the great Leipsic publisher, declined it, but Fritsch, of the same city, put it into type.[1] This book greatly pleased his friends, but the old-line philologists of the time thought it wild and extravagant, and it almost cost Nietzsche his professorship. Students were advised to keep away from him, and during the winter of 1872-3, it is said, he had no pupils at all.

Nevertheless the book, for all its iconoclasm, was an event. It sounded Nietzsche's first, faint battle-cry and put the question mark behind many things that seemed honorable and holy in philology. Most of the philologists of that time were German savants of the comic-paper sort, and their lives were spent in wondering why one Greek poet made the name of a certain plant masculine while another made it feminine. Nietzsche, passing over such scholastic futilities, burrowed down into the heart of Greek literature. Why, he asked himself, did the Greeks take pleasure in witnessing representations of bitter, hopeless conflicts, and how did this form of entertainment arise among them? Later on, his conclusions will be given at length, but in this place it may be well to sketch them in

[1] Begun in 1869, this maiden work was dedicated to Richard Wagner. At Wagner's suggestion Nietzsche eliminated a great deal of matter in the original draft. The full title was "The Birth of Tragedy from the Spirit of Music," but this was changed, in 1886, when a third edition was printed, to "The Birth of Tragedy, or Hellenism and Pessimism." Nietzsche then also added a long preface, entitled "An Attempt at Self-Criticism." The material originally excluded was published in 1896.

outline, because of the bearing they have upon his later
work, and even upon the trend of his life.

In ancient Greece, he pointed out at the start, Apollo
was the god of art — of life as it was recorded and interpreted — and Bacchus Dionysus was the god of life itself
— of eating, drinking and making merry, of dancing and
roistering, of everything that made men acutely conscious
of the vitality and will within them. The difference between the things they represented has been well set forth
in certain homely verses addressed by Rudyard Kipling
to Admiral Robley D. Evans, U. S. N.:

> Zogbaum draws with a pencil
>   And I do things with a pen,
> But you sit up in a conning tower,
>   Bossing eight hundred men.
>
> To him that hath shall be given
>   And that's why these books are sent
> To the man who has *lived* more stories
>   Than Zogbaum or I could *invent*.

Here we have the plain distinction: Zogbaum and
Kipling are apollonic, while Evans is dionysian. Epic
poetry, sculpture, painting and story-telling are apollonic:
they represent, not life itself, but some one man's visualized
idea of life. But dancing, great deeds and, in some cases,
music, are dionysian: they are part and parcel of life as
some actual human being, or collection of human beings,
is living it.

Nietzsche maintained that Greek art was at first
apollonic, but that eventually there appeared a dionysian

influence — the fruit, perhaps, of contact with primitive, barbarous peoples. Ever afterward there was constant conflict between them and this conflict was the essence of Greek tragedy. As Sarcey tells us, a play, to hold our attention, must depict some sort of battle, between man and man or idea and idea. In the melodrama of today the battle is between hero and villain; in the ancient Greek tragedy it was between Apollo and Dionysus, between the life contemplative and the life strenuous, between law and outlaw, between the devil and the seraphim.

Nietzsche, as we shall see, afterward applied this distinction in morals and life as well as in art. He called himself a dionysian and the crowning volume of his system of philosophy, which he had barely started when insanity overtook him, was to have been called " Dionysus."

III

HAVING given birth, in this theory of Greek tragedy, to an idea which, whatever its defects otherwise, was at least original, understandable and workable, Nietzsche began to be conscious, as it were, of his own intellect — or, in his sister's phrase, "to understand what a great man he was." During his first years at Basel he had cut quite a figure in academic society, for he was an excellent musician, he enjoyed dancing and he had plenty of pretty things to say to the ladies. But as his ideas clarified and he found himself more and more in conflict with the pundits about him, he withdrew within himself, and in the end he had few friends save Richard and Cosima Wagner, who lived at Tribschen, not far away. To one of his turn of mind, indeed, the atmosphere of the college town was bound to grow oppressive soon or late. Acutely aware of his own superiority, he showed no patience with the unctuous complacency of dons and dignitaries, and so he became embroiled in various conflicts, and even his admirers among his colleagues seldom ventured upon friendly advances.

There are critics who see in all this proof that Nietzsche showed signs of insanity from early manhood, but as a

matter of fact it was his abnormally accurate vision and
not a vision gone awry, that made him stand so aloof
from his fellows. In the vast majority of those about him
he saw the coarse metal of sham and pretense beneath
the showy gilding of learning. He had before him, at
close range, a good many of the great men of his time —
the intellectuals whose word was law in the schools. He
saw them on parade and he saw them in their shirt sleeves.
What wonder that he lost all false reverence for them and
began to estimate them in terms, not of their dignity and
reputation, but of their actual credibility and worth?
It was inevitable that he should compare his own ideas
to theirs, and it was inevitable that he should perceive the
difference between his own fanatical striving for the truth
and the easy dependence upon precedent and formula
which lay beneath their booming bombast. Thus there
arose in him a fiery loathing for all authority, and a firm
belief that his own opinion regarding any matter to which
he had given thought was as sound, at the least, as any
other man's. Thenceforth the assertive " *ich* " began to
besprinkle his discourse and his pages. " *I* condemn
Christianity. *I* have given to mankind. . . . *I* was never
yet modest. . . . *I* think. . . . *I* say. . . . *I* do. . . ."
Thus he hurled his javelin at authority until the end.

To those about him, perhaps, Nietzsche seemed wild
and impossible, but it is not recorded that any one ever
looked upon him as ridiculous. His high brow, bared by
the way in which he brushed his hair; his keen eyes, with
their monstrous overhanging brows, and his immense, un-
trimmed moustache gave him an air of alarming earnestness. Beside the pedagogues about him — with their

well-barbered, professorial beards, their bald heads and their learned spectacles — he seemed like some incomprehensible foreigner. The exotic air he bore delighted him and he cultivated it assiduously. He regarded himself as a Polish grandee set down by an unkind fate among German shopkeepers, and it gave him vast pleasure when the hotel porters and street beggars, deceived by his disorderly façade, called him " The Polack."

Thus he lived and had his being. The inquisitive boy of old Naumburg, the impudent youth of Pforta and the academic free lance of Bonn and Leipsic had become merged into a man sure of himself and contemptuous of all whose search for the truth was hampered or hedged about by any respect for statute or precedent. He saw that the philosophers and sages of the day, in many of their most gorgeous flights of logic, started from false premises, and he observed the fact that certain of the dominant moral, political and social maxims of the time were mere foolishness. It struck him, too, that all of this faulty ratiocination — all of this assumption of outworn doctrines and dependence upon exploded creeds — was not confined to the confessedly orthodox. There was fallacy no less disgusting in the other camp. The professed apostles of revolt were becoming as bad as the old crusaders and apologists.

Nietzsche harbored a fevered yearning to call all of these false prophets to book and to reduce their fine axioms to absurdity. Accordingly, he planned a series of twenty-four pamphlets and decided to call them " *Unzeitgemässe Betrachtungen*," which may be translated as " Inopportune Speculations," or more clearly, " Essays in Sham-Smashing." In looking about for a head to smash in essay number one, his eye, naturally enough, alighted upon that of David Strauss, the favorite philosopher and fashionable iconoclast of the day. Strauss had been a preacher but had renounced the cloth and set up shop as a critic of Christianity.[1] He had labored with good intentions, no doubt, but the net result of all his smug agnosticism was that his disciples were as self-satisfied, bigoted and prejudiced in the garb of agnostics as they had been before as Christians. Nietzsche's clear eye saw this and in the first of his little pamphlets, " *David Strauss, der Bekenner und der Schriftsteller* " (" David Strauss, the Confessor and the Writer "), he bore down upon Strauss' *bourgeoise* pseudo-skepticism most savagely. This was in 1873.

" Strauss," he said, " utterly evades the question, What is the meaning of life? He had an opportunity to show courage, to turn his back upon the Philistines, and to boldly deduce a new morality from that constant warfare which destroys all but the fittest, but to do this would have required a love of truth infinitely higher than that which spends itself in violent invectives against parsons, miracles and the historical humbug of the resurrection. Strauss had no such courage. Had he worked out the Darwinian doctrine to its last decimal he would have had the Philistines against him to a man. As it is, they are with him. He has wasted his time in combatting Christianity's non-essentials. For the idea at the bottom of it he has pro-

---

[1] David Friedrich Strauss (1808–74) sprang into fame with his " *Das Leben Jesu*," 1835 (Eng. tr. by George Eliot, 1846), but the book which served as Nietzsche's target was " *Der alte und der neue Glaube* " (" The Old Faith and the New "), 1872.

posed no substitute. In consequence, his philosophy is stale." [1]

As a distinguished critic has pointed out, Nietzsche's attack was notable, not only for its keen analysis and ruthless honesty, but also for its courage. It required no little bravery, three years after Sedan, to tell the Germans that the new culture which constituted their pride was rotten, and that, unless it were purified in the fire of absolute truth, it might one day wreck their civilization.

In the year following Nietzsche returned to the attack with a criticism of history, which was then the fashionable science of the German universities, on account, chiefly, of its usefulness in exploding the myths of Christianity. He called his essay "*Vom Nutzen und Nachtheil der Historie für das Leben*" (" On the Good and Bad Effects of History upon Human Life ") and in it he took issue with the reigning pedagogues and professors of the day. There was much hard thinking and no little good writing in this essay and it made its mark. The mere study of history, argued Nietzsche, unless some definite notion regarding the destiny of man were kept ever in mind, was misleading and confusing. There was great danger in assuming that everything which happened was part of some divine and mysterious plan for the ultimate attainment of perfection. As a matter of fact, many historical events were meaningless, and this was particularly true of those expressions of " governments, public opinion and majorities " which historians were prone to accentuate. To Nietzsche the ideas and doings of peoples seemed infinitely less important than the ideas and doings of

[1] " *David Strauss, der Bekenner und der Schriftsteller*," § 7.

exceptional individuals. To put it more simply, he
believed that one man, Hannibal, was of vastly more importance to the world than all the other Carthaginians
of his time taken together. Herein we have a reappearance
of Dionysus and a foreshadowing of the *herrenmoral* and
superman of later days.

Nietzsche's next essay was devoted to Schopenhauer
and was printed in 1874. He called it " *Schopenhauer
als Erzieher* " (" Schopenhauer as a Teacher ") and in it
he laid his burnt offering upon the altar of the great pessimist, who was destined to remain his hero, if no longer
his god, until the end. Nietzsche was already beginning
to read rebellious ideas of his own into " The World as
Will and Idea," but in two things — the theory of will and
the impulse toward truth — he and Schopenhauer were
ever as one. He preached a holy war upon all those
influences which had made the apostle of pessimism, in
his life-time, an unheard outcast. He raged against the
narrowness of university schools of philosophy and denounced all governmental interference in speculation —
whether it were expressed crudely, by inquisitorial laws
and the *Index*, or softly and insidiously, by the bribery of
comfortable berths and public honors.

" Experience teaches us," he said, " that nothing stands
so much in the way of developing great philosophers as
the custom of supporting bad ones in state universities.
. . . It is the popular theory that the posts given to the
latter make them ' free ' to do original work; as a matter
of fact, the effect is quite the contrary. . . . No state
would ever dare to patronize such men as Plato and
Schopenhauer. And why? Because the state is always

afraid of them. . . . It seems to me that there is need
for a higher tribunal outside the universities to critically
examine the doctrines they teach. As soon as philosophers
are willing to resign their salaries, they will constitute such
a tribunal. Without pay and without honors, it will be
able to free itself from the prejudices of the age. Like
Schopenhauer, it will be the judge of the so-called culture
around it." [1]

Years later Nietzsche denied that, in this essay, he
committed himself irretrievably to the whole philosophy
. of Schopenhauer and a fair reading bears him out. He
was not defending Schopenhauer's doctrine of renunciation, but merely asking that he be given a hearing. He
was pleading the case of foes as well as of friends : all he
asked was that the forum be opened to every man who had
something new to say.

Nietzsche regarded Schopenhauer as a king among
philosophers because he shook himself entirely free of the
dominant thought of his time. In an age marked, beyond
everything, by humanity's rising reliance upon human
reason, he sought to show that reason was a puny offshoot
of an irresistible natural law — the law of self-preservation.
Nietzsche admired the man's courage and agreed with
him in his insistence that this law was at the bottom of
all sentient activity, but he was never a subscriber to
Schopenhauer's surrender and despair. From the very
start, indeed, he was a prophet of defiance, and herein
his divergence from Schopenhauer was infinite. As his
knowledge broadened and his scope widened, he expanded
and developed his philosophy, and often he found it

[1] *" Schopenhauer als Erzieher,"* § 8.

necessary to modify it in detail. But that he ever turned upon himself in fundamentals is untrue. Nietzsche at 40 and Nietzsche at 25 were essentially the same. The germ of practically all his writings lies in his first book — nay, it is to be found further back: in the wild speculations of his youth.

The fourth of the " *Unzeitgemässe Betrachtungen* " (and the last, for the original design of the series was not carried out) was " Richard Wagner in Bayreuth." [1] This was published in 1876 and neither it nor the general subject of Nietzsche's relations with Wagner need be considered here. In a subsequent chapter the whole matter will be discussed. For the present, it is sufficient to say that Nietzsche met Wagner through the medium of Ritschl's wife; that they became fast friends; that Nietzsche hailed the composer as a hero sent to make the drama an epitome of the life unfettered and unbounded, of life defiant and joyful; that Wagner, after starting from the Schopenhauer base, travelled toward St. Francis rather than toward Dionysus, and that Nietzsche, after vain expostulations, read the author of " Parsifal " out of meeting and pronounced him anathema. It was all a case of misunderstanding. Wagner was an artist, and not a philosopher. Right or wrong, Christianity was beautiful, and as a thing of beauty it called aloud to him. To Nietzsche beauty seemed a mere phase of truth.

[1] According to Nietzsche's original plan the series was to have included pamphlets on " Literature and the Press," " Art and Painters," " The Higher Education," " German and Counter-German," " War and the Nation," " The Teacher," " Religion," " Society and Trade," " Society and Natural Science," and " The City," with an epilogue entitled " The Way to Freedom."

It was during this period of preliminary skirmishing that Nietzsche's ultimate philosophy began to formulate itself. He saw clearly that there was something radically wrong with the German culture of the day — that many things esteemed right and holy were, in reality, unspeakable, and that many things under the ban of church and state were far from wrong in themselves. He saw, too, that there had grown up a false logic and that its taint was upon the whole of contemporary thought. Men maintained propositions plainly erroneous and excused themselves by the plea that ideals were greater than actualities. The race was subscribing to one thing and practicing another. Christianity was official, but not a single real Christian was to be found in all Christendom. Thousands bowed down to men and ideas that they despised and denounced things that every sane man knew were necessary and inevitable. The result was a flavor of dishonesty and hypocrisy in all human affairs. In the abstract the laws — of the church, the state and society — were looked upon as impeccable, but every man, in so far as they bore upon him personally, tried his best to evade them.

Other philosophers, in Germany and elsewhere, had made the same observation and there was in progress a grand assault-at-arms upon old ideas. Huxley and Spencer, in England, were laboring hard in the vineyard planted by Darwin; Ibsen, in Norway, was preparing for his epoch-making life-work, and in far America Andrew D. White and others were battling to free education from the bonds of theology. Thus it will be seen that, at the start, Nietzsche was no more a pioneer than any one of a dozen other men. Some of these other men, indeed, were far better equipped for the fray than he, and their services, for a long while, seemed a great deal more important. But it was his good fortune, before his working days were over, to press the conflict much further afield than the others. Beginning where they ended, he fought his way into the very citadel of the enemy.

His attack upon Christianity, which is described at length later on, well exemplifies this uncompromising thoroughness. Nietzsche saw that the same plan would have to be pursued in examining all other concepts — religious, political or social. It would be necessary to pass over surface symptoms and go to the heart of things: to tunnel down deep into ideas; to trace out their history and seek out their origins. There were no willing hands to help him in this: it was, in a sense, a work new to the world. In consequence Nietzsche perceived that he would have to go slowly and that it would be needful to make every step plain. It was out of the question to expect encouragement: if the task attracted notice at all, this notice would probably take the form of blundering opposition. But Nietzsche began his clearing and his road cutting with a light heart. The men of his day might call him accursed, but in time his honesty would shame all denial. This was his attitude always: he felt that neglect and opprobrium were all in his day's work and he used to say that if ever the generality of men endorsed any idea that he had advanced he would be convinced at once that he had made an error.

In his preliminary path-finding Nietzsche concerned himself much with the history of specific ideas. He showed how the thing which was a sin in one age became the virtue of the next. He attacked hope, faith and charity in this way, and he made excursions into nearly every field of human thought — from art to primary education. All of this occupied the first half of the 70's. Nietzsche was in indifferent health and his labors tired him so greatly that he thought more than once of giving up his post at Basel, with its dull round of lecturing and quizzing. But his private means at this time were not great enough to enable him to surrender his salary and so he had to hold on. He thought, too, of going to Vienna to study the natural sciences so that he might attain the wide and certain knowledge possessed by Spencer, but the same considerations forced him to abandon the plan. He spent his winters teaching and investigating and his summers at various watering-places — from Tribschen, in Switzerland, where the Wagners were his hosts, to Sorrento, in Italy.

At Sorrento he happened to take lodgings in a house which also sheltered Dr. Paul Rée, the author of " Psychological Observations," " The Origin of Moral Feelings," and other metaphysical works. That Rée gave him great assistance he acknowledged himself in later years, but that his ideas were, in any sense, due to this chance meeting (as Max Nordau would have us believe) is out of the question, for, as we have seen, they were already pretty clear in his mind a long while before. But Rée widened his outlook a great deal, it is evident, and undoubtedly made him acquainted with the English naturalists who had sprung up as spores of Darwin, and with a number of great Frenchmen — Montaigne, La-rochefoucauld, La Bruyère, Fontenelle, Vauvenargues and Chamfort.

Nietzsche had been setting down his thoughts and conclusions in the form of brief memoranda and as he grew better acquainted with the French philosophers, many of whom published their works as collections of aphorisms, he decided to employ that form himself. Thus he began to arrange the notes which were to be given to the world as " *Menschliches allzu Menschliches* " (" Human, All-too Human "). In 1876 he got leave from Basel and gave his whole time to the work. During the winter of 1876-7, with the aid of a disciple named Bernhard Cron (better known as Peter Gast) he prepared the first volume for the press. Nietzsche was well aware that it would make a sensation and while it was being set up his courage apparently forsook him and he suggested to his publisher that it be sent forth anonymously. But the latter would not hear of it and so the first part left the press in 1878.

As the author had expected, the book provoked a fine frenzy of horror among the pious. The first title chosen for it, " *Die Pflugschar* " (" The Plowshare "), and the one finally selected, " Human, All-too Human," indicate that it was an attempt to examine the underside of human ideas. In it Nietzsche challenged the whole of current morality. He showed that moral ideas were not divine, but human, and that, like all things human, they were subject to change. He showed that good and evil were but relative terms, and that it was impossible to say, finally and absolutely, that a certain action was right and another wrong. He applied the acid of critical analysis to a hundred and one specific ideas, and his general conclusion, to put it briefly, was that no human being had a right, in any way or form, to judge or direct the actions of any other being. Herein we have, in a few words, that gospel of individualism which all our sages preach today.[1]

Nietzsche sent a copy of the book to Wagner and the great composer was so appalled that he was speechless. Even the author's devoted sister, who worshipped him as an intellectual god, was unable to follow him. Germany, in general, pronounced the work a conglomeration of crazy fantasies and wild absurdities — and Nietzsche smiled with satisfaction. In 1879 he published the second volume, to which he gave the sub-title of " *Vermischte Meinungen und Sprüche* " (" Miscellaneous Opinions and Aphorisms ") and shortly thereafter he finally resigned his chair at Basel. The third part of the book appeared in 1880 as " *Der Wanderer und sein Schatten* " (" The Wanderer and His Shadow "). The three volumes were published as two in 1886 as " *Menschliches allzu Menschliches,*" with the explanatory sub-title, " *Ein Buch für Freie Geister* " ("A Book for Free Spirits ").

[1] It must be remembered, in considering all of Nietzsche's writings, that when he spoke of a human being, he meant a being of the higher sort — *i. e.* one capable of clear reasoning. He regarded the drudge class, which is obviously unable to think for itself, as unworthy of consideration. Its highest mission, he believed, was to serve and obey the master class. But he held that there should be no artificial barriers to the rise of an individual born to the drudge class who showed an accidental capacity for independent reasoning. Such an individual, he believed, should be admitted, *ipso facto*, to the master class. Naturally enough, he held to the converse too. *Vide* the chapter on " Civilization."

IV

THE PROPHET OF THE SUPERMAN

NIETZSCHE spent the winter of 1879-80 at Naumburg, his old home. During the ensuing year he was very ill, indeed, and for awhile he believed that he had but a short while to live. Like all such invalids he devoted a great deal of time to observing and discussing his condition. He became, indeed, a hypochondriac of the first water and began to take a sort of melancholy pleasure in his infirmities. He sought relief at all the baths and cures of Europe: he took hot baths, cold baths, salt-water baths and mud baths. Every new form of pseudo-therapy found him in its freshman class. To owners of sanitoria and to inventors of novel styles of massage, irrigation, sweating and feeding he was a joy unlimited. But he grew worse instead of better.

After 1880, his life was a wandering one. His sister, after her marriage, went to Paraguay for a while, and during her absence Nietzsche made his progress from the mountains to the sea, and then back to the mountains again. He gave up his professorship that he might spend his winters in Italy and his summers in the Engadine. In the face of all this suffering and travelling about, close application, of course, was out of the question. So he contented himself with working whenever and however his headaches, his doctors and the railway time-tables would permit — on hotel verandas, in cure-houses and in the woods. He would take long, solitary walks and struggle with his problems by the way. He swallowed more and more pills; he imbibed mineral waters by the gallon; he grew more and more moody and ungenial. One of his favorite haunts, in the winter time, was a verdant little neck of land that jutted out into Lake Maggiore. There he could think and dream undisturbed. One day, when he found that some one had placed a rustic bench on the diminutive peninsula, that passersby might rest, he was greatly incensed.

Nietzsche would make brief notes of his thoughts during his daylight rambles, and in the evenings would polish and expand them. As we have seen, his early books were sent to the printer as mere collections of aphorisms, without effort at continuity. Sometimes a dozen subjects are considered in two pages, and then again, there is occasionally a little essay of three or four pages. Nietzsche chose this form because it had been used by the French philosophers he admired, and because it well suited the methods of work that a pain-racked frame imposed upon him.

He was ever in great fear that some of his precious ideas would be lost to posterity — that death, the ever-threatening, would rob him of his rightful immortality and the world of his stupendous wisdom — and so he made efforts, several times, to engage an amanuensis capable of jotting down, after the fashion of Johnson's Boswell, the chance phrases that fell from his lips. His sister was too busy to undertake the task: whenever she was with him her whole time was employed in guarding him from lion-hunters, scrutinizing his daily fare and deftly inveigling him into answering his letters, brushing his clothes and getting his hair cut. Finally, Paul Rée and another friend, Fräulein von Meysenbug, brought to his notice a young Russian woman, Mlle. Lou Salomé, who professed vast interest in his work and offered to help him. But this arrangement quickly ended in disaster, for Nietzsche fell in love with the girl — she was only 20 — and pursued her over half of Europe when she fled. To add to the humors of the situation Rée fell in love with her too, and the two friends thus became foes and there was even some talk of a duel. Mlle. Salomé, however, went to Rée, and with his aid she later wrote a book about Nietzsche.[1] Frau Förster-Nietzsche sneers at that book, but the fact is not to be forgotten that she was very jealous of Mlle. Salomé, and gave constant proof of it by unfriendly word and act. In the end, the latter married one Prof. Andreas and settled down in Göttingen.

Early in 1881 Nietzsche published " *Morgenröte* " (" The Dawn of Day "). It was begun at Venice in 1880 and continued at Marienbad, Lago Maggiore and Genoa. It was, in a broad way, a continuation of " *Menschliches allzu Menschliches.*" It dealt with an infinite variety of subjects, from matrimony to Christianity, and from education to German patriotism. To all the test of fundamental truth was applied: of everything Nietzsche asked, not, Is it respectable or lawful? but, Is it essentially true? These early works, at best, were mere note-books.

[1] " *Friedrich Nietzsche in seinen Werken;* " Vienna, 1894.

Nietzsche saw that the ground would have to be plowed, that people would have to grow accustomed to the idea of questioning high and holy things, before a new system of philosophy would be understandable or possible. In " *Menschliches allzu Menschliches* " and in " *Morgenröte* " he undertook this preparatory cultivation.

The book which followed, " *Die fröhliche Wissenschaft* " (" The Joyful Science ") continued the same task. The first edition contained four parts and was published in 1882. In 1887 a fifth part was added. Nietzsche had now completed his plowing and was ready to sow his crop. He had demonstrated, by practical examples, that moral ideas were vulnerable, and that the Ten Commandments might be debated. Going further, he had adduced excellent historical evidence against the absolute truth of various current conceptions of right and wrong, and had traced a number of moral ideas back to decidedly lowly sources. His work so far had been entirely destructive and he had scarcely ventured to hint at his plans for a reconstruction of the scheme of things. As he himself says, he spent the four years between 1878 and 1882 in preparing the way for his later work.

" I descended," he says, " into the lowest depths, I searched to the bottom, I examined and pried into an old faith on which, for thousands of years, philosophers had built as upon a secure foundation. The old structures came tumbling down about me. I undermined our old faith in morals." [1]

This labor accomplished, Nietzsche was ready to set forth his own notion of the end and aim of existence. He

[1] Preface to " *Morgenröte*," § 2; autumn, 1886.

had shown that the old morality was like an apple rotten
at the core — that the Christian ideal of humility made
mankind weak and miserable; that many institutions
regarded with superstitious reverence, as the direct result
of commands from the creator (such, for instance, as the
family, the church and the state), were mere products
of man's "all-too-human" cupidity, cowardice, stupidity
and yearning for ease. He had turned the searchlight of
truth upon patriotism, charity and self-sacrifice. He
had shown that many things held to be utterly and un-
questionably good or bad by modern civilization were
once given quite different values — that the ancient Greeks
considered hope a sign of weakness, and mercy the attribute
of a fool, and that the Jews, in their royal days, looked
upon wrath, not as a sin, but as a virtue — and in general
he had demonstrated, by countless instances and arguments, that all notions of good and evil were mutable and
that no man could ever say, with utter certainty, that one
thing was right and another wrong.

The ground was now cleared for the work of reconstruction and the first structure that Nietzsche reared
was "Also sprach Zarathustra" ("Thus Spake Zoroaster"). This book, to which he gave the sub-title of
"Ein Buch für Alle und Keinen" ("A book for all and
none"), took the form of a fantastic, half-poetical half-
philosophical rhapsody. Nietzsche had been delving
into oriental mysticism and from the law-giver of the
ancient Persians he borrowed the name of his hero —
Zoroaster. But there was no further resemblance between
the two, and no likeness whatever between Nietzsche's
philosophy and that of the Persians.

The Zoroaster of the book is a sage who lives remote from mankind, and with no attendants but a snake and an eagle. The book is in four parts and all are made up of discourses by Zoroaster. These discourses are delivered to various audiences during the prophet's occasional wanderings and at the conferences he holds with various disciples in the cave that he calls home. They are decidedly oriental in form and recall the manner and phraseology of the biblical rhapsodists. Toward the end Nietzsche throws all restraint to the winds and indulges to his heart's content in the rare and exhilarating sport of blasphemy. There is a sort of parody of the last supper and Zoroaster's backsliding disciples engage in the grotesque and indecent worship of a jackass. Wagner and other enemies of the author appear, thinly veiled, as ridiculous buffoons.

In his discourses Zoroaster voices the Nietzschean idea of the superman — the idea that has come to be associated with Nietzsche more than any other. Later on, it will be set forth in detail. For the present, suffice it to say that it is the natural child of the notions put forward in Nietzsche's first book, " The Birth of Tragedy," and that it binds his entire life work together into one consistent, harmonious whole. The first part of " *Also sprach Zarathustra* " was published in 1883, the second part following in the same year, and the third part was printed in 1884. The last part was privately circulated among the author's friends in 1885, but was not given to the public until 1892, when the entire work was printed in one volume. As showing Nietzsche's wandering life, it may be recorded that the book was conceived in the Engadine and written in Genoa, Sils Maria, Nice and Mentone.

"*Jenseits von Gut und Böse*" ("Beyond Good and Evil") appeared in 1886. In this book Nietzsche elaborated and systematized his criticism of morals, and undertook to show why he considered modern civilization degrading. Here he finally formulated his definitions of master-morality and slave-morality, and showed how Christianity was necessarily the idea of a race oppressed and helpless, and eager to escape the lash of its masters.

"*Zur Genealogie der Moral*" ("The Genealogy of Morals"), which appeared in 1887, developed these propositions still further. In it there was also a partial return to Nietzsche's earlier manner, with its merciless analysis of moral concepts. In 1888 Nietzsche published a most vitriolic attack upon Wagner, under the title of "*Der Fall Wagner*" ("The Case of Wagner"), the burden of which was the author's discovery that the composer, starting, with him, from Schopenhauer's premises, had ended, not with the superman, but with the Man on the cross. "*Götzendämmerung*" ("The Twilight of the Idols") a sort of parody of Wagner's "*Götterdämmerung*" ("The Twilight of the Gods") followed in 1889. "*Nietzsche contra Wagner*" ("Nietzsche versus Wagner") was printed the same year. It was made up of extracts from the philosopher's early works, and was designed to prove that, contrary to the allegations of his enemies, he had not veered completely about in his attitude toward Wagner.

Meanwhile, despite the fact that his health was fast declining and he was approaching the verge of insanity, Nietzsche made plans for a great four volume work that was to sum up his philosophy and stand forever as his *magnum opus.* The four volumes, as he planned them, were to bear the following titles:

1. " *Der Antichrist: Versuch einer Kritik des Christenthums* " (" The Anti-Christ: an Attempt at a Criticism of Christianity ").

2. " *Der freie Geist: Kritik der Philosophie als einer nihilistichen Bewegung* " (" The Free Spirit: a Criticism of Philosophy as a Nihilistic Movement ").

3. " *Der Immoralist: Kritik der verhängnissvollsten Art von Unwissenheit, der Moral* " (" The Immoralist: a Criticism of That Fatal Species of Ignorance, Morality ").

4. " *Dionysus, Philosophie der ewigen Wiederkunft* " (" Dionysus, the Philosophy of Eternal Recurrence ").

This work was to be published under the general title of " *Der Wille zur Macht: Versuch einer Umwerthung aller Werthe* " (" The Will to Power: an Attempt at a Transvaluation of all Values "), but Nietzsche got no further than the first book, " *Der Antichrist,*" and a mass of rough notes for the others. " *Der Antichrist,*" probably the most brilliant piece of writing that Germany had seen in half a century, was written at great speed between September 3rd and September 30th, 1888, but it was not published until 1895, six years after the philosopher had laid down his work forever.

During that same year C. G. Naumann, the Leipsic publisher, began the issue of a definite edition of all his writings, in fifteen volumes, under the editorial direction of Frau Förster-Nietzsche, Dr. Fritz Koegel, Peter

Gast and E. von der Hellen. In this edition his notes for " *Der Wille zur Macht* " and his early philological essays were included. The notes are of great interest to the serious student of Nietzsche, for they show how some of his ideas changed with the years and point out the probable structure of his final system, but the general reader will find them chaotic, and often incomprehensible. In October, 1888, but three months before his breakdown, he began a critical autobiography with the title of " *Ecce Homo*," and it was completed in three weeks. It is an extremely frank and entertaining book, with such chapter headings as " Why I am so Wise," " Why I Write Such Excellent Books " and " Why I am a Fatality." In it Nietzsche sets forth his private convictions regarding a great many things, from cooking to climates, and discusses each of his books in detail. " *Ecce Homo* " was not printed until 1908, when it appeared at Leipsic in a limited edition of 1250 copies.

In January, 1889, at Turin, where he was living alone in very humble quarters, Nietzsche suddenly became hopelessly insane. His friends got news of it from his own hand. " I am Ferdinand de Lesseps," he wrote to Prof. Burckhardt of Basel. To Cosima Wagner: " Ariadne, I love you! " To Georg Brandes, the Danish critic, he sent a telegram signed " The Crucified." Franz Overbeck, an old Basel friend, at once set out for Turin, and there he found Nietzsche thumping the piano with his elbows and singing wild songs. Overbeck brought him back to Basel and he was confined in a private asylum, where his general health greatly improved and hopes were entertained of his recovery. But he never got well enough to be left alone, and so his old mother, with whom he had been on bad terms for years, took him back to Naumburg. When, in 1893, his sister Elizabeth returned from Paraguay, where her husband had died, he was well enough to meet her at the railroad station. Four years later, when their mother died, Elizabeth removed him to Weimar, where she bought a villa called " *Silberblick* " (Silver View) in the suburbs. This villa had a garden overlooking the hills and the lazy river Ilm, and a wide, sheltered veranda for the invalid's couch. There he would sit day after day, receiving old friends but saying little. His mind never became clear enough for him to resume work, or even to read. He had to grope for words, slowly and painfully, and he retained only a cloudy memory of his own books. His chief delight was in music and he was always glad when someone came who could play the piano for him.

There is something poignantly pathetic in the picture of this valiant fighter — this arrogant *ja-sager* — this foe of men, gods and devils — being nursed and coddled like a little child. His old fierce pride and courage disappeared and he became docile and gentle. " You and I, my sister — we are happy! " he would say, and then his hand would slip out from his coverings and clasp that of the tender and faithful Lisbeth. Once she mentioned Wagner to him. " *Den habe ich sehr geliebt!* " he said. All his old fighting spirit was gone. He remembered only the glad days and the dreams of his youth.

Nietzsche died at Weimar on August 25, 1900, the immediate cause of death being pneumonia. His ashes are buried in the little village of Röcken, his birthplace.

THE PHILOSOPHER AND THE MAN

" My brother," says Frau Förster-Nietzsche, in her biography, " was stockily and broadly built and was anything but thin. He had a rather dark, healthy, ruddy complexion. In all things he was tidy and orderly, in speech he was soft-spoken, and in general, he was inclined to be serene under all circumstances. All in all, he was the very antithesis of a nervous man.

" In the fall of 1888, he said of himself, in a reminiscent memorandum: ' My blood moves slowly. A doctor who treated me a long while for what was at first diagnosed as a nervous affection said: " No, your trouble cannot be in your nerves. I myself am much more nervous than you." ' . . .

" My brother, both before and after his long illness seized him, was a believer in natural methods of healing. He took cold baths, rubbed down every morning and was quite faithful in continuing light, bed-room gymnastics."

At one time, she says, Nietzsche became a violent vegetarian and afflicted his friends with the ancient vegetarian horror of making a sarcophagus of one's stomach. It seems surprising that a man so quick to perceive errors, saw none in the silly argument that, because an ape's organs are designed for a vegetarian diet, a man's are so planned also. An acquaintance with elementary anatomy and physiology would have shown him the absurdity of this, but apparently he knew little about the human body, despite his uncanny skill at unearthing the secrets of the human mind. Nietzsche had read Emerson in his youth, and those Emersonian seeds which have come to full flower in the United States as the so-called New Thought movement — with Christian Science, osteopathy, mental telepathy, occultism, pseudo-psychology and that grand lodge of credulous *comiques*, the Society for Psychical Research, as its final blossoms — all of this probably made its mark on the philosopher of the superman, too.

Frau Förster-Nietzsche, in her biography, seeks to prove the impossible thesis that her brother, despite his constant illness, was ever well-balanced in mind. It is but fair to charge that her own evidence is against her. From his youth onward, Nietzsche was undoubtedly a neurasthenic, and after the Franco-Prussian war he was a constant sufferer from all sorts of terrible ills — some imaginary, no doubt, but others real enough. In many ways, his own account of his symptoms recalls vividly the long catalogue of aches and pains given by Herbert Spencer in his autobiography. Spencer had queer pains in his head and so did Nietzsche. Spencer roved about all his life in search of health and so did Nietzsche. Spencer's working hours were limited and so were Nietzsche's. The latter tells us himself that, in a single year, 1878, he was disabled 118 days by headaches and pains in the eyes.

Dr. Gould, the prophet of eye-strain, would have us believe that both of these great philosophers suffered because they had read too much during adolescence. It is more likely, however, that each was the victim of some definite organic malady, and perhaps of more than one. In Nietzsche's case things were constantly made worse by his fondness for self-medication, that vice of fools. Preparatory to his service as a hospital steward in 1870 he had attended a brief course of first-aid lectures at the military hospital at Erlangen, and thereafter he regarded himself as a finished pathologist and was forever taking his own doses. The amount of medicine he thus swallowed was truly appalling, and the only way he could break his appetite for one drug was by acquiring an appetite for another. Chloral, however, was his favorite, and toward the end he took it daily and in staggering quantities.

Meanwhile, his mental disturbances grew more and more visible. At times he would be highly excited and exalted, denouncing his foes, and proclaiming his own genius. This was his state when his friends were finally forced to put him under restraint. At other times he would show symptoms of melancholia — a feeling of isolation and friendlessness, a great sadness, a foreboding of death. The hostility with which his books were received gave sharpness and plausibility to this mood, and it pursued him through many a despairing day.

" An animal, when it is sick," he wrote to Baron von Seydlitz, in 1888, " slinks away to some dark cavern, and so, too, does the *bête philosophe*. I am alone — absurdly alone — and in my unflinching and toilsome struggle against all that men have hitherto held sacred and ven-

erable, I have become a sort of dark cavern myself —
something hidden and mysterious, which is not to be
explored. . . ." But the mood vanished as the words
were penned, and the defiant dionysian roared his challenge at his foes. " It is not impossible," he said, " that
I am the greatest philosopher of the century — perhaps
even more than that ! I may be the decisive and fateful
link between two thousand centuries ! " [1]

Max Nordau [2] says that Nietzsche was crazy from birth,
but the facts do not bear him out. It is much more reasonable to hold that the philosopher came into the world a
sound and healthy animal, and that it remained for over-
study in his youth, over-work and over drugging later on,
exposure on the battle field, functional disorders and
constant and violent strife to undermine and eventually
overthrow his intellect.

But if we admit the indisputable fact that Nietzsche
died a madman and the equally indisputable fact that his
insanity was not sudden, but progressive, we by no means
read him out of court as a thinker. A man's reasoning
is to be judged, not by his physical condition, but by its
own ingenuity and accuracy. If a raving maniac says
that twice two make four, it is just as true as it would be
if Pope Pius X or any other undoubtedly sane man were
to maintain it. Judged in this way Nietzsche's philosophy
is very far from insane. Later on we shall consider it as
a workable system, and point out its apparent truths and
apparent errors, but in no place (saving, perhaps, one)

[1] Thomas Common: " Nietzsche as Critic, Philosopher, Poet and
Prophet ; " London, 1901, p. 54.
[2] " Degeneration ; " Eng. tr. : New York, 1895 ; pp. 415–472.

is his argument to be dismissed as the phantasm of a lunatic.

Nietzsche's sister says that, in the practical affairs of life, the philosopher was absurdly impractical. He cared nothing for money and during the better part of his life had little need to do so. His mother, for a country pastor's widow, was well-to-do, and when he was twenty-five his professorship at Basel brought him 3,000 francs a year. At Basel, in the late sixties, 3,000 francs was the income of an independent, not to say opulent man. Nietzsche was a bachelor and lived very simply. It was only upon books and music and travel that he was extravagant.

After two years' service at Basel, the university authorities raised his wage to 4,000 francs, and in 1879, when ill health forced him to resign, they gave him a pension of 3,000 francs a year. Besides that, he inherited 30,000 marks from one of his aunts, and so, altogether, he had an income of $900 or $1,000 a year — the sum which Herbert Spencer regarded, all his life, as an insurance of perfect tranquillity and happiness.

Nietzsche's passion and dissipation, throughout his life, was music. In all his books musical terms and figures of speech are constantly encountered. He played the piano very well, indeed, and was especially fond of performing transcriptions of the Wagner opera scores. " My three solaces," he wrote home from Leipsic, " are Schopenhauer's philosophy, Schumann's music and solitary walks." In his late youth, Wagner engrossed him, but his sympathies were broad enough to include Bach, Schubert and Mendelssohn. His admiration for the last named, in fact, helped to alienate him from Wagner, who regarded the Mendelssohn scheme of things as unspeakable.

Nietzsche's own compositions were decidedly heavy and scholastic. He was a skillful harmonist and contrapuntalist, but his musical ideas lacked life. Into the simplest songs he introduced harsh and far-fetched modulations. The music of Richard Strauss, who professes to be his disciple and has found inspiration in his " *Also sprach Zarathustra* " would have delighted him. Strauss has achieved the uncanny feat of writing in two keys at once. Such an effort would have enlisted Nietzsche's keen interest.

All the same, his music was not a mere creature of the study and of rules, and we have evidence that he was frequently inspired to composition by bursts of strong emotion. On his way to the Franco-Prussian war, he wrote a patriotic song, words and music, on the train. He called it " Adieu! I Must Go! " and arranged it for men's chorus, *a capella*. It would be worth while to hear a German *männerchor*, with its high, beery tenors, and ponderous basses, sing this curious composition. Certainly no more grotesque music was ever put on paper by mortal man.

Much has been written by various commentators about the strange charm of Nietzsche's prose style. He was, indeed, a master of the German language, but this mastery was not inborn. Like Spencer he made a deliberate effort, early in life, to acquire ease and force in writing. His success was far greater than Spencer's. Toward the end — in " *Der Antichrist*," for instance — he attained a degree of powerful and convincing utterance almost comparable to Huxley's. But his style never exhibited quite that wonderful air of clearness, of utter certainty, of inevitableness which makes the "Lay Sermons" so tremendously impressive. Nietzsche was ever nearer to Carlyle than to Addison. "His style," says a writer in the *Athenæum,* "is a shower of sparks, which scatter, like fireworks, all over the sky."

"My sense for form," says Nietzsche himself, "awakened on my coming in contact with Sallust." Later on he studied the great French stylists, particularly Larochefaucauld, and learned much from them. He became a master of the aphorism and the epigram, and this skill, very naturally, led him to descend, now and then, to mere violence and invective. He called his opponents all sorts of harsh names — liar, swindler, counterfeiter, ox, ass, snake and thief. Whatever he had to say, he hammered in with gigantic blows, and to the accompaniment of fearsome bellowing and grimacing. "Nervous, vivid and picturesques, full of fire and a splendid vitality," says one critic, "his style flashed and coruscated like a glowing flame, and had a sort of dithyrambic movement that at times recalls the swing of the Pindaric odes." Naturally, this very *abandon* made his poetry formless and grotesque. He scorned metres and rhymes and raged on in sheer savagery. Reading his verses one is forced irresistibly into the thought that they should be printed in varied fonts of type and in a dozen brilliant inks.

Nietzsche never married, but he was by no means a misogynist. His sister tells us, indeed, that he made a formal proposal of marriage to a young Dutch woman, Fräulein Tr——, at Geneva in 1876, and the story of his melodramatic affair with Mlle. Lou Salomé, six years later, was briefly rehearsed in the last chapter. There were also other women in his life, early and late, and certain scandal-mongers do not hesitate to accuse him of a passion for Cosima Wagner, apparently on the ground that he wrote to her, in his last mad days, " Ariadne, I love thee! " But his intentions were seldom serious. Even when he pursued Mlle. Salomé from Rome to Leipsic and quarrelled with his sister about her, and threatened poor Rée with fire-arms, there is good reason to believe that he shied at bell and book. His proposal, in brief, was rather one of a free union than one of marriage. For the rest, he kept safely to impossible flirtations. During all his wanderings he was much petted by the belles of pump room and hotel parlor, not only because he was a mysterious and romantic looking fellow, but also because his philosophy was thought to be blasphemous and indecent, particularly by those who knew nothing about it. But the fair admirers he singled out were either securely married or hopelessly antique. " For me to marry," he soliloquized in 1887, " would probably be sheer asininity."

There are sentimental critics who hold that Nietzsche's utter lack of geniality was due to his lack of a wife. A good woman — alike beautiful and sensible — would have rescued him, they say, from his gloomy fancies. He would have expanded and mellowed in the sunshine of her smiles, and children would have civilized him. The defect in this theory lies in the fact that philosophers do not seem to flourish amid scenes of connubial joy. High thinking, it would appear, presupposes boarding house

fare and hall bed-rooms. Spinoza, munching his solitary
herring up his desolate backstairs, makes a picture that
pains us, perhaps, but it must be admitted that it also
satisfies our sense of eternal fitness. A married Spinoza,
with two sons at college, another managing the family
lens business, a daughter busy with her trousseau and a
wife growing querulous and fat — the vision, alas, is
preposterous, outrageous and impossible! We must
think of philosophers as beings alone but not lonesome.
A married Schopenhauer or Kant or Nietzsche would be
unthinkable.

That a venture into matrimony might have somewhat
modified Nietzsche's view of womankind is not at all improbable, but that this change would have been in the direction of greater accuracy does not follow. He would have
been either a ridiculously henpecked slave or a violent domestic tyrant. As a bachelor he was comparatively well-
to-do, but with a wife and children his thousand a year
would have meant genteel beggary. His sister had her
own income and her own affairs. When he needed her,
she was ever at his side, but when his working fits were
upon him — when he felt efficient and self-sufficient — she
discreetly disappeared. A wife's constant presence, day
in and day out, would have irritated him beyond measure
or reduced him to a state of compliance and sloth. Nietzsche himself sought to show, in more than one place, that
a man whose whole existence was colored by one woman
would inevitably acquire some trace of her feminine outlook, and so lose his own sure vision. The ideal state
for a philosopher, indeed, is celibacy tempered by polyg-
amy. He must study women, but he must be free, when

he pleases, to close his note book and go away and digest its contents with an open mind.

Toward the end of his life, when increasing illness made him helpless, Nietzsche's faithful sister took the place of wife and mother in his clouding world. She made a home for him and she sat by and watched him. They talked for hours — Nietzsche propped up with pillows, his old ruddiness faded into a deathly white, and his Niagara of a moustache showing dark against his pallid skin. They talked of Naumburg and the days of long ago and the fiery prophet of the superman became simple Brother Fritz. We are apt to forget that a great man is thus not only great, but also a man: that a philosopher, in a life time, spends less hours pondering the destiny of the race than he gives over to wondering if it will rain to-morrow and to meditating upon the toughness of steaks, the dustiness of roads, the stuffiness of railway coaches and the brigandage of gas companies.

Nietzsche's sister was the only human being that ever saw him intimately, as a wife might have seen him. Her affection for him was perfect and her influence over him perfect, too. Love and understanding, faith and gentleness — these are the things which make women the angels of joyous illusion. Lisbeth, the calm and trusting, had all in boundless richness. There was, indeed, something noble, and almost holy in the eagerness with which she sought her brother's comfort and peace of mind during his days of stress and storm, and magnified his virtues after he was gone.

NIETZSCHE THE PHILOSOPHER

I

DIONYSUS VERSUS APOLLO

IN one of the preceding chapters Nietzsche's theory of Greek tragedy was given in outline and its dependence upon the data of Schopenhauer's philosophy was indicated. It is now in order to examine this theory a bit more closely and to trace cut its origin and development with greater dwelling upon detail. In itself it is of interest only as a step forward in the art of literary criticism, but in its influence upon Nietzsche's ultimate inquiries it has colored, to a measurable extent, the whole stream of modern thought.

Schopenhauer laid down, as his cardinal principle, it will be recalled, the idea that, in all the complex whirl-pool of phenomena we call human life, the mere will to survive is at the bottom of everything, and that intelligence, despite its seeming kingship in civilization, is nothing more, after all, than a secondary manifestation of this primary will. In certain purely artificial situations, it may seem to us that reason stands alone (as when, for example, we essay to solve an abstract problem in mathematics), but in everything growing out of our relations as human beings, one to the other, the old instinct of race-and-self-preservation is plainly discernible. All of our

acts, when they are not based obviously and directly
upon our yearning to eat and take our ease and beget our
kind, are founded upon our desire to appear superior, in
some way or other, to our fellow men about us, and this
desire for superiority, reduced to its lowest terms, is
merely a desire to face the struggle for existence — to eat
and beget — under more favorable conditions than those
the world accords the average man. " Happiness is the
feeling that power increases — that resistance is being
overcome." [1]

Nietzsche went to Basel firmly convinced that these
fundamental ideas of Schopenhauer were profoundly
true, though he soon essayed to make an amendment
to them. This amendment consisted in changing Schopenhauer's " will to live " into " will to power." That which
does not live, he argued, cannot exercise a will to live, and
when a thing is already in existence, how can it strive
after existence? Nietzsche voiced the argument many
times, but its vacuity is apparent upon brief inspection.
He started out, in fact, with an incredibly clumsy mis-
interpretation of Schopenhauer's phrase. The philosopher of pessimism, when he said " will to live " obviously
meant, not will to begin living, but will to continue living.
Now, this will to continue living, if we are to accept words
at their usual meaning, is plainly identical, in every respect,
with Nietzsche's will to power. Therefore, Nietzsche's
amendment was nothing more than the coinage of a new
phrase to express an old idea. The unity of the two
philosophers and the identity of the two phrases are proved
a thousand times by Nietzsche's own discourses. Like

[1] " *Der Antichrist*," § 2.

Schopenhauer he believed that all human ideas were the
direct products of the unconscious and unceasing effort
of all living creatures to remain alive. Like Schopenhauer
he believed that abstract ideas, in man, arose out of
concrete ideas, and that the latter arose out of experience,
which, in turn, was nothing more or less than an ordered
remembrance of the results following an endless series
of endeavors to meet the conditions of existence and so
survive. Like Schopenhauer, he believed that the criminal
laws, the poetry, the cookery and the religion of a race were
alike expressions of this unconscious groping for the line
of least resistance.

As a philologist, Nietzsche's interest, very naturally,
was fixed upon the literature of Greece and Rome, and
so it was but natural that his first tests of Schopenhauer's
doctrines should be made in that field. Some time before
this, he had asked himself (as many another man had
asked before him) why it was that the ancient Greeks,
who were an efficient and vigorous people, living in a green
and sunny land, should so delight in gloomy tragedies.
One would fancy that a Greek, when he set out to spend
a pleasant afternoon, would seek entertainment that was
frivolous and gay. But instead, he often preferred to
see one of the plays of Thespis, Æschylus, Phrynichus
or Pratinus, in which the heroes fought hopeless battles
with fate and died miserably, in wretchedness and despair. Nietzsche concluded that the Greeks had this
liking for tragedy because it seemed to them to set forth,
truthfully and understandably, the conditions of life as
they found it: that it appeared to them as a reasonable
and accurate picture of human existence. The gods or-

dered the drama on the real stage of the world; the dramatist ordered the drama on the mimic stage of the theatre — and the latter attained credibility and verisimilitude in proportion as it approached an exact imitation or reproduction of the former. Nietzsche saw that this quality of realism was the essence of all stage plays. " Only insofar as the dramatist," he said, " coalesces with the priordial dramatist of the world, does he reach the true function of his craft." [1] " Man posits himself as the standard . . . A race cannot do otherwise than thus acquiesce in itself." [2] In other words, man is interested in nothing whatever that has no bearing upon his own fate: he himself is his own hero. Thus the ancient Greeks were fond of tragedy because it reflected their life in miniature. In the mighty warriors who stalked the boards and defied the gods each Greek recognized himself. In the conflicts on the stage he saw replicas of that titanic conflict which seemed to him to be the eternal essence of human existence.

But why did the Greeks regard life as a conflict? In seeking an answer to this Nietzsche studied the growth of their civilization and of their race ideas. These race ideas, as among all other peoples, were visualized and crystallized in the qualities, virtues and opinions attributed to the racial gods. Therefore, Nietzsche undertook an inquiry into the nature of the gods set up by the Greeks, and particularly into the nature of the two gods who controlled the general scheme of Greek life, and, in consequence, of Greek art, — for art, as we have seen, is

[1] " *Die Geburt der Tragödie*," § 5.
[2] " *Götzendämmerung*," ix, § 19.

nothing more or less than a race's view or opinion of itself, *i. e.* an expression of the things it sees and the conclusions it draws when it observes and considers itself.   These gods were Apollo and Dionysus.

Apollo, according to the Greeks, was the inventor of music, poetry and oratory, and as such, became the god of all art.   Under his beneficent sway the Greeks became a race of artists and acquired all the refinement and culture that this implies.   But the art that he taught them was essentially contemplative and subjective.   It depicted, not so much things as they were, as things as they had been.   Thus it became a mere record, and as such, exhibited repose as its chief quality.   Whether it were expressed as sculpture, architecture, painting or epic poetry, this element of repose, or of action translated into repose, was uppermost.   A painting of a man running, no matter how vividly it suggests the vitality and activity of the runner, is itself a thing inert and lifeless.   Architecture, no matter how much its curves suggest motion and its hard lines the strength which may be translated into energy, is itself a thing immovable.   Poetry, so long as it takes the form of the epic and is thus merely a chronicle of past actions, is as lifeless, at bottom, as a tax list.

The Greeks, during Apollo's reign as god of art, thus turned art into a mere inert fossil or record — a record either of human life itself or of the emotions which the vicissitudes of life arouse in the spectator.   This notion of art was reflected in their whole civilization.   They became singers of songs and weavers of metaphysical webs rather than doers of deeds, and the man who could carve a flower was more honored among them than the

man who could grow one. In brief, they began to degenerate and go stale. Great men and great ideas grew few.
They were on the downward road.

What they needed, of course, was the shock of contact
with some barbarous, primitive people — an infusion of
good red blood from some race that was still fighting for
its daily bread and had had no time to grow contemplative and retrospective and fat. This infusion of red blood
came in good time, but instead of coming from without
(as it did years afterward in Rome, when the Goths
swooped down from the North), it came from within. That
is to say, there was no actual invasion of barbarian hordes,
but merely an auto-reversion to simpler and more primitive ideas, which fanned the dormant energy of the Greeks
into flame and so allowed them to accomplish their own
salvation. This impulse came in the form of a sudden
craze for a new god — Bacchus Dionysus.

Bacchus was a rude, boisterous fellow and the very
antithesis of the quiet, contemplative Apollo. We remember him today merely as the god of wine, but in his
time he stood, not only for drinking and carousing, but
also for a whole system of art and a whole notion of
civilization. Apollo represented the life meditative;
Bacchus Dionysus represented the life strenuous. The
one favored those forms of art by which human existence
is halted and embalmed in some lifeless medium —
sculpture, architecture, painting or epic poetry. The
other was the god of life in process of actual being, and so
stood for those forms of art which are not mere records or
reflections of past existence, but brief snatches of present
existence itself — dancing, singing, music and the drama.

It will be seen that this barbarous invasion of the new god and his minions made a profound change in the whole of Greek culture. Instead of devoting their time to writing epics, praising the laws, splitting philosophical hairs and hewing dead marble, the Greeks began to question all things made and ordained and to indulge in riotous and gorgeous orgies, in which thousands of maidens danced and hundreds of poets chanted songs of love and war, and musicians vied with cooks and vintners to make a grand delirium of joy. The result was that the entire outlook of the Greeks, upon history, upon morality and upon human life, was changed. Once a people of lofty introspection and elegant repose, they became a race of violent activity and strong emotions. They began to devote themselves, not to writing down the praises of existence as they had found it, but to the task of improving life and of widening the scope of present and future human activity and the bounds of possible human happiness.[1]

But in time there came a reaction and Apollo once more triumphed. He reigned for awhile, unsteadily and uncertainly, and then, again, the pendulum swung to the other side. Thus the Greeks swayed from one god to the other. During Apollo's periods of ascendancy they were contemplative and imaginative, and man, to them, seemed to reach his loftiest heights when he was most the historian. But when Dionysus was their best-beloved,

[1] "This enrichment of consciousness among the Greeks . . . showed itself first in the development of lyric poetry, in which the gradual transition from the expression of universal religious and political feeling to that which is personal and individual formed a typical process." Dr. Wilhelm Windelband, "A History of Ancient Philosophy," tr. by H E. Cushman; p. 18; New York, 1901.

they bubbled over with the joy of life, and man seemed, not an historian, but a maker of history — not an artist, but a work of art. In the end, they verged toward a safe middle ground and began to weigh, with cool and calm, the ideas represented by the two gods. When they had done so, they came to the conclusion that it was not well to give themselves unreservedly to either. To attain the highest happiness, they decided, humanity required a dash of both. There was need in the world for dionysians, to give vitality an outlet and life a purpose, and there was need, too, for apollonians, to build life's monuments and read its lessons. They found that true civilization meant a constant conflict between the two — between the dreamer and the man of action, between the artist who builds temples and the soldier who burns them down, between the priest and policeman who insist upon the permanence of laws and customs as they are and the criminal and reformer and conqueror who insist that they be changed.

When they had learned this lesson, the Greeks began to soar to heights of culture and civilization that, in the past, had been utterly beyond them, and so long as they maintained the balance between Apollo and Dionysus they continued to advance. But now and again, one god or the other grew stronger, and then there was a halt. When Apollo had the upper hand, Greece became too contemplative and too placid. When Dionysus was the victor, Greece became wild and thoughtless and careless of the desires of others, and so turned a bit toward bar-barism. This seesawing continued for a long while, but Apollo was the final victor — if victor he may be called. In the eternal struggle for existence Greece became a mere looker-on. Her highest honors went to Socrates, a man who tried to reduce all life to syllogisms. Her favorite sons were rhetoricians, dialecticians and philosophical cobweb-spinners. She placed ideas above deeds. And in the end, as all students of history know, the state that once ruled the world descended to senility and decay, and dionysians from without overran it, and it perished in anarchy and carnage. But with this we have nothing to do.

Nietzsche noticed that tragedy was most popular in Greece during the best days of the country's culture, when Apollo and Dionysus were properly balanced, one against the other. This ideal balancing between the two gods was the result, he concluded, not of conscious, but of unconscious impulses. That is to say, the Greeks did not call parliaments and discuss the matter, as they might have discussed a question of taxes, but acted entirely in obedience to their racial instinct. This instinct — this will to live or desire for power — led them to feel, without putting it into words, or even, for awhile, into definite thoughts, that they were happiest and safest and most vigorous, and so best able to preserve their national existence, when they kept to the golden mean. They didn't reason it out; they merely felt it.

But as Schopenhauer shows us, instinct, long exercised, means experience, and the memory of experience, in the end, crystallizes into what we call intelligence or reason. Thus the unconscious Greek feeling that the golden mean best served the race, finally took the form of an idea: i. e. that human life was an endless conflict between two forces, or impulses. These, as the Greeks saw them, were the dionysian impulse to destroy, to burn the candle, to "use up" life; and the apollonian impulse to preserve. Seeing life in this light, it was but natural that the Greeks should try to exhibit it in the same light on their stage. And so their tragedies were invariably founded upon some deadly and unending conflict — usually between a human hero and the gods. In a word, they made their stage plays set forth life as they saw it and found it, for, like all other human beings, at all times and everywhere, they were more interested in life as they found it than in anything else on the earth below or in the vasty void above.

When Nietzsche had worked out this theory of Greek tragedy and of Greek life, he set out, at once, to apply it to modern civilization, to see if it could explain certain ideas of the present as satisfactorily as it had explained one great idea of the past. He found that it could: that men were still torn between the apollonian impulse to conform and moralize and the dionysian impulse to exploit and explore. He found that all mankind might be divided into two classes: the apollonians who stood for permanence and the dionysians who stood for change. It was the aim of the former to live in strict obedience to certain invariable rules, which found expression as religion, law and morality. It was the aim of the latter to live under the most favorable conditions possible; to adapt themselves to changing circumstances, and to avoid the snares of artificial, permanent rules.

Nietzsche believed that an ideal human society would be one in which these two classes of men were evenly balanced — in which a vast, inert, religious, moral slave class stood beneath a small, alert, iconoclastic, immoral,

progressive master class. He held that this master class —
this aristocracy of efficiency — should regard the slave
class as all men now regard the tribe of domestic beasts:
as an order of servitors to be exploited and turned to account. The aristocracy of Europe, though it sought to do
this with respect to the workers of Europe, seemed to him
to fail miserably, because it was itself lacking in true
efficiency. Instead of practising a magnificent opportunism and so adapting itself to changing conditions, it stood
for formalism and permanence. Its fetish was property
in land and the worship of this fetish had got it into such
a rut that it was becoming less and less fitted to survive,
and was, indeed, fast sinking into helpless parasitism.
Its whole color and complexion were essentially apollonic. [1]

Therefore Nietzsche preached the gospel of Dionysus,
that a new aristocracy of efficiency might take the place of
this old aristocracy of memories and inherited glories.
He believed that it was only in this way that mankind
could hope to forge ahead. He believed that there was
need in the world for a class freed from the handicap
of law and morality, a class acutely adaptable and immoral; a class bent on achieving, not the equality of all
men, but the production, at the top, of the superman.

[1] *Vide* the chapter on " Civilization."

II

THE ORIGIN OF MORALITY

It may be urged with some reason, by those who have read the preceding chapter carefully, that the Nietzschean argument, so far, has served only to bring us face to face with a serious contradiction. We have been asked to believe that all human impulses are merely expressions of the primary instinct to preserve life by meeting the changing conditions of existence, and in the same breath we have been asked to believe, too, that the apollonian idea — which, like all other ideas, must necessarily be a result of this instinct — destroys adaptability and so tends to make life extra hazardous and difficult and progress impossible. Here we have our contradiction: the will to live is achieving, not life, but death. How are we to explain it away? How are we to account for the fact that the apollonian idea at the bottom of Christian morality, for example, despite its origin in the will to live, has an obvious tendency to combat free progress? How are we to account for the fact that the church, which is based upon this Christian morality, is, always has been and ever will be a bitter and implacable foe of good health, intellectual freedom, self-defense and every other essential factor of efficiency?

Nietzsche answers this by pointing out that an idea, while undoubtedly an effect or expression of the primary life instinct, is by no means identical with it. The latter manifests itself in widely different acts as conditions change: it is necessarily opportunistic and variable. The former, on the contrary, has a tendency to survive unchanged, even after its truth is transformed into falsity. That is to say, an idea which arises from a true and healthy instinct may survive long after this instinct itself, in consequence of the changing conditions of existence, has disappeared and given place to an instinct diametrically opposite. This survival of ideas we call morality. By its operation the human race is frequently saddled with the notions of generations long dead and forgotten. Thus we modern Christians still subscribe to the apollonian morality of the ancient Jews — our moral forebears — despite the fact that their ideas were evolved under conditions vastly different from those which confront us today. Thus the expressions of the life instinct, by obtaining an artificial and unnatural permanence, turn upon the instinct itself and defeat its beneficent purpose. Thus our contradiction is explained.

To make this rather complicated reasoning more clear it is necessary to follow Nietzsche through the devious twists and windings of his exhaustive inquiry into the origin of moral codes. In making this inquiry he tried to rid himself of all considerations of authority and reverence, just as a surgeon, in performing a difficult and painful operation, tries to rid himself of all sympathy and emotion. Adopting this plan, he found that a code of morals was nothing more than a system of customs.

laws and ideas which had its origin in the instinctive desire of some definite race to live under conditions which best subserved its own welfare. The morality of the Egyptians, he found, was one thing, and the morality of the Goths was another. The reason for the difference lay in the fact that the environment of the Egyptians — the climate of their land, the nature of their food supply and the characteristics of the peoples surrounding them — differed from the environment of the Goths. The morality of each race was, in brief, its consensus of instinct, and once having formulated it and found it good, each sought to give it force and permanence. This was accomplished by putting it into the mouths of the gods. What was once a mere expression of instinct thus became the mandate of a divine law-giver. What was once a mere attempt to meet imminent — and usually temporary — conditions of existence, thus became a code of rules to be obeyed forever, no matter how much these conditions of existence might change. Wherefore, Nietzsche concluded that the chief characteristic of a moral system was its tendency to perpetuate itself unchanged, and to destroy all who questioned it or denied it.[1]

Nietzsche saw that practically all members of a given race, including the great majority of those who violated these rules, were influenced into believing them

[1] II Thess. II, 15: "Hold the tradition which ye have been taught." Eusebius Pamphilus: "Those things which are written believe; those things which are not written, neither think upon nor inquire after." St. Austin: "Whatever ye hear from the holy scriptures let it favor well with you; whatever is without them refuse." See also St. Basil, Tertullian and every other professional moralist since, down to John Alexander Dowie and Emperor William of Germany.

— or at least into professing to believe them — utterly
and unchangeably correct, and that it was the main
function of all religions to enforce and support them by
making them appear as laws laid down, at the beginning
of the world, by the lord of the universe himself, or at
some later period, by his son, messiah or spokesman.
" Morality," he said, " not only commands innumerable
terrible means for preventing critical hands being laid
upon her: her security depends still more upon a sort of
enchantment at which she is phenomenally skilled. That
is to say, she knows how to *enrapture*. She appeals to the
emotions; her glance paralyzes the reason and the will.
. . . Ever since there has been talking and persuading on
earth, she has been the supreme mistress of seduction."[1]
Thus " a double wall is put up against the continued testing, selection and criticism of values. On one hand is
revelation, and on the other, veneration and tradition.
The authority of the law is based upon two assumptions
— first, that God gave it, and secondly, that the wise men
of the past obeyed it." [2] Nietzsche came to the conclusion
that this universal tendency to submit to moral codes —
this unreasonable, emotional faith in the invariable truth
of moral regulations — was a curse to the human race and
the chief cause of its degeneration, inefficiency and un-
happiness. And then he threw down the gauntlet by
denying that an ever-present deity had anything to do with
framing such codes and by endeavoring to prove that,
far from being eternally true, they commonly became
false with the passing of the years. Starting out as expressions of the primary life-instinct's effort to adapt

[1] " *Morgenröte*," preface, § 3.   [2] " *Der Antichrist*," § 57.

some individual or race to certain given conditions of existence, they took no account of the fact that these conditions were constantly changing, and that the thing which was advantageous at one time and to one race was frequently injurious at some other time and to another race.

This reduction of all morality to mere expressions of expedience engaged the philosopher during what he calls his " tunneling " period. To exhibit his precise method of " tunneling " let us examine, for example, a moral idea which is found in the code of every civilized country. This is the notion that there is something inherently and fundamentally wrong in the act of taking human life. We have good reason to believe that murder was as much a crime 5,000 years ago as it is today and that it took rank at the head of all conceivable outrages against humankind at the very dawn of civilization. And why? Simply because the man who took his neighbor's life made the life of everyone else in his neighborhood precarious and uncomfortable. It was plain that what he had done once he could do again, and so the peace and security of the whole district were broken.

Now, it is apparent that the average human being desires peace and security beyond all things, because it is only when he has them that he may satisfy his will to live — by procuring food and shelter for himself and by becoming the father of children. He is ill-fitted to fight for his existence; the mere business of living and begetting his kind consumes all of his energies: " the world, as a world," as Horace Greeley said, " barely makes a living." Therefore, it came to be recognized at the very beginning of civilization, that the man who killed other men was a foe to those conditions which the average man had to seek in order to exist — to peace and order and quiet and security. Out of this grew the doctrine that it was immoral to commit murder, and as soon as mankind became imaginative enough to invent personal gods, this doctrine was put into their mouths and so attained the force and authority of divine wisdom. In some such manner, said Nietzsche, the majority of our present moral concepts were evolved. At the start they were mere echoes of a protest against actions which made existence difficult and so outraged and opposed the will to live.

As a rule, said Nietzsche, such familiar protests as that against murder, which laid down the maxim that the community had rights superior to those of the individual, were voiced by the weak, who found it difficult to protect themselves, as individuals, against the strong. One strong man, perhaps, was more than a match, in the struggle for existence, for ten weak men and so the latter were at a disadvantage. But fortunately for them they could overcome this by combination, for they were always in an overwhelming majority, numerically, and in consequence they were stronger, taken together, than the phalanx of the strong. Thus it gradually became possible for them to enforce the rules that they laid down for their own protection — which rules always operated against the wishes — and, as an obvious corollary, against the best interests of — the strong.[1] When the time arrived

---

[1] The fact that the state is founded, not upon a mysterious " social impulse " in man, but upon each individual's regard for his own interest, was first pointed out by Thomas Hobbes (1588–1679), in his argument against Aristotle and Grotius.

for fashioning religious systems, these rules were credited to the gods, and again the weak triumphed. Thus the desire of the weak among the world's early races of men, to protect their crops and wives against the forays of the strong, by general laws and divine decrees instead of by each man fighting for his own, has come down to us in the form of the Christian commandments: " Thou shalt not steal. . . . Thou shalt not covet thy neighbor's house. . . . Thou shalt not covet thy neighbor's wife, nor his manservant, nor his maidservant, nor his ox, nor his ass, nor anything that is thy neighbor's."

Nietzsche shows that the device of putting man-made rules of morality into the mouths of the gods — a device practiced by every nation in history — has vastly increased the respectability and force of all moral ideas. This is well exhibited by the fact that, even today and among thinking men, offenses which happen to be included in the scope of the Ten Commandments, either actually or by interpretation, are regarded with a horror which seldom, if ever, attaches to offenses obviously defined and delimited by merely human agencies. Thus, theft is everywhere looked upon as dishonorable, but cheating at elections, which is fully as dangerous to the body politic, is commonly pardoned by public opinion as a normal consequence of enthusiasm, and in some quarters is even regarded as an evidence of courage, not to say of a high and noble sense of gratitude and honor.

Nietzsche does not deny that human beings have a right to construct moral codes for themselves, and neither does he deny that they are justified, from their immediate standpoint, at least, in giving these codes the authority and force

of divine commands. But he points out that this procedure
is bound to cause trouble in the long run, for the reason
that divine commands are fixed and invariable, and do
not change as fast as the instincts and needs of the race.
Suppose, for instance, that all acts of Parliament and
Congress were declared to be the will of God, and that,
as a natural consequence, the power to repeal or modify
them were abandoned. It is apparent that the world
would outgrow them as fast as it does today, but it is also
apparent that the notion that they were infallible would
paralyze and block all efforts, by atheistic reformers, to
overturn or amend them. As a result, the British and
American people would be compelled to live in obedience
to rules which, on their very face, would often seem
illogical and absurd.

Yet the same thing happens to notions of morality.
They are devised, at the start, as measures of expediency,
and then given divine sanction in order to lend them
authority. In the course of time, perhaps, the race out-
grows them, but none the less, they continue in force —
at least so long as the old gods are worshipped. Thus
human laws become divine — and inhuman. Thus morality itself becomes immoral. Thus the old instinct whereby
society differentiates between good things and bad, grows
muddled and uncertain, and the fundamental purpose of
morality — that of producing a workable scheme of
living — is defeated. Thereafter it is next to impossible
to distinguish between the laws that are still useful and
those that have outlived their usefulness, and the man
who makes the attempt — the philosopher who endeavors
to show humanity how it is condemning as bad a thing

that, in itself, is now good, or exalting as good a thing that, for all its former goodness, is now bad — this man is damned as a heretic and anarchist, and according as fortune serves him, is burned at the stake or merely read out of the human race.[1]

Nietzsche found that all existing moral ideas might be divided into two broad classes, corresponding to the two broad varieties of human beings — the masters and the slaves. Every man is either a master or a slave, and the same is true of every race. Either it rules some other race or it is itself ruled by some other race. It is impossible to think of a man or of a people as being utterly isolated, and even were this last possible, it is obvious that the community would be divided into those who ruled and those who obeyed. The masters are strong and are capable of doing as they please; the slaves are weak and must obtain whatever rights they crave by deceiving, cajoling or collectively intimidating their masters. Now, since all moral codes, as we have seen, are merely collections of the rules laid down by some definite group of human beings for their comfort and protection, it is evident that the morality of the master class has for its main object the preservation of the authority and kingship of that class, while the morality of the slave class seeks to make slavery as bearable as possible and to exalt and dignify those things in which the slave can hope to become the apparent equal or superior of his master.

The civilization which existed in Europe before the

---

[1] The risk of such idol-smashing is well set forth at length by G. Bernard Shaw in the preface to "The Quintessence of Ibsenism;" London, 1904.

dawn of Christianity was a culture based upon master-morality, and so we find that the theologians and moralists of those days esteemed a certain action as right only when it plainly subserved the best interests of strong, resourceful men. The ideal man of that time was not a meek and lowly sufferer, bearing his cross uncomplainingly, but an alert, proud and combative being who knew his rights and dared maintain them. In consequence we find that in many ancient languages, the words "good" and "aristocratic" were synonymous. Whatever served to make a man a nobleman — cunning, wealth, physical strength, eagerness to resent and punish injuries — was considered virtuous, praiseworthy and moral,[1] and on the other hand, whatever tended to make a man sink to the level of the great masses — humility, lack of ambition, modest desires, lavish liberality and a spirit of ready forgiveness — was regarded as immoral and wrong.

"Among these master races," says Nietzsche, "the antithesis 'good and bad' signified practically the same as 'noble and contemptible!' The despised ones were the cowards, the timid, the insignificant, the self-abasing — the dog-species of men who allowed themselves to be misused — the flatterers and, above all, the liars. It is a fundamental belief of all true aristocrats that the common people are deceitful. 'We true ones,' the ancient Greek nobles called themselves.

[1] Henry Bradley, in a lecture at the London Institution, in Jan 1907, showed that this was true of the ancient Britons, as is demonstrated by their liking for bestowing such names as Wolf and Bear upon themselves. It was true, also, of the North American Indians and of all primitive races conscious of their efficiency.

"It is obvious that the designations of moral worth were at first applied to individual men, and not to actions or ideas in the abstract. The master type of man regards himself as a sufficient judge of worth. He does not seek approval: his own feelings determine his conduct. 'What is injurious to me,' he reasons, 'is injurious in itself.' This type of man honors whatever qualities he recognizes in himself: his morality is self-glorification. He has a feeling of plentitude and power and the happiness of high tension. He helps the unfortunate, perhaps, but it is not out of sympathy. The impulse, when it comes at all, rises out of his superabundance of power — his thirst to function. He honors his own power, and he knows how to keep it in hand. He joyfully exercises strictness and severity over himself and he reverences all that is strict and severe. 'Wotan has put a hard heart in my breast,' says an old Scandinavian saga. There could be no better expression of the spirit of a proud viking. . . .

"The morality of the master class is irritating to the taste of the present day because of its fundamental principle that a man has obligations only to his equals; that he may act to all of lower rank and to all that are foreign as he pleases. . . . The man of the master class has a capacity for prolonged gratitude and prolonged revenge, but it is only among his equals. He has, too, great resourcefulness in retaliation; great capacity for friendship, and a strong need for enemies, that there may be an outlet for his envy, quarrelsomeness and arrogance, and that by spending these passions in this manner, he may be gentle towards his friends."[1]

[1] "*Jenseits von Gut und Böse,*" § 260.

By this ancient *herrenmoral,* or master-morality, Napoleon Bonaparte would have been esteemed a god and the Man of Sorrows an enemy to society. It was the ethical scheme, indeed, of peoples who were sure of themselves and who had no need to make terms with rivals or to seek the good will or forbearance of anyone. In its light, such things as mercy and charity seemed pernicious and immoral, because they meant a transfer of power from strong men, whose proper business it was to grow stronger and stronger, to weak men, whose proper business it was to serve the strong. In a word, this master-morality was the morality of peoples who knew, by experience, that it was pleasant to rule and be strong. They knew that the nobleman was to be envied and the slave to be despised, and so they came to believe that everything which helped to make a man noble was good and everything which helped to make him a slave was evil. The idea of nobility and the idea of good were expressed by the same word, and this verbal identity survives in the English language today, despite the fact that our present system of morality, as we shall see, differs vastly from that of the ancient master races.

In opposition to this master-morality of the strong, healthy nations there was the *sklavmoral,* or slave-morality, of the weak nations. The Jews of the four or five centuries preceding the birth of Christ belonged to the latter class. Compared to the races around them, they were weak and helpless. It was out of the question for them to conquer the Greeks or Romans and it was equally impossible for them to force their laws, their customs or their religion upon their neighbors on other sides. They were, indeed, in the position of an army surrounded by a horde of irresistible enemies. The general of such an army, with the instinct of self-preservation strong within him, does not attempt to cut his way out. Instead he tries to make the best terms he can, and if the leader of the enemy insists upon making him and his vanquished force prisoners, he endeavors to obtain concessions which will make this imprisonment as bearable as possible. The strong man's object is to take as much as he can from his victim; the weak man's is to save as much as he can from his conqueror.

The fruit of this yearning of weak nations to preserve as much of their national unity as possible is the thing Nietzsche calls slave-morality. Its first and foremost purpose is to discourage, and if possible, blot out, all those traits and actions which are apt to excite the ire, the envy, or the cupidity of the menacing enemies round about. Revenge, pride and ambition are condemned as evils. Humility, forgiveness, contentment and resignation are esteemed virtues. The moral man is the man who has lost all desire to triumph and exult over his fellow-men — the man of mercy, of charity, of self-sacrifice.

" The impotence which does not retaliate for injuries," says Nietzsche, " is falsified into ' goodness;' timorous abjectness becomes ' humility;' subjection to those one hates is called ' obedience,' and the one who desires and commands this impotence, abjectness and subjection is called God. The inoffensiveness of the weak, their cowardice (of which they have ample store); their standing at the door, their unavoidable time-serving and waiting — all these things get good names. The inability to get revenge is translated into an *unwillingness* to get revenge, and becomes forgiveness, a virtue.

" They are wretched — these mutterers and forgers — but they say that their wretchedness is of God's choosing and even call it a distinction that he confers upon them. The dogs which are liked best, they say, are beaten most. Their wretchedness is a test, a preparation, a schooling — something which will be paid for, one day, in happiness. They call that ' bliss.' " [1]

By the laws of this slave-morality the immoral man is he who seeks power and eminence and riches — the millionaire, the robber, the fighter, the schemer. The act of acquiring property by conquest — which is looked upon as a matter of course by master-morality — becomes a crime and is called theft. The act of mating in obedience to natural impulses, without considering the desire of others, becomes adultery; the quite natural act of destroying one's enemies becomes murder.

[1] " *Zur Geneologie der Moral,*" I, § 14.

III

DESPITE the divine authority which gives permanence
to all moral codes, this permanence is constantly opposed
by the changing conditions of existence, and very often
the opposition is successful. The slave-morality of the
ancient Jews has come down to us, with its outlines little
changed, as ideal Christianity, but such tenacious persistence of a moral scheme is comparatively rare. As a
general rule, in truth, races change their gods very much
oftener than we have changed ours, and have less faith
than we in the independence of intelligence. In consequence they constantly revamp and modify their moral
concepts. The same process of evolution affects even our
own code, despite the extraordinary tendency to permanence just noted. Our scheme of things, in its fundamentals, has persisted for 2,500 years, but in matters of
detail it is constantly in a state of flux. We still call ourselves Christians, but we have evolved many moral ideas
that are not to be found in the scriptures and we have
sometimes denied others that are plainly there. Indeed,
as will be shown later on, the beatitudes would have wiped
us from the face of the earth centuries ago had not our
forefathers devised means of circumventing them without

openly questioning them. Our progress has been made, not as a result of our moral code, but as a result of our success in dodging its inevitable blight.

All morality, in fact, is colored and modified by opportunism, even when its basic principles are held sacred and kept more or less intact. The thing that is a sin in one age becomes a virtue in the next. The ancient Persians, who were Zoroastrians, regarded murder and suicide, under any circumstances, as crimes. The modern Persians, who are Mohammedans, think that ferocity and foolhardiness are virtues. The ancient Japanese, to whom the state appeared more important than the man, threw themselves joyously upon the spears of the state's enemies. The modern Japanese, who are fledgling individualists, armor their ships with nickel steel and fight on land from behind bastions of earth and masonry. And in the same way the moral ideas that have grown out of Christianity, and even some of its important original doctrines, are being constantly modified and revised, despite the persistence of the fundamental notion of self-sacrifice at the bottom of them. In Dr. Andrew D. White's monumental treatise " On the Warfare of Science with Theology in Christendom " there are ten thousand proofs of it. Things that were crimes in the middle ages are quite respectable at present. Actions that are punishable by excommunication and ostracism in Catholic Spain today, are sufficient to make a man honorable in freethinking England. In France, where the church once stood above the king, it is now stripped of all rights not inherent in the most inconsequential social club. In Germany it is a penal offense to poke fun at the head of the state; in the

United States it is looked upon by many as an evidence of independence and patriotism. In some of the American states a violation of the seventh commandment, in any form, is a felony; in Maryland, it is, in one form, a mere misdemeanor, and another form, no crime at all.

" Many lands did I see," says Zarathustra, " and many peoples, and so I discovered the good and bad of many peoples. . . . Much that was regarded as good by one people was held in scorn and contempt by another. I found many things called bad here and adorned with purple honors there. . . . A catalogue of blessings is posted up for every people. Lo! it is the catalogue of their triumphs — the voice of their will to power! . . . Whatever enables them to rule and conquer and dazzle, to the dismay and envy of their neighbors, is regarded by them as the summit, the head, the standard of all things. . . . Verily, men have made for themselves all their good and bad. Verily they did not find it so: it did not come to them as a voice from heaven. . . . It is only through valuing that there comes value." [1]

To proceed from the concrete to the general, and to risk a repetition, it is evident that all morality, as Nietzsche pointed out, is nothing more than an expression of expediency. [2] A thing is called wrong solely because a definite group of people, at some specific stage of their career, have found it injurious to them. The fact that

---

[1] " *Also sprach Zarathustra* " I.

[2] " The word *mos*, from signifying what is customary, has come to signify what is right." Sir Wm. Markby : " Elements of Law Considered with Reference to General Principles of Jurisprudence: " pp. 118, 5th ed., London, 1896.

they have discovered grounds for condemning it in some pronunciamento of their god signifies nothing, for the reason that the god of a people is never anything more than a reflection of their ideas for the time being. As Prof. Otto Pfleiderer has shown,[1] Jesus Christ was a product of his age, mentally and spiritually as well as physically. Had there been no Jewish theology before him, he could not have sought or obtained recognition as a messiah, and the doctrines that he expressed — had he ever expressed them at all — would have fallen upon unheeding and uncomprehending ears.

Therefore it is plain that the Ten Commandments are no more immortal and immutable, in the last analysis, than the acts of Parliament. They have lasted longer, it is true, and they will probably continue in force for many years, but this permanence is only relative. Fundamentally they are merely expressions of expedience, like the rules of some great game, and it is easily conceivable that there may arise upon the earth, at some future day, a race to whom they will appear injurious, unreasonable and utterly immoral. " The time may come, indeed, when we will prefer the *Memorabilia* of Socrates to the Bible."[2]

Admitting this, we must admit the inevitable corollary that morality in the absolute sense has nothing to do with truth, and that it is, in fact, truth's exact antithesis. Absolute truth necessarily implies eternal truth. The statement that a man and a woman are unlike was true on the day the first man and woman walked the earth

[1] In his masterly treatise, " Christian Origins," tr. by David A. Huebsch: New York, 1906.
[2] " *Menschliches allzu Menschliches* " III.

and it will be true so long as there are men and women. Such a statement approaches very near our ideal of an absolute truth. But the theory that humility is a virtue is not an absolute truth, for while it was undoubtedly true in ancient Judea, it was not true in ancient Greece and is debatable, to say the least, in modern Europe and America. The Western Catholic Church, despite its extraordinarily successful efforts at permanence, has given us innumerable proofs that laws, in the long run, always turn upon themselves. The popes were infallible when they held that the earth was flat and they were infallible when they decided that it was round — and so we reach a palpable absurdity. Therefore, we may lay it down as an axiom that morality, in itself, is the enemy of truth, and that, for at least half of the time, by the mathematical doctrine of probabilities, it is necessarily untrue.

If this is so, why should any man bother about moral rules and regulations? Why should any man conform to laws formulated by a people whose outlook on the universe probably differed diametrically from his own? Why should any man obey a regulation which is denounced, by his common-sense, as a hodge-podge of absurdities, and why should he model his whole life upon ideals invented to serve the temporary needs of a forgotten race of some past age? These questions Nietzsche asked himself. His conclusion was a complete rejection of all fixed codes of morality, and with them of all gods, messiahs, prophets, saints, popes, bishops, priests, and rulers.

The proper thing for a man to do, he decided, was to formulate his own morality as he progressed from lower to higher things. He should reject the old conceptions of good and evil and substitute for them the human valuations, good and bad. In a word, he should put behind him the morality invented by some dead race to make its own progress easy and pleasant, and credited to some man-made god to give it authority, and put in the place of this a workable personal morality based upon his own power of distinguishing between the things which benefit him and the things which injure him. He should (to make the idea clearer) judge a given action solely by its effect upon his own welfare; his own desire or will to live; and that of his children after him. All notions of sin and virtue should be banished from his mind. He should weigh everything in the scales of individual expedience.

Such a frank wielding of a razor-edged sword in the struggle for existence is frowned upon by our Jewish slave-morality. We are taught to believe that the only true happiness lies in self-effacement; that it is wrong to profit by the misfortune or weakness of another. But against this Nietzsche brings the undeniable answer that all life, no matter how much we idealize it, is, at bottom, nothing more or less than exploitation. The gain of one man is inevitably the loss of some other man. That the emperor may die of a surfeit the peasant must die of starvation. Among human beings, as well as among the bacilli in the hanging drop and the lions in the jungle, there is ever in progress this ancient struggle for existence. It is waged decently, perhaps, but it is none the less savage and unmerciful, and the devil always takes the hindmost.

" Life," says Nietzsche, "is essentially the appropriation, the injury, the vanquishing of the unadapted and weak. Its object is to obtrude its own forms and insure its own unobstructed functioning. Even an organization whose individuals forbear in their dealings with one another (a healthy aristocracy, for example) must, if it would live and not die, act hostilely toward all other organizations. It must endeavor to gain ground, to obtain advantages, to acquire ascendancy. And this is not because it is *immoral*, but because it lives, and all life is will to power." [1]

Nietzsche argues from this that it is absurd to put the stigma of evil upon the mere symptoms of the great struggle. " In itself," he says, " an act of injury, violation, exploitation or annihilation cannot be wrong, for life operates, essentially and fundamentally, by injuring, violating, exploiting and annihilating, and cannot even be conceived of out of this character. One must admit, indeed, that, from the highest biological standpoint, conditions under which the so-called rights of others are recognized must ever be regarded as exceptional conditions — that is to say, as partial restrictions of the instinctive power-seeking will-to-live of the individual, made to satisfy the more powerful will-to-live of the mass. Thus small units of power are sacrificed to create large units of power. To regard the rights of others as being inherent in them, and not as mere compromises for the benefit of the mass-unit, would be to enunciate a principle hostile to life itself." [2]

Nietzsche holds that the rights of an individual may

---

[1] " *Jenseits von Gut und Böse*," § 259.
[2] " *Zur Geneologie der Moral*," II, § 11.

be divided into two classes: those things he is able to do despite the opposition of his fellow men, and those things he is enabled to do by the grace and permission of his fellow men. The second class of rights may be divided again into two groups: those granted through fear and foresight, and those granted as free gifts. But how do fear and foresight operate to make one man concede rights to another man? It is easy enough to discern two ways. In the first place, the grantor may fear the risks of a combat with the grantee, and so give him what he wants without a struggle. In the second place, the grantor, while confident of his ability to overcome the grantee, may forbear because he sees in the struggle a certain diminution of strength on both sides, and in consequence, an impaired capacity for joining forces in effective opposition to some hostile third power.

And now for the rights obtained under the second head — by bestowal and concession. " In this case," says Nietzsche, " one man or race has enough power, and more than enough, to be able to bestow some of it on another man or race." [1] The king appoints one subject viceroy of a province, and so gives him almost regal power, and makes another cup-bearer and so gives him a perpetual right to bear the royal cup. When the power of the grantee, through his inefficiency, decreases, the grantor either restores it to him or takes it away from him altogether. When the power of the grantee, on the contrary, increases, the grantor, in alarm, commonly seeks to undermine it and encroach upon it. When the power of the grantee remains at a level for a considerable time, his rights become

[1] "*Morgenröte*," § 112.

" vested " and he begins to believe that they are inherent in him — that they constitute a gift from the gods and are beyond the will and disposal of his fellow men. As Nietzsche points out, this last happens comparatively seldom. More often, the grantor himself begins to lose power and so comes into conflict with the grantee, and not infrequently they exchange places. "National rights," says Nietzsche, " demonstrate this fact by their constant lapse and regenesis." [1]

Nietzsche believed that a realization of all this would greatly benefit the human race, by ridding it of some of its most costly delusions. He held that so long as it sought to make the struggle for existence a parlor game, with rules laid down by some blundering god — that so long as it regarded its ideas of morality, its aspirations and its hopes as notions implanted by the creator in the mind of Father Adam — that so long as it insisted upon calling things by fanciful names and upon frowning down all effort to reach the ultimate verities — that just so long its progress would be fitful and slow. It was morality that burned the books of the ancient sages, and morality that halted the free inquiry of the Golden Age and substituted for it the credulous imbecility of the Age of Faith. It was a fixed moral code and a fixed theology which robbed the human race of a thousand years by wasting them upon alchemy, heretic-burning, witchcraft and sacerdotalism.

Nietzsche called himself an immoralist. He believed that all progress depended upon the truth and that the truth could not prevail while men yet enmeshed themselves in a web of gratuitous and senseless laws fashioned by

[1] " *Morgenröte*," § 112.

their own hands. He was fond of picturing the ideal immoralist as " a magnificent blond beast " — innocent of " virtue " and " sin " and knowing only " good " and " bad." Instead of a god to guide him, with commandments and the fear of hell, this immoralist would have his own instincts and intelligence. Instead of doing a given thing because the church called it a virtue or the current moral code required it, he would do it because he knew that it would benefit him or his descendants after him. Instead of refraining from a given action because the church denounced it as a sin and the law as a crime, he would avoid it only if he were convinced that the action itself, or its consequences, might work him or his an injury.

Such a man, were he set down in the world today, would bear an outward resemblance, perhaps, to the most pious and virtuous of his fellow-citizens, but it is apparent that his life would have more of truth in it and less of hypocrisy and cant and pretense than theirs. He would obey the laws of the land frankly and solely because he was afraid of incurring their penalties, and for no other reason, and he would not try to delude his neighbors and himself into believing that he saw anything sacred in them. He would have no need of a god to teach him the difference between right and wrong and no need of priests to remind him of this god's teachings. He would look upon the woes and ills of life as inevitable and necessary results of life's conflict, and he would make no effort to read into them the wrath of a peevish and irrational deity at his own or his ancestors' sins. His mind would be absolutely free of thoughts of sin and hell, and in consequence, he would be vastly happier than the majority of persons about him.

All in all, he would be a powerful influence for truth in his community, and as such, would occupy himself with the most noble and sublime task possible to mere human beings: the overthrow of superstition and unreasoning faith, with their long train of fears, horrors, doubts, frauds, injustice and suffering. [1]

Under an ideal government — which Herbert Spencer defines as a government in which the number of laws has reached an irreducible minimum — such a man would prosper a great deal more than the priest-ridden, creed-barnacled masses about him. In a state wherein communistic society, with its levelling usages and customs, had ceased to exist, and wherein each individual of the master class was permitted to live his life as much as possible in accordance with his own notions of good and bad, such a man would stand forth from the herd in proportion as his instincts were more nearly healthy and infallible than the instincts of the herd. Ideal anarchy, in brief, would insure the success of those men who were wisest mentally and strongest physically, and the race would make rapid progress.

It is evident that the communistic and socialistic forms of government at present in fashion in the world oppose such a consummation as often as they facilitate it. Civilization, as we know it, makes more paupers than millionaires,

----

[1] "It is my experience," said Thomas H. Huxley, "that, aside from a few human affections, the only thing that gives lasting and untainted pleasure in the world, is the pursuit of truth and the destruction of error." See "The Life and Letters of T. H. Huxley," by Leonard Huxley; London, 1900.

[2] "Read the suicide tables and see how many despairing men, hopeless of keeping their homes together, pay with their lives the toil im-

and more cripples than Sandows. Its most **conspicuous** products, the church and the king, stand unalterably opposed to all progress. Like the frog of the fable, which essayed to climb out of a well, it slips back quite as often as it goes ahead.

And for these reasons Nietzsche was an anarchist — in the true meaning of that much-bespattered word — just as Herbert Spencer and Arthur Schopenhauer were anarchists before him.

IV

THE SUPERMAN

No doubt the reader who has followed the argument in the preceding chapters will have happened, before now, upon the thought that Nietzsche's chain of reasoning, so far, still has a gap in it. We have seen how he started by investigating Greek art in the light of the Schopenhauerean philosophy, how this led him to look into morality, how he revealed the origin of morality in transitory manifestations of the will to power, and how he came to the conclusion that it was best for a man to reject all ready-made moral ideas and to so order his life that his every action would be undertaken with some notion of making it subserve his own welfare or that of his children or children's children. But a gap remains and it may be expressed in the question: How is a man to define and determine his own welfare and that of the race after him?

Here, indeed, our dionysian immoralist is confronted by a very serious problem, and Nietzsche himself well understood its seriousness. Unless we have in mind some definite ideal of happiness and some definite goal of progress we had better sing the doxology and dismiss our congregation. Christianity has such an ideal and such a goal. The one is a Christ-like life on earth and the other is a place at the right hand of Jehovah in the hereafter. Mohammedanism, a tinsel form of Christianity, paints pictures of the same sort. Buddhism holds out the tempting bait of a race set free from the thrall of earthly desires, with an eternity of blissful nothingness. [1] The other oriental faiths lead in the same direction and Schopenhauer, in his philosophy, laid down the doctrine that humanity would attain perfect happiness only when it had overcome its instinct of self-preservation — that is to say, when it had ceased to desire to live. Even Christian Science — that most grotesque child of credulous faith and incredible denial — offers us the double ideal of a mortal life entirely free from mortal pain and a harp in the heavenly band for all eternity.

What had Nietzsche to offer in place of these things? By what standard was his immoralist to separate the good — or beneficial — things of the world from the bad — or damaging — things? And what was the goal that the philosopher had in mind for his immoralist? The answer to the first question is to be found in Nietzsche's definition of the terms " good " and " bad." " All that elevates the sense of power, the will to power, and power itself " — this is how he defined " good." " All that proceeds from weakness " — this is how he defined " bad." Happiness, he held, is " the feeling that power increases — that resistance is being overcome." " I preach not contentedness," he said, " but more power; not peace, but war; not virtue, but efficiency. The weak

[1] " Nirvana is a cessation of striving for individual existence " — that is, after death. See " Dictionary of Philosophy and Psychology," vol. II, pp. 178 ; New York, 1902.

and defective must go to the wall: that is the first principle of the dionysian charity. And we must help them to go." [1]

To put it more simply, Nietzsche offers the gospel of prudent and intelligent selfishness, of absolute and utter individualism. " One must learn," sang Zarathustra, " how to love oneself, with a whole and hearty love, that one may find life with oneself endurable, and not go gadding about. This gadding about is familiar: it is called ' loving one's neighbor.' " [2] His ideal was an aristocracy which regarded the proletariat merely as a conglomeration of draft animals made to be driven, enslaved and exploited. " A good and healthy aristocracy," he said, " must acquiesce, with a good conscience, in the sacrifice of a legion of individuals, who, for its benefit, must be reduced to slaves and tools. The masses have no right to exist on their own account: their sole excuse for living lies in their usefulness as a sort of superstructure or scaffolding, upon which a more select race of beings may be elevated." [3] Rejecting all permanent rules of good and evil and all notions of brotherhood, Nietzsche held that the aristocratic individualist — and it was to the aristocrat only that he gave, unreservedly, the name of human being — must seek every possible opportunity to increase and exalt his own sense of efficiency, of success, of mastery, of power. Whatever tended to impair him, or to decrease his efficiency, was bad. Whatever tended to increase it — at no matter what cost to others — was good. There must be a complete surrender to the law of natural selection —

---

[1] " *Der Antichrist,*" § 2.
[2] " *Also sprach Zarathustra,*" III.
[3] " *Jenseits von Gut und Böse,*" § 258.

that invariable natural law which ordains that the fit shall survive and the unfit shall perish. All growth must occur at the top. The strong must grow stronger, and that they may do so, they must waste no strength in the vain task of trying to lift up the weak.

The reader may interrupt here with the question we encountered at the start : how is the dionysian individualist to know whether a given action will benefit him or injure him? The answer, of course, lies in the obvious fact that, in every healthy man, instinct supplies a very reliable guide, and that, when instinct fails or is uncertain, experiment must solve the problem. As a general thing, nothing is more patent than the feeling of power — the sense of efficiency, of capacity, of mastery. Every man is constantly and unconsciously measuring himself with his neighbors, and so becoming acutely aware of those things in which he is their superior. Let two men clash in the stock market and it becomes instantly apparent that one is richer, or more resourceful or more cunning than the other. Let two men run after an omnibus and it becomes instantly apparent that one is swifter than the other. Let two men come together as rivals in love, war, drinking or holiness, and one is bound to feel that he has bested the other. Such contests are infinite in variety and in number, and all life, in fact, is made up of them. Therefore, it is plain that every man is conscious of his power, and aware of it when this power is successfully exerted against some other man. In such exertions, argues Nietzsche, lies happiness, and so his prescription for happiness consists in unrestrained yielding to the will to power. That all men worth discussing so yield, despite the moral demand for humility, is so plain that it scarcely needs statement. It is the desire to attain and manifest efficiency and superiority which makes one man explore the wilds of Africa and another pile up vast wealth and another write books of philosophy and another submit to pain and mutilation in the prize ring. It is this yearning which makes men take chances and risk their lives and limbs for glory. Everybody knows, indeed, that in the absence of such a primordial and universal emulation the world would stand still and the race would die. Nietzsche asks nothing more than that the fact be openly recognized and admitted; that every man yield to the yearning unashamed, without hypocrisy and without wasteful efforts to feed and satisfy the yearning of other men at the expense of his own.

It is evident, of course, that the feeling of superiority has a complement in the feeling of inferiority. Every man, in other words, sees himself, in respect to some talent possessed in common by himself and a rival, in one of three ways: he knows that he is superior, he knows that he is inferior, or he is in doubt. In the first case, says Nietzsche, the thing for him to do is to make his superiority still greater by yielding to its stimulation: to make the gap between himself and his rival wider and wider. In the second case, the thing for him to do is to try to make the gap smaller: to lift himself up or to pull his rival down until they are equal or the old disproportion is reversed. In the third case, it is his duty to plunge into a contest and risk his all upon the cast of the die. " I do not exhort you to peace," says Zarathustra, " but to victory!"[1]

[1] "*Also sprach Zarathustra*," I.

If victory comes not, let it be defeat, death and annihilation — but, in any event, let there be a fair fight. Without this constant strife — this constant testing — this constant elimination of the unfit — there can be no progress. " As the smaller surrenders himself to the greater, so the greater must surrender himself to the will to power and stake life upon the issue. It is the mission of the greatest to run risk and danger — to cast dice with death." [1] Power, in a word, is never infinite: it is always becoming.

Practically and in plain language, what does all this mean? Simply that Nietzsche preaches a mighty crusade against all those ethical ideas which teach a man to sacrifice himself for the theoretical good of his inferiors. A culture which tends to equalize, he says, is necessarily a culture which tends to rob the strong and so drag them down, for the strong cannot give of their strength to the weak without decreasing their store. There must be an unending effort to widen the gap; there must be a constant search for advantage, an infinite alertness. The strong man must rid himself of all idea that it is disgraceful to yield to his acute and ever present yearning for still more strength. There must be an abandonment of the old slave-morality and a transvaluation of moral values. The will to power must be emancipated from the bonds of that system of ethics which brands it with infamy, and so makes the one all-powerful instinct of every sentient creature loathsome and abominable.

It is only the under-dog, he says, that believes in equality. It is only the groveling and inefficient mob that seeks to reduce all humanity to one dead level, for it is only the

[1] " *Also sprach Zarathustra,*" II.

mob that would gain by such leveling. " ' There are nc higher men,' says the crowd in the market place. ' We are all equal; man is man; in the presence of God we are all equal!' In the presence of God, indeed! But I tell you that God is dead!" So thunders Zarathustra.[1] That is to say, our idea of brotherhood is part of the mob-morality of the ancient Jews, who evolved it out of their own helplessness and credited it to their god. We have inherited their morality with their god and so we find it difficult — in the mass — to rid ourselves of their point of view. Nietzsche himself rejected utterly the Judaic god and he believed that the great majority of intelligent men of his time were of his mind. That he was not far wrong in this assumption is evident to everyone. At the present time, indeed, it is next to impossible to find a sane man in all the world who believes in the actual existence of the deity described in the old testament. All theology is now an effort to explain away this god. Therefore, argues Nietzsche, it is useless to profess an insincere con-currence in a theistic idea at which our common sense revolts, and ridiculous to maintain the inviolability of an ethical scheme grounded upon this idea.

It may be urged here that, even if the god of Judea is dead, the idea of brotherhood still lives, and that, as a matter of fact, it is an idea inherent in the nature of man, and one that owes nothing to the rejected supernaturalism which once fortified and enforced it. That is to say, it may be argued that the impulse to self-sacrifice and mutual help is itself an instinct. The answer to this lies in the very patent fact that it is not. Nothing, indeed, is more

[1] " *Also sprach Zarathustra*," IV.

apparent than the essential selfishness of man. In so far
as they are able to defy or evade the moral code without
shame or damage, the strong always exploit the weak.
The rich man puts up the price of the necessities of life
and so makes himself richer and the poor poorer. The
emperor combats democracy. The political boss opposes
the will of the people for his own advantage. The inventor
patents his inventions and so increases his relative superiority to the common run of men. The ecclesiastic leaves
a small parish for a larger one — because the pay is better
or "the field offers wider opportunities," *i. e.* gives him
a better chance to "save souls" and so increases his
feeling of efficiency. The philanthropist gives away
millions because the giving visualizes and makes evident
to all men his virtue and power. It is ever the same in
this weary old world: every slave would be a master if
he could. Therefore, why deny it? Why make it a crime
to do what every man's instincts prompt him to do? Why
call it a sin to do what every man does, insofar as he can?
The man who throws away his money or cripples himself
with drink, or turns away from his opportunities — we
call him a lunatic or a fool. And yet, wherein does he
differ from the ideal holy man of our slave-morality —
the holy man who tortures himself, neglects his body,
starves his mind and reduces himself to parasitism, that
the weak, the useless and unfit may have, through his
ministrations, some measure of ease? Such is the argument of the dionysian philosophy. It is an argument
for the actual facts of existence — however unrighteous
and ugly those facts may be.

That the lifting up of the weak, in the long run, is an

unprofitable and useless business is evident on very brief
reflection. Philanthropy, considered largely, is inevitably
a failure. Now and then we may transform an individual
pauper or drunkard into a useful, producing citizen, but
this happens very seldom. Nothing is more patent, indeed,
than the fact that charity merely converts the unfit — who,
in the course of nature, would soon die out and so cease
to encumber the earth — into parasites — who live on
indefinitely, a nuisance and a burden to their betters.
The " reformed " drunkard always goes back to his cups :
drunkardness, as every physician knows, is as essentially
incurable as congenital insanity. And it is the same
with poverty. We may help a pauper to survive by giving
him food and drink, but we cannot thereby make an
efficient man of him — we cannot rid him of the unfitness
which made him a pauper. There are, of course, ex-
ceptions to this, as to other rules, but the validity of the
rule itself will not be questioned by any observant man.
It goes unquestioned, indeed, by those who preach the
doctrine of charity the loudest. They know it would be
absurd to argue that helping the unfit is profitable to
the race, and so they fall back, soon or late, upon the
argument that charity is ordained of God and that the
impulse to it is implanted in every decent man. Nietzsche
flatly denies this. Charity, he says, is a man-made idea,
with which the gods have nothing to do. Its sole effect
is to maintain the useless at the expense of the strong. In
the mass, the helped can never hope to discharge in full
their debt to the helpers. The result upon the race is
thus retrogression.

   And now for our second question. What was the goal

Nietzsche had in mind for his immoralist? What was
to be the final outcome of his overturning of all morality?
Did he believe the human race would progress until men
became gods and controlled the sun and stars as they
now control the flow of great rivers? Or did he believe that
the end of it all would be annihilation? After the publication of Nietzsche's earlier books, with their ruthless
tearing down of the old morality, these questions were
asked by critics innumerable in all the countries of Europe.
The philosopher was laughed at as a crazy iconoclast
who destroyed without rebuilding. He was called a
visionary and a lunatic, and it was reported and believed
that he had no answer: that his philosophy was doomed
to bear itself to the earth, like an arch without a keystone.
But in April, 1883, he began the publication of " *Also
sprach Zarathustra* " and therein his reply was written
large.

"I teach you," cries Zarathustra, " the superman!
Man is something that shall be surpassed. What, to
man, is the ape? A joke or a shame. Man shall be the
same to the superman: a joke or shame. . . . Man is
a bridge connecting ape and superman. . . . The superman will be the final flower and ultimate expression of the
earth. I conjure you to be faithful to the earth. . . to
cease looking beyond the stars for your hopes and rewards.
You must sacrifice yourself to the earth that one day it
may bring forth the superman." [1]

Here we hearken unto the materialist, the empiricist,
the monist *par excellence*. And herein we perceive dimly
the outlines of the superman. He will be rid of all delu-

[1] "*Also sprach Zarathustra*," I.

sions that hamper and oppress the will to power. He will
be perfect in body and perfect in mind. He will know
everything worth knowing and have strength and skill
and cunning to defend himself against any conceivable
foe. Because the prospect of victory will feed his will to
power he will delight in combat, and his increasing capacity
for combat will decrease his sensitiveness to pain. Conscious of his efficiency, he will be happy; having no illusions regarding a heaven and a hell, he will be content.
He will see life as something pleasant — something to be
faced gladly and with a laugh. He will say " yes " alike
to its pleasures and to its ills. Rid of the notion that there
is anything filthy in living — that the flesh is abominable [1]
and life an affliction [2] — he will grow better and better
fitted to meet the conditions of actual existence. He will
be scornful, merciless and supremely fit. He will be set
free from man's fear of gods and of laws, just as man has
been set free from the ape's fear of lions and of open
places.

To put it simply, the superman's thesis will be this:
that he has been put into the world without his consent,
that he must live in the world, that he owes nothing to the
other people there, and that he knows nothing whatever
of existence beyond the grave. Therefore, it will be his
effort to attain the highest possible measure of satisfaction
for the only unmistakable and genuinely healthy instinct
within him: the yearning to live — to attain power —
to meet and overcome the influences which would weaken
or destroy him. " Keep yourselves up, my brethren,"

---

[1] Galatians V, 19, 20, 21.
[2] Job V, 7; XIV, 1; Ecclesiastes I, 1.

cautions Zarathustra, " learn to keep yourselves up! The
sea is stormy and many seek to keep afloat by your aid.
The sea is stormy and all are overboard. Well, cheer up
and save yourselves, ye old seamen! . . . What is your
fatherland? The land wherein your children will dwell.
. . . Thus does your love to these remote ones speak:
' Disregard your neighbors! Man is something to be
surpassed!' Surpass yourself at the expense of your
neighbor. What you cannot seize, let no man *give* you.
. . . Let him who can command, obey!"[1] The idea,
by this time, should be plain. The superman, in the
struggle for existence, asks and gives no quarter. He
believes that it is the destiny of sentient beings to progress
upward, and he is willing to sacrifice himself that his race
may do so. But his sacrifice must benefit, not his neighbor — not the man who should and must look out for
himself — but the generations yet unborn.

It must be borne in mind that the superman will make a
broad distinction between instinct and passion — that
he will not mistake the complex thing we call love, with
its costly and constant hurricanes of emotion, for the
instinct of reproduction — that he will not mistake mere
anger for war —that he will not mistake patriotism, with
all its absurdities and illusions, for the homing instinct.
The superman, in brief, will know how to renounce as well
as how to possess, but his renunciation will be the child,
not of faith or of charity, but of expediency. " Will
nothing beyond your capacity," says Zarathustra. " Demand nothing of yourself that is beyond achievement!
. . . The higher a thing is, the less often does it succeed.

[1] " *Also sprach Zarathustra,*" I.

Be of good cheer! What matter! Learn to laugh at
yourselves! . . . Suppose you have failed? Has not
the future gained by your failure?"[1]   The superman,
as Nietzsche was fond of putting it, must play at dice
with death. He must have ever in mind no other goal
but the good of the generations after him. He must be
willing to battle with his fellows, as with illusions, that
those who came after may not be afflicted by these enemies.
He must be supremely unmoral and unscrupulous. His
must be the gospel of eternal defiance.

Nietzsche, it will be observed, was unable to give any
very definite picture of this proud, heaven-kissing superman. It is only in Zarathustra's preachments to "the
higher man," a sort of bridge between man and superman,
that we may discern the philosophy of the latter. On one
occasion Nietzsche penned a passage which seemed to
compare the superman to "the great blond beasts"
which ranged Europe in the days of the mammoth, and
from this fact many commentators have drawn the conclusion that he had in mind a mere two-legged brute, with
none of the higher traits that we now speak of as distinctly
human. But, as a matter of fact, he harbored no such idea.
In another place, wherein he speaks of three metamor-
phoses of the race, under the allegorical names of the camel,
the lion and the child, he makes this plain. The camel,
a hopeless beast of burden, is man. But when the camel
goes into the solitary desert, it throws off its burden and
becomes a lion. That is to say, the heavy and hampering
load of artificial dead-weight called morality is cast aside
and the instinct to live — or, as Nietzsche insists upon

[1] "*Also sprach Zarathustra*," IV.

regarding it, the will to power — is given free rein. The lion is the " higher man " — the intermediate stage between man and superman. The latter appears neither as camel nor lion, but as a little child. He knows a little child's peace. He has a little child's calm. Like a babe *in utero,* he is ideally adapted to his environment.

Zarathustra sees man " like a camel kneeling down to be heavy laden." What are his burdens? One is " to humiliate oneself." Another is " to love those who despise us." In the desert comes the first metamorphosis, and the " thou shalt " of the camel becomes the " I will " of the lion. And what is the mission of the lion? " To create for itself freedom for new creating." After the lion comes the child. It is " innocence and oblivion, a new starting, a play, a wheel rolling by itself, a prime motor, a holy asserting." The thought here is cast in the heightened language of mystic poetry, but its meaning, I take it, is not lost. [1]

Nietzsche, even more than Schopenhauer, recognized the fact that great mental progress — in the sense that mental progress means an increased capacity for grappling with the conditions of existence — necessarily has to depend upon physical efficiency. In exceptional cases a great mind may inhabit a diseased body, but it is obvious that this is not the rule. A nation in which the average man had but one hand and the duration of life was but 20 years could not hope to cope with even the weakest nation of modern Europe. So it is plain that the first step in the improvement of the race must be the improvement of the body. Jesus Christ gave expression to this need

[1] " *Also sprach Zarathustra.*" I.

by healing the sick, and the chief end and aim of all modern science is that of making life more and more bearable. Every labor-saving machine ever invented by man has no other purpose than that of saving bodily wear and tear. Every religion aims to rescue man from the racking fear of hell and the strain of trying to solve the great problems of existence for himself. Every scheme of government that we know is, at bottom, a mere device for protecting human beings from injury and death.

Thus it will be seen that Nietzsche's program of progress does not differ from other programs quite so much as, at first sight, it may seem to do. He laid down the principle that, before anything else could be accomplished, we must have first looked to the human machine. As we have seen, the intellect is a mere symptom of the will to live. Therefore whatever removes obstacles to the free exercise of this will to live, necessarily promotes and increases intelligence. A race that was never incapacitated by illness would be better fitted than any other race for any conceivable intellectual pursuit: from making money to conjugating Greek verbs. Nietzsche merely states this obvious fact in an unaccustomed form.

His superman is to give his will to live — or will to power, as you please — perfect freedom. As a result, those individuals in whom this instinct most accurately meets the conditions of life on earth will survive, and in their offspring, by natural laws, the instinct itself will become more and more accurate. That is to say, there will appear in future generations individuals in whom this instinct will tend more and more to order the performance of acts of positive benefit and to forbid the perform-

ance of acts likely to result in injury. This injury, it is
plain, may take the form of unsatisfied wants as well as
of broken skulls.   Therefore, the man — or superman —
in whom the instinct reaches perfection will unconsciously
steer clear of all the things which harass and batter mankind today — exhausting self-denials as well as exhausting
passions.   Whatever seems likely to benefit him, he will
do; whatever seems likely to injure him he will avoid.
When he is in doubt, he will dare — and accept defeat or
victory with equal calm.   His attitude, in brief, will be
that of a being who faces life as he finds it, defiantly and
unafraid — who knows how to fight and how to forbear
— who sees things as they actually are, and not as they
might or should be, and so wastes no energy yearning for
the moon or in butting his head against stone walls.
" This new table, O my brethren, I put over you: *Be
hard!* " [1]

Such was the goal that Nietzsche held before the human
race.   Other philosophers before him had attempted
the same thing.   Schopenhauer had put forward his idea
of a race that had found happiness in putting away its
desire to live.   Comte had seen a vision of a race whose
every member sought the good of all.   The humanitarians
of all countries had drawn pictures of Utopias peopled
by beings who had outgrown all human instincts — who
had outgrown the *one* fundamental, unquenchable and
eternal instinct of every living thing: the desire to conquer,
to live, to remain alive.   Nietzsche cast out all these fine
ideals as essentially impossible.   Man was of the earth,
earthy, and his heavens and hells were creatures of his

[1] *Also sprach Zarathustra,"* III.

own vaporings. Only after he had ceased dreaming of them and thrown off his crushing burden of transcendental morality — only thus and then could he hope to rise out of the slough of despond in which he wallowed.

V

IN the superman Nietzsche showed the world a conceivable and possible goal for all human effort. But there
still remained a problem and it was this: When the superman at last appears on earth, what then? Will there be
another super-superman to follow and a super-super-
superman after that? In the end, will man become the
equal of the creator of the universe, whoever or whatever
He may be? Or will a period of decline come after, with
a return down the long line, through the superman to
man again, and then on to the anthropoid ape, to the
lower mammals, to the asexual cell, and, finally, to mere
inert matter, gas, ether and empty space?

Nietzsche answered these questions by offering the
theory that the universe moves in regular cycles and that
all which is now happening on earth, and in all the stars,
to the uttermost, will be repeated, again and again,
throughout eternity. In other words, he dreamed of a
cosmic year, corresponding, in some fashion, to the ter-
restrial year. Man, who has sprung from the elements,
will rise into superman, and perhaps infinitely beyond,
and then, in the end, by catastrophe or slow decline, he
will be resolved into the primary elements again, and the
whole process will begin anew.

This notion, it must be admitted, was not original with
Nietzsche and it would have been better for his philosophy
and for his repute as an intelligent thinker had he never
sought to elucidate it. In his early essay on history he first
mentioned it and there he credited it to its probable inventors — the Pythagoreans.[1] It was their belief that,
whenever the heavenly bodies all returned to certain fixed
relative positions, the whole history of the universe began
anew. The idea seemed to fascinate Nietzsche, in whom,
despite his worship of the actual, there was an ever-
evident strain of mysticism, and he referred to it often
in his later books. The pure horror of it — of the notion
that all the world's suffering would have to be repeated
again and again, that men would have to die over and over
again for all infinity, that there was no stopping place or
final goal — the horror of all this appealed powerfully to
his imagination. Frau Andreas-Salomé tells us that he
" spoke of it only in a low voice and with every sign of the
profoundest emotion " and there is reason to believe that,
at one time, he thought there might be some confirmation
of it in the atomic theory, and that his desire to go to Vienna
to study the natural sciences was prompted by a wish to
investigate this notion. Finally he became convinced
that there was no ground for such a belief in any of the
known facts of science, and after that, we are told, his
shuddering horror left him.

[1] Pythagoras (B. C. 570?–500?) was a Greek who brought the doctrine of the transmigration of souls from Asia Minor to Greece. In
Magna Graecia he founded a mystical brotherhood, half political party
and half school of philosophy. It survived him for many years and its
members revered him as the sage of sages. He was a bitter foe to democracy and took part in wars against its spread.

It was then possible for him to deal with the doctrine of eternal recurrence as a mere philosophical speculation, without the uncomfortable reality of a demonstrated scientific fact, and thereafter he spent much time considering it. In "*Also sprach Zarathustra*" he puts it into the brain of his prophet-hero, and shows how it wellnigh drove the latter mad.

"I will come back," muses Zarathustra, "with this sun, with this earth, with this eagle, with this serpent — *not* for a new life or a better life, but to the same life I am now leading. I will come back unto this same old life, in the greatest things and in the smallest, in order to teach once more the eternal recurrence of all things." [1]

In the end, Nietzsche turned this fantastic idea into a device for exalting his superman. The superman is one who realizes that all of his struggles will be in vain, and that, in future cycles, he will have to go through them over and over again. Yet he has attained such a superhuman immunity to all emotion — to all ideas of pleasure and pain — that the prospect does not daunt him. Despite its horror, he faces it unafraid. It is all a part of life, and in consequence it is good. He has learned to agree to everything that exists — even to the ghastly necessity for living again and again. In a word, he does not fear an endless series of lives, because life, to him, has lost all the terrors which a merely human man sees in it.

"Let us not only endure the inevitable," says Nietzsche, "and still less hide it from ourselves: *let us love it!*"

---

[1] "*Also sprach Zarathustra*," III.

As Vernon Lee (Miss Violet Paget) [1] has pointed out, this idea is scarcely to be distinguished from the fundamental tenet of stoicism.   Miss Paget also says that it bears a close family resemblance to that denial of pain which forms the basis of Christian Science, but this is not true, for a vast difference exists between a mere denial of pain and a willingness to admit it, face it, and triumph over it. But the notion appears, in endless guises, in many philosophies and Goethe voiced it, after a fashion, in his maxim, " *Entbehren sollst du* " (" Man must do without "). The idea of eternal recurrence gives point, again, to a familiar anecdote.   This concerns a joker who goes to an inn, eats his fill and then says to the innkeeper: " You and I will be here again in a million years: let me pay you then."   " Very   well,"   replies   the   quick-witted innkeeper, " but first pay me for the beefsteak you ate the last time you were here — a million years ago."

Despite Nietzsche's conclusion that the known facts of existence do not bear it out, and the essential impossibility of discussing it to profit, the doctrine of eternal recurrence is by no means unthinkable.   The celestial cycle put forward, as an hypothesis, by modern astronomy — the progression, that is, from gas to molten fluid, from fluid to solid, and from solid, by catastrophe, back to gas again — is easily conceivable, and it is easily conceivable, too, that the earth, which has passed through an uninhabitable state into a habitable state, may one day become uninhabitable again, and so keep see-sawing back and forth through all eternity.

But what will be the effect of eternal recurrence upon

[1] *North American Review*, Dec., 1904.

the superman? The tragedy of it, as we have seen, will merely serve to make him heroic. He will defy the universe and say "yes" to life. Putting aside all thought of conscious existence beyond the grave, he will seek to live as nearly as possible in exact accordance with those laws laid down for the evolution of sentient beings on earth when the cosmos was first set spinning. But how will he know when he has attained this end? How will he avoid going mad with doubts about his own knowledge? Nietzsche gave much thought, first and last, to this epistemological problem, and at different times he leaned toward different schools, but his writing, taken as a whole, indicates that the fruit of his meditations was a thorough-going empiricism. The superman, indeed, is an empiricist who differs from Bacon only in the infinitely greater range of his observation and experiment. He learns by bitter experience and he generalizes from this knowledge. An utter and unquestioning materialist, he knows nothing of mind except as a function of body. To him speculation seems vain and foolish: his concern is ever with imminent affairs. That is to say, he believes a thing to be true when his eyes, his ears, his nose and his hands tell him it is true. And in this he will be at one with all those men who are admittedly above the mass today. Reject empiricism and you reject at one stroke, the whole sum of human knowledge.

When a man stubs his toe, for example, the facts that the injured member swells and that it hurts most frightfully appear to him as absolute certainties. If we deny that he actually knows these things and maintain that the spectacle of the swelling and the sensation of pain are mere creatures of his mind, we cast adrift from all order and common-sense in the universe and go sailing upon a stormy sea of crazy metaphysics and senseless contradictions. There are many things that we do not know, and in the nature of things, never can know. We do not know *why* phosphorus has a tendency to combine with oxygen, but the fact that it *has* we *do* know — and if we try to deny we *do* know it, we must deny that we are sentient beings, and in consequence, must regard life and the universe as mere illusions. No man with a sound mind makes any such denial. The things about us are real, just as our feeling that we are alive is real.[1]

From this it must be plain that the superman will have the same guides that we have, viz. : his instincts and senses. But in him they will be more accurate and more acute than in us, because the whole tendency of his scheme of things will be to fortify and develop them.[2] If any race

---

[1] *Vide* the chapter on " Truth."

[2] It is very evident, I take it, that the principal function of all science is the widening of our perceptions. The chief argument for idealism used to be the axiom that our power of perception was necessarily limited and that it would be limited forever. This may be true still, but it is now apparent that these limits are being indefinitely extended, and may be extended, in future, almost infinitely. A thousand years ago, if any one had laid down the thesis that malaria was caused by minute animals, he would have been dismissed as a lunatic, because it was evident that no one could see these animals, and it was evident, too — that is to say, the scientists of that time held it to be evident — that this inability to see them would never be removed, because the human eye would always remain substantially as it was. But now we know that the microscope may increase the eye's power of perception a thousandfold. When we consider the fact that the spectroscope has enabled us to make a chemical analysis of the sun, that the telephone has enabled us to hear 2,000 miles and that the x-rays have enabled us to see through

of Europe devoted a century to exercising its right arms, its descendants, in the century following, would have right arms like piston-rods. In the same way, the superman, by subordinating everything else to his instinct to live, will make it evolve into something very accurate and efficient. His whole concern, in brief, will be to live as long as possible and so to avoid as much as possible all of those things which shorten life — by injuring the body from without or by using up energy within. As a result he will cease all effort to learn *why* the world exists and will devote himself to acquiring knowledge *how* it exists. This knowledge *how* will be within his capacity even more than it is within our capacity today. Our senses, as we have seen, have given us absolute knowledge that stubbing the toe results in swelling and pain. The superman's developed senses will give him absolute knowledge about everything that exists on earth. He will know exactly *how* a tubercle bacillus attacks the lung tissue, he will know exactly *how* the blood fights the bacillus, and he will know exactly *how* to interfere in this battle in such a manner that the blood shall be invariably victorious. In a word, he will be the possessor of exact and complete knowledge regarding the working of all the benign and malignant forces in the world about him, but he will not bother himself about insoluble problems. He will waste no time speculating as to *why* tubercle bacilli were sent into the world: his instinct to live will be satisfied by his success in stamping them out.

flesh and bone, we must admit without reservation, that our power of perception, at some future day, may be infinite. And if we admit this we must admit the essential possibility of the superman.

The ideal superman then is merely a man in whom instinct works without interference — a man who feels that it is right to live and that the only knowledge worth while is that which makes life longer and more bearable. The superman's instinct for life is so strong that its mere exercise satisfies him, and so makes him happy. He doesn't bother about the unknown void beyond the grave: it is sufficient for him to know that he is alive and that being alive is pleasant. He is, in the highest sense, a utilitarian, and he believes to the letter in Auguste Comte's[1] dictum that the only thing living beings can ever hope to accomplish on earth is to adapt themselves perfectly to the natural forces around them — to the winds and the rain, the hills and the sea, the thunderbolt and the germ of disease.

" I am a dionysian! " cries Nietzsche. " I am an immoralist! " He means simply that his ideal is a being capable of facing the horrors of life unafraid, of meeting great enemies and slaying them, of gazing down upon the earth in pride and scorn, of making his own way and bearing his own burdens. In the profane folk-philosophy of every healthy and vigorous people, we find some trace of this dionysian idea. " Let us so live day by day," says a distinguished American statesman, " that we can look any man in the eye and tell him to go to hell! " We get a subtle sort of joy out of this saying because it voices our racial advance toward individualism and away from servility and oppression. We believe in freedom, in

---

[1] "*Cours de philosophie positive*," tr. by Helen Martineau; London., 1853.

toleration, in moral anarchy.   We have put this notion into innumerable homely forms.

> Things have come to a hell of a pass
> When a man can't wallop his own jackass!

So we phrase it.   The superman, did he stalk the earth, would say the same thing

VI

CHRISTIANITY

Nietzsche's astonishingly keen and fearless criticism of Christianity has probably sent forth wider ripples than any other stone he ever heaved into the pool of philistine contentment. He opened his attack in " *Menschliches allzu Menschliches*," the first book of his maturity, and he was still at it, in full fuming and fury, in " *Der Antichrist*," the last thing he was destined to write. The closing chapter of " *Der Antichrist* " — his swan song — contains his famous phillipic, beginning " I condemn." It recalls Zola's " *j'accuse* " letter in the Dreyfus case, but it is infinitely more sweeping and infinitely more uproarious and daring.

" I condemn Christianity," it begins. " I bring against it the most terrible of accusations that ever an accuser put into words. It is to me the greatest of all imaginable corruptions. . . . It has left nothing untouched by its depravity. It has made a worthlessness out of every value, a lie out of every truth, a sin out of everything straightforward, healthy and honest. Let anyone dare to speak to me of its humanitarian blessings! To do away with pain and woe is contrary to its principles. It lives by pain and woe: it has created pain and woe in order to perpetuate itself. It invented the idea of original sin.[1] It invented ' the equality of souls before God ' — that cover for all the rancour of the useless and base. . . . It has bred the art of self-violation — repugnance and contempt for all good and cleanly instincts. . . . Parasitism is its praxis. It combats all good red-blood, all love and all hope for life, with its anæmic ideal of holiness. It sets up ' the other world ' as a negation of every reality. The cross is the rallying post for a conspiracy against health, beauty, well-being, courage, intellect, benevolence — against life itself. . . .

" This eternal accusation I shall write upon all walls: I call Christianity the one great curse, the one great intrinsic depravity, . . . for which no expedient is sufficiently poisonous, secret, subterranean, mean ! I call it the one immortal shame and blemish upon the human race ! " [2]

So much for the philosopher's vociferous hurrah at the close of his argument. In the argument itself it is apparent that his indictment of Christianity contains two chief counts. The first is the allegation that it is essentially untrue and unreasonable, and the second is the theory that it is degrading. The first of these counts is not unfamiliar to the students of religious history. It was first voiced by that high priest who " rent his clothes " and cried " What need have we of any further witnesses? Ye have heard the blasphemy." [3] It was voiced again by the Romans who threw converts to the lions, and after the

---

[1] *Vide* the chapter on " Crime and Punishment."
[2] " *Der Antichrist,*" § 62.
[3] St. Mark XIV, 63, 64.

long silence of the middle ages, it was piped forth
again by Voltaire, Hume, the encyclopedists and Paine.
After the philosophers and scientists who culminated in
Darwin had rescued reason for all time from the transcendental nonsense of the cobweb-spinners and metaphysicians, Huxley came to the front with his terrific heavy
artillery and those who still maintained that Christianity
was historically true — Gladstone and the rest of the
forlorn hope — were mowed down. David Strauss,
Lessing, Eichhorn, Michaelis, Bauer, Meyer, Ritschl, [1]
Pfleiderer and a host of others joined in the chorus and in
Nietzsche's early manhood the battle was practically won.
By 1880 no reasonable man actually believed that there
were devils in the swine, and it was already possible to
deny the physical resurrection and still maintain a place
in respectable society. Today a literal faith in the gospel
narrative is confined to ecclesiastical reactionaries, pious
old ladies and men about to be hanged.

Therefore, Nietzsche did not spend much time examining the historical credibility of Christianity. He did not
try to prove, like Huxley, that the witnesses to the resurrection were superstitious peasants and hysterical women,
nor did he seek to show, like Huxley again, that Christ
might have been taken down from the cross before he was

---

[1] Albrecht Ritschl (1822-89), who is not to be confused with Nietzsche's teacher at Bonn and Leipsic. Ritschl founded what is called the
Ritschlian movement in theology. This has for its object the abandonment of supernaturalism and the defence of Christianity as a mere scheme
of living. It admits that the miracle stories are fables and even con-
cedes that Christ was not divine, but maintains that his teachings
represent the best wisdom of the human race. See Denny: "Studies
in Theology," New York, 1894.

dead. He was intensely interested in all such inquiries, but he saw that, in the last analysis, they left a multitude of problems unsolved. The solution of these unsolved problems was the task that he took unto himself. Tunneling down, in his characteristic way, into the very foundations of the faith, he endeavored to prove that it was based upon contradictions and absurdities; that its dogmas were illogical and its precepts unworkable; and that its cardinal principles presupposed the acceptance of propositions which, to the normal human mind, were essentially unthinkable. This tunneling occupied much of Nietzsche's energy in " *Menschliches allzu Menschliches*," and he returned to it again and again, in all of the other books that preceded " *Der Antichrist*." His method of working may be best exhibited by a few concrete examples.

Prayer, for instance, is an exceedingly important feature of Christian worship and any form of worship in which it had no place would be necessarily unchristian.[1] But upon what theory is prayer based? Examining the matter from all sides you will have to conclude that it is reasonable only upon two assumptions: first, that it is possible to change the infallible will and opinion of the deity, and secondly, that the petitioner is capable of judging what he needs. Now, Christianity maintains, as one of its main dogmas, that the deity is omniscient and all-wise,[2] and,

---

[1] Ph. IV, 6: "Be careful for nothing; but in everything by prayer and supplication, with thanksgiving, let your requests be made known to God."

[2] Deut. XXXII, 4: "He is the rock, his work is perfect." See also a hundred similar passages in the Old and New Testaments.

as another fundamental doctrine, that human beings are absolutely unable to solve their problems without heavenly aid [1] *i. e.* that the deity necessarily knows what is best for any given man better than that man can ever hope to know it himself. Therefore, Christianity, in ordaining prayer, orders, as a condition of inclusion in its communion, an act which it holds to be useless. This contradiction, argues Nietzsche, cannot be explained away in terms comprehensible to the human intelligence.

Again Christianity holds that man is a mere creature of the deity's will, and yet insists that the individual be judged and punished for his acts. In other words, it tries to carry free will on one shoulder and determinism on the other, and its doctors and sages have themselves shown that they recognize the absurdity of this by their constant, but futile efforts to decide which of the two shall be abandoned. This contradiction is a legacy from Judaism, and Mohammedanism suffers from it, too. Those sects which have sought to remove it by an entire acceptance of determinism — under the name of predestination, fatalism, or what not — have become bogged in hopeless morasses of unreason and dogmatism. It is a cardinal doctrine of Presbyterianism, for instance, that " by the decree of God, for the manifestation of his glory, some men and angels are predestinated unto everlasting life and others foreordained to everlasting death . . . without any foresight of faith or good works, or perseverance in either of them, or any other thing in the creature, as con-

---

[1] Isaiah XLIV, 8 : " Now, O Lord, thou art our Father ; we are the clay and thou our potter ; and we all are the work of thy hand."

ditions. . . ." [1] In other words, no matter how faithfully one man tries to follow in the footsteps of Christ, he may go to hell, and no matter how impiously another sins, he may be foreordained for heaven. That such a belief makes all religion, faith and morality absurd is apparent. That it is, at bottom, utterly unthinkable to a reasoning being is also plain.

Nietzsche devoted a great deal of time during his first period of activity to similar examinations of Christian ideas and he did a great deal to supplement the historical investigations of those English and German savants whose ruthless exposure of fictions and frauds gave birth to what we now call the higher criticism. But his chief service was neither in the field of historical criticism nor in that of the criticism of dogmas. Toward the end of his life he left the business of examining biblical sources to the archeologists and historians, whose equipment for the task was necessarily greater than his own, and the business of reducing Christian logic to contradiction and absurdity to the logicians. Thereafter, his own work took him a step further down and in the end he got to the very bottom of the subject. The answer of the theologians had been that, even if you denied the miracles, the gospels, the divinity of Christ and his very existence as an actual man, you would have to admit that Christianity itself was sufficient excuse for its own existence; that it had made the world better and that it provided a workable scheme of life by which men could live and die and rise to higher things. This answer, for awhile, staggered the agnostics

[1] "The Constitution of the Presbyterian Church in the United States," pp. 16 to 20 : Philadelphia, 1841.

and Huxley himself evidently came near being convinced that it was beyond rebuttal.[1] But it only made Nietzsche spring into the arena more confident than ever. " Very well," he said, " we will argue it out. You say that Christianity has made the world better? I say that it has made it worse! You say that it is comforting and up-lifting? I say that it is cruel and degrading! You say that it is the best religion mankind has ever invented? I say it is the most dangerous! "

Having thus thrown down the gage of battle, Nietzsche proceeded to fight like a Tartar, and it is but common fairness to say that, for a good while, he bore the weight of his opponents' onslaught almost unaided. The world was willing enough to abandon its belief in Christian supernaturalism and as far back as the early 80's the dignitaries of the Church of England — to employ a blunt but expressive metaphor — had begun to get in out of the wet. But the pietists still argued that Christianity remained the fairest flower of civilization and that it met a real and ever-present human want and made mankind better. To deny this took courage of a decidedly unusual sort — courage that was willing to face, not only ecclesi-astical anathema and denunciation, but also the almost automatic opposition of every so-called respectable man.

---

[1] To the end of his days Huxley believed that, to the average human being, even of the highest class, some sort of faith would always be necessary. "My work in the London hospitals," he said, "taught me that the preacher often does as much good as the doctor." It would be interesting to show how this notion has been abandoned in recent years. The trained nurse, who was unknown in Huxley's hospital days, now takes the place of the confessor, and as Dr. Osler has shown us in "Science and Immortality," men die just as comfortably as before.

But Nietzsche, whatever his deficiencies otherwise, certainly was not lacking in assurance, and so, when he came to write " *Der Antichrist* " he made his denial thunderous and uncompromising beyond expression. No medieval bishop ever pronounced more appalling curses. No backwoods evangelist ever laid down the law with more violent eloquence. The book is the shortest he ever wrote, but it is by long odds the most compelling. Beginning *allegro*, it proceeds from *forte*, by an uninterrupted *crescendo* to *allegro con moltissimo molto fortissimo.* The sentences run into mazes of italics, dashes and asterisks. It is German that one cannot read aloud without roaring and waving one's arm.

Christianity, says Nietzsche, is the most dangerous system of slave-morality the world has ever known. " It has waged a deadly war against the highest type of man. It has put a ban on all his fundamental instincts. It has distilled evil out of these instincts. It makes the strong and efficient man its typical outcast man. It has taken the part of the weak and the low ; it has made an ideal out of its antagonism to the very instincts which tend to preserve life and well-being. . . . It has taught men to regard their highest impulses as sinful — as temptations." [1] In a word, it tends to rob mankind of all those qualities which fit any living organism to survive in the struggle for existence.

As we shall see later on, civilization obscures and even opposes this struggle for existence, but it is in progress all the same, at all times and under all conditions. Every one knows, for instance, that one-third of the human

[1] *" Der Antichrist,"* § 5.

beings born into the world every year die before they are five years old. The reason for this lies in the fact that they are, in some way or other, less fitted to meet the conditions of life on earth than the other two-thirds. The germ of cholera infantum is an enemy to the human race, and so long as it continues to exist upon earth it will devote all of its activity to attacking human infants and seeking to destroy them. It happens that some babies recover from cholera infantum, while others die of it. This is merely another way of saying that the former, having been born with a capacity for resisting the attack of the germ, or having been given the capacity artificially, are better fitted to survive, and that the latter, being incapable of making this resistance, are unfit.

All life upon earth is nothing more than a battle with the enemies of life. A germ is such an enemy, cold is such an enemy, lack of food is such an enemy, and others that may be mentioned are lack of water, ignorance of natural laws, armed foes and deficient physical strength. The man who is able to get all of the food he wants, and so can nourish his body until it becomes strong enough to combat the germs of disease; who gets enough to drink, who has shelter from the elements, who has devised means for protecting himself against the desires of other men— who yearn, perhaps, who take for themselves some of the things that he has acquired — such a man, it is obvious, is far better fitted to live than a man who has none of these things. He is far better fitted to survive, in a purely physical sense, because his body is nourished and protected, and he is far better fitted to attain happiness, because most of his powerful wants are satisfied.

Nietzsche maintains that Christianity urges a man to make no such efforts to insure his personal survival in the struggle for existence. The beatitudes require, he says, that, instead of trying to do so, the Christian shall devote his energies to helping others and shall give no thought to himself. Instead of exalting himself as much as possible above the common herd and thus raising his chances of surviving, and those of his children, above those of the average man, he is required to lift up this average man. Now, it is plain that every time he lifts up some one else, he must, at the same time, decrease his own store, because his own store is the only stock from which he can draw. Therefore, the tendency of the Christian philosophy of humility is to make men voluntarily throw away their own chances of surviving, which means their own sense of efficiency, which means their own " feeling of increasing power," which means their own happiness. As a substitute for this natural happiness, Christianity offers the happiness derived from the belief that the deity will help those who make the sacrifice and so restore them to their old superiority. This belief, as Nietzsche shows, is no more borne out by known facts than the old belief in witches. It is, in fact, proved to be an utter absurdity by all human experience.

" I call an animal, a species, an individual, depraved," he says, " when it loses its instincts, when it selects, when it *prefers* what is injurious to it. . . . Life itself is an instinct for growth, for continuance, for accumulation of forces, for *power:* where the will to power is wanting there is decline." [1] Christianity, he says, squarely opposes

[1] " *Der Antichrist*," § 6.

this will to power in the Golden Rule, the cornerstone of the faith. The man who confines his efforts to attain superiority over his fellow men to those acts which he would be willing to have them do toward him, obviously abandons all such efforts entirely. To put it in another form, a man can't make himself superior to the race in general without making every other man in the world, to that extent, his inferior. Now, if he follows the Golden Rule, he must necessarily abandon all efforts to make himself superior, because if he didn't he would be suffering all the time from the pain of seeing other men — whose standpoint the Rule requires him to assume — grow inferior. Thus his activity is restricted to one of two things: standing perfectly still or deliberately making himself inferior. The first is impossible, but Nietzsche shows that the latter is not, and that, in point of fact, it is but another way of describing the act of sympathy — one of the things ordered by the fundamental dogma of Christianity.

Sympathy, says Nietzsche, consists merely of a strong man giving up some of his strength to a weak man. The strong man, it is evident, is debilitated thereby, while the weak man, very often, is strengthened but little. If you go to a hanging and sympathize with the condemned, it is plain that your mental distress, without helping that gentleman, weakens, to a perceptible degree, your own mind and body, just as all other powerful emotions weaken them, by consuming energy, and so you are handicapped in the struggle for life to the extent of this weakness. You may get a practical proof of it an hour later by being overcome and killed by a foot-pad whom you might have been able to conquer, had you been feeling perfectly well, or by losing money to some financial rival for whom, under normal conditions, you would have been a match; and then again you may get no immediate or tangible proof of it at all. But your organism will have been weakened to some measurable extent, all the same, and at some time — perhaps on your death bed — this minute drain will make itself evident, though, of course, you may never know it.

" Sympathy," says Nietzsche, " stands in direct antithesis to the tonic passions which elevate the energy of human beings and increase their feeling of efficiency and power. It is a depressant. One loses force by sympathizing and any loss of force which has been caused by other means — personal suffering, for example — is increased and multiplied by sympathy. Suffering itself becomes contagious through sympathy and under certain circumstances it may lead to a total loss of life. If a proof of that is desired, consider the case of the Nazarene, whose sympathy for his fellow men brought him, in the end, to the cross.

" Again, sympathy thwarts the law of development, of evolution, of the survival of the fittest. It preserves what is ripe for extinction, it works in favor of life's condemned ones, it gives to life itself a gloomy aspect by the number of the ill-constituted it *maintains* in life. . . . It is both a multiplier of misery and a conservator of misery. It is the principal tool for the advancement of decadence. It leads to nothingness, to the negation of all those instincts which are at the basis of life. . . . But one does not say 'nothingness;' one says instead 'the other world' or 'the better life.' . . . This innocent rhetoric, out of the

domain of religio-moral fantasy, becomes far from innocent when one realizes what tendency it conceals: the
tendency *hostile to life.*" [1]

The foregoing makes it patent that Nietzsche was a
thorough-going and uncompromising biological monist.
That is to say, he believed that man, while superior to all
other animals because of his greater development, was,
after all, merely an animal, like the rest of them; that the
struggle for existence went on among human beings exactly as it went on among the lions in the jungle and the
protozoa in the sea ooze, and that the law of natural selection ruled all of animated nature — mind and matter —
alike. Indeed, it is but just to credit him with being the
pioneer among modern monists of this school, for he
stated and defended the doctrine of morphological universality at a time when practically all the evolutionists
doubted it, and had pretty well proved its truth some years
before Haeckel wrote his " Monism " and " The Riddle
of the Universe."

To understand all of this, it is necessary to go back to
Darwin and his first statement of the law of natural
selection. Darwin proved, in " The Origin of the Species," that a great many more individuals of any given
species of living being are born into the world each year
than can possibly survive. Those that are best fitted to
meet the condition of existence live on; those that are
worst fitted die. The result is that, by the influence of
heredity, the survivors beget a new generation in which
there is a larger percentage of the fit. One might think
that this would cause a greater number to survive, but

[1] " *Der Antichrist,*" § 7.

inasmuch as the food and room on earth are limited, a large number must always die. But all the while the half or third, or whatever the percentage may be, which actually do survive become more and more fit. In consequence, a species, generation after generation, tends to become more and more adapted to meet life's vicissitudes, or, as the biologists say, more and more adapted to its environment.

Darwin proved that this law was true of all the lower animals and showed that it was responsible for the evolution of the lower apes into anthropoid apes, and that it could account, theoretically, for a possible evolution of anthropoid apes into man. But in " The Descent of Man " he argued that the law of natural selection ceased when man became an intelligent being. Thereafter, he said, man's own efforts worked against those of nature. Instead of letting the unfit of his race die, civilization began to protect and preserve them. The result was that nature's tendency to make all living beings more and more sturdy was set aside by man's own conviction that mere sturdiness was not the thing most to be desired. From this Darwin argued that if two tribes of human beings lived side by side, and if, in one of them, the unfit were permitted to perish, while in the other there were many " courageous, sympathetic and faithful members, who were always ready to warn each other of danger, and to aid and defend one another " — that in such a case, the latter tribe would make the most progress, despite its concerted effort to defy a law of nature.

Darwin's disciples agreed with him in this and some of them went to the length of asserting that civilization, in its essence, was nothing more or less than a successful defiance of this sort. [1] Herbert Spencer was much troubled by the resultant confusion and as one critic puts it,[2] the whole drift of his thought "appears to be inspired by the question: how to evade and veil the logical consequence of evolutionarism for human existence?" John Fiske, another Darwinian, accepted the situation without such disquieting doubt. "When humanity began to be evolved," he said, "an entirely new chapter in the history of the universe was opened. Henceforth the life of the nascent soul came to be first in importance and the bodily life became subordinated to it."[3] Even Huxley believed that man would have to be excepted from the operation of the law of natural selection. "The ethical progress of society," he said, "depends, not on imitating the cosmic process and still less on running away from it, but in combating it." He saw that it was audacious thus to pit man against nature, but he thought that man was sufficiently important to make such an attempt and hoped "that the enterprise might meet with a certain measure of success."[4] And the other Darwinians agreed with him. [5]

[1] Alfred Russell Wallace: "Darwinism," London, 1889.

[2] Alexander Tille, introduction to the Eng. tr. of "The Works of Friedrich Nietzsche," vol. XI; New York, 1896.

[3] John Fiske: "The Destiny of Man;" London, 1884.

[4] Romanes Lecture on "Evolution and Ethics," 1893.

[5] As a matter of fact this dualism still lives. Thus it was lately defended by a correspondent of the New York *Sun:* "If there can be such a thing as an essential difference there surely is one between the animal evolution discovered by Darwin and the self-culture, progress and spiritual aspiration of man." Many other writers on the subject take the same position.

As all the best critics of philosophy have pointed out,[1] any philosophical system which admits such a great contradiction fails utterly to furnish workable standards of order in the universe, and so falls short of achieving philosophy's first aim. We must either believe with the scholastics that intelligence rules, or we must believe, with Haeckel, that all things happen in obedience to invariable natural laws. We cannot believe both. A great many men, toward the beginning of the 90's, began to notice this fatal defect in Darwin's idea of human progress. In 1891 one of them pointed out the conclusion toward which it inevitably led.[2] If we admitted, he said, that humanity had set at naught the law of natural selection, we must admit that civilization was working against nature's efforts to preserve the race, and that, in the end, humanity would perish. To put it more succinctly, man might defy the law of natural selection as much as he pleased, but he could never hope to set it aside. Soon or late, he would awaken to the fact that he remained a mere animal, like the rabbit and the worm, and that, if he permitted his body to degenerate into a thing entirely lacking in strength and virility, not all the intelligence conceivable could save him.

Nietzsche saw all this clearly as early as 1877.[3] He

[1] See the article on "Monism" in the New International Encyclopedia.

[2] A. J. Balfour: "Fragment on Progress;" London, 1891.

[3] He was a monist, indeed, as early as 1873, at which time he had apparently not yet noticed Darwin's notion that the human race could successfully defy the law of natural selection. "The absence of any cardinal distinction between man and beast," he said, "is a doctrine which I consider true." ("*Unzeitgemässe Betrachtungen*," I, 189.) Nev-

saw that what passed for civilization, as represented by
Christianity, was making such an effort to defy and
counteract the law of natural selection, and he came to
the conclusion that the result would be disaster. Christianity, he said, ordered that the strong should give part
of their strength to the weak, and so tended to weaken the
whole race. Self-sacrifice, he said, was an open defiance
of nature, and so were all the other Christian virtues, in
varying degree. He proposed, then, that before it was too
late, humanity should reject Christianity, as the " greatest
of all imaginable corruptions," and admit freely and fully
that the law of natural selection was universal and that
the only way to make real progress was to conform to it.

It may be asked here how Nietzsche accounted for the
fact that humanity had survived so long — for the fact
that the majority of men were still physically healthy and
that the race, as a whole, was still fairly vigorous. He
answered this in two ways. First, he denied that the race
was maintaining to the full its old vigor. " The European
of the present," he said, " is far below the European of
the Renaissance." It would be absurd, he pointed out, to
allege that the average German of 1880 was as strong and
as healthy — *i. e.* as well fitted to his environment —

ertheless, in a moment of sophistry, late in life, he undertook to
criticize the law of natural selection and even to deny its effects (*vide*
" Roving Expeditions of an Inopportune Philosopher," § 14, in " The
Twilight of the Idols "). It is sufficient to say, in answer, that the law
itself is inassailable and that all of Nietzsche's work, saving this single
unaccountable paragraph, helps support it. His frequent sneers at
Darwin, in other places, need not be taken too seriously. Everything
English, toward the close of his life, excited his ire, but the fact remains that he was a thorough Darwinian and that, without Darwin's
work, his own philosophy would have been impossible.

as the " blond beast " who roamed the Saxon lowlands in the days of the mammoth. It would be equally absurd to maintain that the highest product of modern civilization — the town-dweller — was as vigorous and as capable of becoming the father of healthy children as the intelligent farmer, whose life was spent in approximate accordance with all the more obvious laws of health.

Nietzsche's second answer was that humanity had escaped utter degeneration and destruction because, despite its dominance as a theory of action, few men actually practiced Christianity. It was next to impossible, he said, to find a single man who, literally and absolutely, obeyed the teachings of Christ.[1] There were plenty of men who thought they were doing so, but all of them were yielding in only a partial manner. Absolute Christianity meant absolute disregard of self. It was obvious that a man who reached this state of mind would be unable to follow any gainful occupation, and so would find it impossible to preserve his own life or the lives of his children. In brief, said Nietzsche, an actual and utter Christian would perish today just as Christ perished, and so, in his own fate, would provide a conclusive argument against Christianity.

Nietzsche pointed out further that everything which makes for the preservation of the human race is diametrically opposed to the Christian ideal. Thus Christianity becomes the foe of science. The one argues that man should sit still and let God reign; the other that man

---

[1] This observation is as old as Montaigne, who said: " After all, the stoics were actually stoical, but where in all Christendom will you find a Christian ? "

should battle against the tortures which fate inflicts upon him, and try to overcome them and grow strong. Thus all science is unchristian, because, in the last analysis, the whole purpose and effort of science is to arm man against loss of energy and death, and thus make him self-reliant and unmindful of any duty of propitiating the deity. That this antagonism between Christianity and the search for truth really exists has been shown in a practical way time and again. Since the beginning of the Christian era the church has been the bitter and tireless enemy of all science, and this enmity has been due to the fact that every member of the priest class has realized that the more a man learned the more he came to depend upon his own efforts, and the less he was given to asking help from above. In the ages of faith men prayed to the saints when they were ill. Today they send for a doctor. In the ages of faith battles were begun with supplications, and it was often possible to witness the ridiculous spectacle of both sides praying to the same God. Today every sane person knows that the victory goes to the wisest generals and largest battalions.

Nietzsche thus showed, first, that Christianity (and all other ethical systems having self-sacrifice as their basis) tended to oppose the law of natural selection and so made the race weaker; and secondly, that the majority of men, consciously or unconsciously, were aware of this, and so made no effort to be absolute Christians. If Christianity were to become universal, he said, and every man in the world were to follow Christ's precepts to the letter in all the relations of daily life, the race would die out in a genera-tion. This being true — and it may be observed in passing that no one has ever successfully controverted it — there follows the converse: that the human race had best abandon the idea of self-sacrifice altogether and submit itself to the law of natural selection. If this is done, says Nietzsche, the result will be a race of supermen — of proud, strong dionysians — of men who will say " yes " to the world and will be ideally capable of meeting the conditions under which life must exist on earth.

In his efforts to account for the origin of Christianity, Nietzsche was less happy, and indeed came very near the border-line of the ridiculous. The faith of modern Europe, he said, was the result of a gigantic effort on the part of the ancient Jews to revenge themselves upon their masters. The Jews were helpless and inefficient and thus evolved a slave-morality. Naturally, as slaves, they hated their masters, while realizing, all the while, the unmanliness of the ideals they themselves had to hold to in order to survive. So they crucified Christ, who voiced these same ideals, and the result was that the outside world, which despised the Jews, accepted Christ as a martyr and prophet and thus swallowed the Jewish ideals without realizing it. In a word, the Jews detested the slave-morality which circumstances thrust upon them, and got their revenge by foisting it, in a sugar-coated pill, upon their masters.

It is obvious that this idea is sheer lunacy. That the Jews ever realized the degenerating effect of their own slave-morality is unlikely, and that they should take counsel together and plan such an elaborate and complicated revenge, is impossible. The reader of Nietzsche must expect to encounter such absurdities now and then.

The mad German was ordinarily a most logical and orderly thinker, but sometimes the traditional German tendency to indulge in wild and imbecile flights of speculation cropped up in him.

VII

TRUTH

A⊤ the bottom of all philosophy, of all science and of all thinking, you will find the one all-inclusive question: How is man to tell truth from error? The ignorant man solves this problem in a very simple manner: he holds that whatever he believes, he *knows;* and that whatever he knows is true. This is the attitude of all amateur and professional theologians, politicians and other numbskulls of that sort. The pious old maid, for example, who believes in the doctrine of the immaculate conception looks upon her faith as proof, and holds that all who disagree with her will suffer torments in hell. Opposed to this childish theory of knowledge is the chronic doubt of the educated man. He sees daily evidence that many things held to be true by nine-tenths of all men are, in reality, false, and he is thereby apt to acquire a doubt of everything, including his own beliefs.

At different times in the history of man, various methods of solving or evading the riddle have been proposed. In the age of faith it was held that, by his own efforts alone, man was unable, even partly, to distinguish between truth and error, but that he could always go for enlightenment to an infallible encyclopedia: the word of god, as set forth, through the instrumentality of inspired scribes, in the holy scriptures. If these scriptures said that a certain proposition was true, it *was* true, and any man who doubted it was either a lunatic or a criminal.[1] This doctrine prevailed in Europe for many years and all who ventured to oppose it were in danger of being killed, but in the course of time the number of doubters grew so large that it was inconvenient or impossible to kill all of them, and so, in the end, they had to be permitted to voice their doubts unharmed.

The first man of this new era to inflict any real damage upon the ancient churchly idea of revealed wisdom was Nicolas of Cusa, a cardinal of the Roman Catholic Church, who lived in the early part of the fifteenth century.[2] Despite his office and his time, Nicolas was an independent and intelligent man, and it became apparent to him, after long reflection, that mere belief in a thing was by no means a proof of its truth. Man, he decided was prone to err, but in the worst of his errors, there was always some kernel of truth, else he would revolt against it as inconceivable. Therefore, he decided, the best thing for man to do was to hold all of his beliefs lightly and to reject them whenever they began to appear as errors. The real danger, he said, was not in making mistakes, but in clinging to them after they were known to be mistakes.

It seems well nigh impossible that a man of Nicolas' age and training should have reasoned so clearly, but

[1] J. W. Draper, " A History of the Conflict Between Religion and Science;" New York, 1874.

[2] Richard Falckenberg: " A History of Modern Philosophy," tr. by A. C. Armstrong, Jr.; New York, 1897; Chap. I.

the fact remains that he did, and that all of modern
philosophy is built upon the foundations he laid. Since
his time a great many other theories of knowledge have
been put forward, but all have worked, in a sort of circle,
back to Nicolas. It would be interesting, perhaps, to
trace the course and history of these variations and denials,
but such an enterprise is beyond the scope of the present
inquiry. Nicolas by no means gave the world a complete and wholly credible system of philosophy. Until
the day of his death scholasticism was dominant in the
world that he knew, and it retained its old hold upon
human thought, in fact, for nearly two hundred years
thereafter. Not until Descartes, in 1619, made his
famous resolution " to take nothing for the truth without
clear knowledge that it is such," did humanity in general
begin to realize, as Huxley says, that there was sanctity
in doubt. And even Descartes could not shake himself
free of the supernaturalism and other balderdash which
yet colored philosophy. He laid down, for all time, the
emancipating doctrine that " the profession of belief
in propositions, of the truth of which there is no sufficient evidence, is immoral " — a doctrine that might
well be called the Magna Charta of human thought [1] — but
it should not be forgotten that he also laid down other
doctrines and that many of them were visionary and
silly. The philosophers after him rid their minds of the
old ideas but slowly and there were frequent reversions
to the ancient delusion that a man's mind is a function
of his soul — whatever that may be — and not of his
body. It was common, indeed, for a philosopher to

[1] T. H. Huxley: " Hume," preface; London, 1879.

set out with sane, debatable, conceivable ideas — and then to go soaring into the idealistic clouds.[1] Only in our own time have men come to understand that the ego, for all its seeming independence, is nothing more than the sum of inherited race experience — that a man's soul, his conscience and his attitude of mind are things he has inherited from his ancestors, just as he has inherited his two eyes, his ten toes and his firm belief in signs, portents and immortality. Only in our own time have men ceased seeking a golden key to all riddles, and sat themselves down to solve one riddle at a time.

Those metaphysicians who fared farthest from the philosopher of Cusa evolved the doctrine that, in themselves, things have no existence at all, and that we can think of them only in terms of our impressions of them. The color green, for example, may be nothing but a delusion, for all we can possibly know of it is that, under certain conditions, our optic nerves experience a sensation of greenness. Whether this sensation of greenness is a mere figment of our imagination or the reflection of an actual physical state, is something that we cannot tell. It is impossible, in a word, to determine whether there are actual things around us, which produce real impressions upon us, or whether our idea of these things is the mere result of subjective impressions or conditions. We know that a blow on the eyes may cause us to see a flash of light which does not exist and that a nervous person may feel the touch of hands and hear noises which are purely imaginary. May it not be possible, also, that all

[1] Comte and Kant, for example.

other sensations have their rise within us instead of without, and that in saying that objects give us impressions we have been confusing cause and effect?

Such is the argument of those metaphysicians who doubt, not only the accuracy of human knowledge, but also the very capacity of human beings to acquire knowledge. It is apparent, on brief reflection, that this attitude, while theoretically admissible, is entirely impracticable, and that, as a matter of fact, it gives us no more substantial basis for intelligent speculation than the old device of referring all questions to revelation. To say that nothing exists save in the imagination of living beings is to say that this imagination itself does not exist. This, of course, is an absurdity, because every man is absolutely certain that he himself is a real thing and that his mind is a real thing, too, and capable of thought. In place of such cob-web spinning, modern philosophers — driven to it, it may be said, in parenthesis, by the scientists — have gone back to the doctrine that, inasmuch as we can know nothing of anything save through the impressions it makes upon us, these impressions must be accepted provisionally as accurate, so long as they are evidently normal and harmonize one with the other.

That is to say, our perceptions, corrected by our experience and our common sense, must serve as guides for us, and we must seize every opportunity to widen their range and increase their accuracy. For millions of years they have been steadily augmenting our store of knowledge. We know, for instance, that when fire touches us it causes an impression which we call pain and that this impression is invariably the same, and always leads to the same results, in all normal human beings. Therefore, we accept it as an axiom that fire causes pain. There are many other ideas that may be and have been established in the same manner: by the fact that they are universal among sane men. But there is also a multitude of things which produce different impressions upon different men, and here we encounter the problem of determining which of these impressions is right and which is wrong. One man, observing the rising and setting of the sun, concludes that it is a ball of fire revolving about the earth. Another man, in the face of the same phenomena, concludes that the earth revolves around the sun. How, then, are we to determine which of these men has drawn the proper conclusion?

As a matter of fact, it is impossible in such a case, to come to any decision which can be accepted as utterly and absolutely true. But all the same the scientific empiric method enables us to push the percentage of error nearer and nearer to the irreducible minimum. We can observe the phenomenon under examination from a multitude of sides and compare the impression it produces with the impressions produced by kindred phenomena regarding which we know more. Again, we can put this examination into the hands of men specially trained and fitted for such work — men whose conclusions we know, by previous experience, to be above the average of accuracy. And so, after a long time, we can formulate some idea of the thing under inspection which violates few or none of the other ideas held by us. When we have accomplished this, we have come as near to the absolute truth as it is possible for human beings to come.

I need not point out that this method does not contemplate a mere acceptance of the majority vote. Its actual effect, indeed, is quite the contrary, for it is only a small minority of human beings who may be said, with any truth, to be capable of thought. It is probable, for example, that nine-tenths of the people in Christendom today believe that Friday is an unlucky day, while only the remaining tenth hold that one day is exactly like another. But despite this, it is apparent that the idea of the latter will survive and that, by slow degrees, it will be forced upon the former. We know that it is true, not because it is accepted by all men or by the majority of men — for, as a matter of fact, we have seen that it isn't — but because we realize that the few who hold to it are best capable of distinguishing between actual impressions and mere delusions.

Again, the scientific method tends to increase our knowledge by the very fact that it discourages unreasoning faith. The scientist realizes that most of his so-called facts are probably errors and so he is willing to harbor doubts of their truth and to seek for something better. Like Socrates he boldly says " I know that I am ignorant." He realizes, in fact, that error, when it is constantly under fire, is bound to be resolved in the long run into something approximating the truth. As Nicolas pointed out 500 years ago, nothing is utterly and absolutely true and nothing is utterly and absolutely false. There is always a germ of truth in the worst error, and there is always a residuum of error in the soundest truth. Therefore, an error is fatal only when it is hidden from the white light of investigation. Herein lies the difference between the

modern scientist and the moralist. The former holds
nothing sacred, not even his own axioms; the latter lays
things down as law and then makes it a crime to doubt
them.

It is in this way — by submitting every idea to a searching, pitiless, unending examination — that the world is
increasing its store of what may be called, for the sake of
clearness, absolute knowledge. Error always precedes
truth, and it is extremely probable that the vast majority
of ideas held by men of today — even the sanest and
wisest men — are delusions, but with the passing of the
years our stock of truth grows larger and larger. " A
conviction," says Nietzsche, " always has its history —
its previous forms, its tentative forms, its states of error.
It becomes a conviction, indeed, only after having been
not a conviction, and then *hardly* a conviction. No doubt
falsehood is one of these embryonic forms of conviction.
Sometimes only a change of persons is needed to transform one into the other. That which, in the son, is a conviction, was, in the father, still a falsehood." [1] The
tendency of intelligent men, in a word, is to approach
nearer and nearer the truth, by the processes of rejection,
revision and invention. Many old ideas are rejected by
each new generation, but there always remain a few that
survive. We no longer believe with the cave-men that the
thunder is the voice of an angry god and the lightning
the flash of his sword, but we·still believe, as they did, that
wood floats upon water, that seeds sprout and give forth
plants, that a roof keeps off the rain and that a child, if
it lives long enough, will inevitably grow into a man or a

[1] " *Der Antichrist*," § 55.

woman. Such ideas may be called truths. If we deny them we must deny at once that the world exists and that we exist ourselves.

Nietzsche's discussion of these problems is so abstruse and so much complicated by changes in view that it would be impossible to make an understandable summary of it in the space available here. In his first important book, "*Menschliches allzu Menschliches*," he devoted himself, in the main, to pointing out errors made in the past, without laying down any very definite scheme of thought for the future. In the early stages of human progress, he said, men made the mistake of regarding everything that was momentarily pleasant or beneficial as absolutely and eternally true. Herein they manifested the very familiar human weakness for rash and hasty generalization, and the equally familiar tendency to render the ideas of a given time and place perpetual and permanent by erecting them into codes of morality and putting them into the mouths of gods. This, he pointed out, was harmful, for a thing might be beneficial to the men of today and fatal to the men of tomorrow. Therefore, he argued that while a certain idea's effect was a good criterion, humanly speaking, of its present or current truth, it was dangerous to assume that this effect would be always the same, and that, in consequence, the idea itself would remain true forever.

Not until the days of Socrates, said Nietzsche, did men begin to notice this difference between imminent truth and eternal truth. The notion that such a distinction existed made its way very slowly, even after great teachers began to teach it, but in the end it was accepted by enough men to give it genuine weight. Since that day philosophy and science, which were once merely different names for the same thing, have signified two separate things. It is the object of philosophy to analyze happiness, and by means of the knowledge thus gained, to devise means for safeguarding and increasing it. In consequence, it is necessary for philosophy to generalize — to assume that the thing which makes men happy today will make them happy tomorrow. Science, on the contrary, concerns itself, not with things of the uncertain future, but with things of the certain present. Its object is to examine the world as it exists today, to uncover as many of its secrets as possible, and to study their effect upon human happiness. In other words, philosophy first constructs a scheme of happiness and then tries to fit the world to it, while science studies the world with no other object in view than the increase of knowledge, and with full confidence that, in the long run, this increase of knowledge will increase efficiency and in consequence happiness.

It is evident, then, that science, for all its contempt for fixed schemes of happiness, will eventually accomplish with certainty what philosophy — which most commonly swims into the ken of the average man as morality — is now trying to do in a manner that is not only crude and unreasonable, but also necessarily unsuccessful. In a word, just so soon as man's store of knowledge grows so large that he becomes complete master of the natural forces which work toward his undoing, he will be perfectly happy. Now, Nietzsche believed, as we have seen in past chapters, that man's instinctive will to power had this same complete mastery over his environment as its ultimate object, and so he concluded that the will to power

might be relied upon to lead man to the truth. That is
to say, he believed that there was, in every man of the
higher type (the only type he thought worth discussing)
an instinctive tendency to seek the true as opposed to the
false, that this instinct, as the race progressed, grew more
and more accurate, and that its growing accuracy explained
the fact that, despite the opposition of codes of morality
and of the iron hand of authority, man constantly increased his store of knowledge. A thought, he said, arose
in a man without his initiative or volition, and was nothing
more or less than an expression of his innate will to obtain
power over his environment by accurately observing and
interpreting it. It was just as reasonable, he said, to say *It*
thinks as to say *I* think,¹ because every intelligent person
knew that a man couldn't control his thoughts. Therefore,
the fact that these thoughts, in the long run and considering the human race as a whole, tended to uncover more and
more truths proved that the will to power, despite the danger of generalizing from its manifestations, grew more and
more accurate and so worked in the direction of absolute
truth. Nietzsche believed that mankind was ever the
slave of errors, but he held that the number of errors
tended to decrease. When, at last, truth reigned supreme
and there were no more errors, the superman would walk
the earth.

Now it is impossible for any man to note the workings
of the will to power save as it is manifested in his own
instincts and thoughts, and therefore Nietzsche, in his
later books, urges that every man should be willing, at all
times, to pit his own feelings against the laws laid down

¹ *"Jenseits von Gut und Böse,"* VII.

by the majority. A man should steer clear of rash generalization from his own experience, but he should be doubly careful to steer clear of the generalizations of others. The greatest of all dangers lies in subscribing to a thesis without being certain of its truth. " This not-wishing-to-see what one sees . . . is a primary requisite for membership in a party, in any sense whatsoever. Therefore, the party man becomes a liar by necessity." The proper attitude for a human being, indeed, is chronic dissent and skepticism. " Zarathustra is a skeptic. . . . Convictions are prisons. . . . The freedom from every kind of permanent conviction, the ability to search freely, belong to strength. . . . The need of a belief, of something that is unconditioned . . . is a sign of weakness. The man of belief is necessarily a dependent man. . . . His instinct gives the highest honor to self-abnegation. He does not belong to himself, but to the author of the idea he believes." [1] It is only by skepticism, argues Nietzsche, that we can hope to make any progress. If all men accepted without question, the *dicta* of some one supreme sage, it is plain that there could be no further increase of knowledge. It is only by constant turmoil and conflict and exchange of views that the minute granules of truth can be separated from the vast muck heap of superstition and error. Fixed truths, in the long run, are probably more dangerous to intelligence than falsehoods.[2]

This argument, I take it, scarcely needs greater elucidation. Every intelligent man knows that if there had been no brave agnostics to defy the wrath of the church in the

[1] " *Der Antichrist*," § 54.
[2] " *Menschliches allzu Menschliches*," § 483.

middle ages, the whole of Christendom would still wallow in the unspeakably foul morass of ignorance which had its center, during that black time, in an infallible sovereign of sovereigns. Authority, at all times and everywhere, means sloth and degeneration. It is only doubt that creates. It is only the minority that counts.

The fact that the great majority of human beings are utterly incapable of original thought, and so must, perforce, borrow their ideas or submit tamely to some authority, explains Nietzsche's violent loathing and contempt for the masses. The average, self-satisfied, conservative, orthodox, law-abiding citizen appeared to him to be a being but little raised above the cattle in the barn-yard. So violent was this feeling that every idea accepted by the majority excited, for that very reason, his suspicion and opposition. "What everybody believes," he once said, "is never true." This may seem like a mere voicing of brobdingnagian egotism, but as a matter of fact, the same view is held by every man who has spent any time investigating the history of ideas. "Truth," said Dr. Osler a while ago, "scarcely ever carries the struggle for acceptance at its first appearance." The masses are always a century or two behind. They have made a virtue of their obtuseness and call it by various fine names: conservatism, piety, respectability, faith. The nineteenth century witnessed greater human progress than all the centuries before it saw or even imagined, but the majority of white men of today still believe in ghosts, still fear the devil, still hold that the number 13 is unlucky and still picture the deity as a patriarch in a white beard, surrounded by a choir of resplendent amateur musicians. "We think a thing," says Prof. Henry Sedgwick, "because all other people think so; or because, after all, we *do* think so; or because we are told so, and think we must think so; or because we once thought so, and think we still think so; or because, having thought so, we think we *will* think so."

Naturally enough, Nietzsche was an earnest opponent of the theological doctrine of free will. He held, as we have seen, that every human act was merely the effect of the will to power reacting against environment, and in consequence he had to reject absolutely the notion of volition and responsibility. A man, he argued, was not an object *in vacuo* and his acts, thoughts, impulses and motives could not be imagined without imagining some cause for them. If this cause came from without, it was clearly beyond his control, and if it came from within it was no less so, for his whole attitude of mind, his instinctive habits of thoughts, his very soul, so-called, were merely attributes that had been handed down to him, like the shape of his nose and the color of his eyes, from his ancestors. Nietzsche held that the idea of responsibility was the product and not the cause of the idea of punishment, and that the latter was nothing more than a manifestation of primitive man's will to power — to triumph over his fellows by making them suffer the handicap and humiliation of pain. "Men were called free," he said, "in order that they might be condemned and punished. . . . When we immoralists try to cleanse psychology, history, nature and sociology of these notions, we find that our chief enemies are the theologians, who, with their preposterous idea of 'a moral order of the world,' go on tainting the innocence of man's struggle upward with talk of punishment and guilt. Christianity is, indeed, a hangman's metaphysic."[1] As a necessary corollary of this, Nietzsche denied the existence of any plan in the cosmos. Like Haeckel, he believed that but two things existed — energy and matter; and that all the phenomena which made us conscious of the universe were nothing more than symptoms of the constant action of the one upon the other. Nothing ever happened without a cause, he said, and no cause was anything other than the effect of some previous cause. "The destiny of man," he said, "cannot be disentangled from the destiny of everything else in existence, past, present and future. . . . We are a part of the whole, we exist in the whole. . . . There is nothing which could judge, measure or condemn our being, for that would be to judge, measure and condemn the whole. . . . But there is nothing outside of the whole. . . . The concept of God has hitherto made our existence a crime. . . . We deny God, we deny responsibility by denying God: it is only thereby that we save man."[2]

Herein, unluckily, Nietzsche fell into the trap which has snapped upon Haeckel and every other supporter of atheistic determinism. He denied that the human will was free and argued that every human action was inevitable, and yet he spent his whole life trying to convince his fellow men that they should do otherwise than as they did in fact. In a word, he held that they had no control whatever over their actions, and yet, like Moses, Mohammed and St. Francis, he thundered at them uproariously and urged them to turn from their errors and repent.

[1] "*Götzendämmerung,*" VI.   [2] "*Götzendämmerung,*" VI.

VIII

CIVILIZATION

On the surface, at least, the civilization of today seems to be moving slowly toward two goals. One is the eternal renunciation of war and the other is universal brotherhood: one is " peace on earth " and the other is " good will to men." Five hundred years ago a statesman's fame rested frankly and solely upon the victories of his armies; today we profess to measure him by his skill at keeping these armies in barracks. And in the internal economy of all civilized states we find today some pretence at unrestricted and equal suffrage. In times past it was the chief concern of all logicians and wiseacres to maintain the proposition that God reigned. At present, the dominant platitude of Christendom — the cornerstone of practically every political party and the stock-in-trade of every politician — is the proposition that the people rule.

Nietzsche opposed squarely both the demand for peace and the demand for equality, and his opposition was grounded upon two arguments. In the first place, he said, both demands were rhetorical and insincere and all intelligent men knew that neither would ever be fully satisfied. In the second place, he said, it would be ruinous to the race if they were. That is to say, he believed that war was not only necessary, but also beneficial, and that the natural system of castes was not only beneficent, but also inevitable. In the demand for universal peace he saw only the yearning of the weak and useless for protection against the righteous exploitation of the useful and strong. In the demand for equality he saw only the same thing. Both demands, he argued, controverted and combated that upward tendency which finds expression in the law of natural selection.

" The order of castes," said Nietzsche, " is the dominating law of nature, against which no merely human agency may prevail. In every healthy society there are three broad classes, each of which has its own morality, its own work, its own notion of perfection and its own sense of mastery. The first class comprises those who are obviously superior to the mass intellectually; the second includes those whose eminence is chiefly muscular, and the third is made up of the mediocre. The third class, very naturally, is the most numerous, but the first is the most powerful.

" To this highest caste belongs the privilege of representing beauty, happiness and goodness on earth. . . . Its members accept the world as they find it and make the best of it. . . . They find their happiness in those things which, to lesser men, would spell ruin — in the labyrinth, in severity toward themselves and others, in effort. Their delight is self-governing: with them asceticism becomes naturalness, necessity, instinct. A difficult task is regarded by them as a privilege; to play with burdens which would crush others to death is their recreation.

They are the most venerable species of men. They are the most cheerful, the most amiable. They rule because they are what they are. They are not at liberty to be second in rank.

" The second caste includes the guardians and keepers of order and security — the warriors, the nobles, the king — above all, as the highest types of warrior, the judges and defenders of the law. They execute the mandates of the first caste, relieving the latter of all that is coarse and menial in the work of ruling.

" At the bottom are the workers — the men of handicraft, trade, agriculture and the greater part of art and science. It is the law of nature that they should be public utilities — that they should be wheels and functions. T. e only kind of happiness of which they are capable makes intelligent machines of them. For the mediocre, it is happiness to be mediocre. In them the mastery of one thing — *i. e.* specialism — is an instinct.

" It is unworthy of a profound intellect to see in mediocrity itself an objection. It is, indeed, a necessity of human existence, for only in the presence of a horde of average men is the exceptional man a possibility. . . .

" Whom do I hate most among the men of today? The socialist who undermines the workingman's healthy instincts, who takes from him his feeling of contentedness with his existence, who makes him envious, who teaches him revenge. . . . There is no wrong in unequal rights : it lies in the vain pretension to equal rights." [1]

It is obvious from this that Nietzsche was an ardent believer in aristocracy, but it is also obvious that he was

" *Der Antichrist,*" § 57.

not a believer in the thing which passes for aristocracy in the world today. The nobility of Europe belongs, not to his first class, but to his second class. It is essentially military and legal, for in themselves its members are puny and inefficient, and it is only the force of law that maintains them in their inheritance.

The fundamental doctrine of civilized law, as we know it today, is the proposition that what a man has once acquired shall belong to him and his heirs forever, without need on his part or theirs to defend it personally against predatory rivals. This transfer of the function of defense from the individual to the state naturally exalts the state's professional defenders — that is, her soldiers and judges — and so it is not unnatural to find the members of this class, and their parasites, in control of most of the world's governments and in possession of a large share of the world's wealth, power and honors.[1] To Nietzsche this seemed grotesquely illogical and unfair. He saw that this ruling class expended its entire energy in combating

[1] In " The Governance of England," (London: 1904) Sidney Low points out (chap. X) that, despite the rise of democracy, the government of Great Britain is still entirely in the hands of the landed gentry and nobility. The members of this class plainly owe their power to the military prowess of their ancestors, and their identity with the present military and judicial class is obvious. The typical M. P., in fact, also writes " J. P." after his name and " Capt." or " Col." before it. The examples of Russia, Germany, Japan, Austria, Italy, Spain and the Latin-American republics scarcely need be mentioned. In China the military, judicial and legislative-executive functions are always combined, and in the United States, while the military branch of the second caste is apparently impotent, it is plain that the balance of legislative power in every state and in the national legislature is held by lawyers, just as the final determination of all laws rests with judges.

experiment and change and that the aristocracy it begot and protected — an aristocracy often identical, very naturally, with itself — tended to become more and more unfit and helpless and more and more a bar to the ready recognition and unrestrained functioning of the only true aristocracy — that of efficiency.

Nietzsche pointed out that one of the essential absurdities of a constitutional aristocracy was to be found in the fact that it hedged itself about with purely artificial barriers. Next only to its desire to maintain itself without actual personal effort was its jealous endeavor to prevent accessions to its ranks. Nothing, indeed, disgusts the traditional belted earl quite so much as the ennobling of some upstart brewer or iron-master. This exclusiveness, from Nietzsche's point of view, seemed ridiculous and pernicious, for a true aristocracy must be ever willing and eager to welcome to its ranks — and to enroll in fact, automatically — all who display those qualities which make a man extraordinarily fit and efficient. There should always be, he said, a free and constant interchange of individuals between the three natural castes of men. It should be always possible for an abnormally efficient man of the slave class to enter the master class, and, by the same token, accidental degeneration or incapacity in the master class should be followed by swift and merciless reduction to the ranks of slaves. Thus, those aristocracies which presented the incongruous spectacle of imbeciles being intrusted with the affairs of government seemed to him utterly abhorrent, and those schemes of caste which made a mean birth an offset to high intelligence seemed no less so.

So long as man's mastery of the forces of nature is

incomplete, said Nietzsche, it will be necessary for the vast majority of human beings to spend their lives in either supplementing those natural forces which are partly under control or in opposing those which are still unleashed. The business of tilling the soil, for example, is still largely a matter of muscular exertion, despite the vast improvement in farm implements, and it will probably remain so for centuries to come. Since such labor is necessarily mere drudgery, and in consequence unpleasant, it is plain that it should be given over to men whose realization of its unpleasantness is least acute. Going further, it is plain that this work will be done with less and less revolt and less and less driving, as we evolve a class whose ambition to engage in more inviting pursuits grows smaller and smaller. In a word, the ideal plough-man is one who has no thought of anything higher and better than ploughing. Therefore, argued Nietzsche, the proper performance of the manual labor of the world makes it necessary that we have a laboring class, which means a class content to obey without fear or question.

This doctrine brought down upon Nietzsche's head the pious wrath of all the world's humanitarians, but empiric experiment has more than once proved its truth. The history of the hopelessly futile and fatuous effort to improve the negroes of the Southern United States by education affords one such proof. It is apparent, on brief reflection, that the negro, no matter how much he is educated, must remain, as a race, in a condition of subservience; that he must remain the inferior of the stronger and more intelligent white man so long as he retains racial differentiation. Therefore, the effort to educate

him has awakened in his mind ambitions and aspirations
which, in the very nature of things, must go unrealized,
and so, while gaining nothing whatever materially, he has
lost all his old contentment, peace of mind and happiness.
Indeed, it is a commonplace of observation in the United
States that the educated and refined negro is invariably
a hopeless, melancholy, embittered and despairing man.

Nietzsche, to resume, regarded it as absolutely essential
that there be a class of laborers or slaves — his " third
caste "— and was of the opinion that such a class would
exist upon earth so long as the human race survived. Its
condition, compared to that of the ruling class, would
vary but slightly, he thought, with the progress of the
years. As man's mastery of nature increased, the laborer
would find his task less and less painful, but he would
always remain a fixed distance behind those who ruled
him. Therefore, Nietzsche, in his philosophy, gave no
thought to the desires and aspirations of the laboring class,
because, as we have just seen, he held that a man could
not properly belong to this class unless his desires and
aspirations were so faint or so well under the control of
the ruling class that they might be neglected. All of the
Nietzschean doctrines and ideas apply only to the ruling
class. It was at the top, he argued, that mankind grew.
It was only in the ideas of those capable of original thought
that progress had its source. William the Conqueror
was of far more importance, though he was but a single
man, than all the other Normans of his generation taken
together.

Nietzsche was well aware that his " first caste " was
necessarily small in numbers and that there was a strong

tendency for its members to drop out of it and seek ease and peace in the castes lower down. " Life," he said, " is always hardest toward the summit — the cold increases, the responsibility increases." [1] But to the truly efficient man these hardships are but spurs to effort. His joy is in combating and in overcoming — in pitting his will to power against the laws and desires of the rest of humanity. " I do not advise you to labor," says Zarathustra, " but to fight. I do not advise you to compromise and make peace, but to conquer. Let your labor be fighting and your peace victory. . . . You say that a good cause will hallow even war? I tell you that a good war hallows every cause. War and courage have done more great things than charity. Not your pity, but your bravery lifts up those about you. Let the little girlies tell you that ' good ' means ' sweet ' and ' touching.' I tell you that ' good ' means ' brave.' . . . The slave rebels against hardships and calls his rebellion superiority. Let your superiority be an acceptance of hardships. Let your commanding be an obeying. . . . Let your highest thought be: ' Man is something to be surpassed.' . . . I do not advise you to love your neighbor — the nearest human being. I advise you rather to flee from the nearest and love the furthest human being. Higher than love to your neighbor is love to the higher man that is to come in the future. . . . Propagate yourself upward. Thus live your life. What are many years worth? I do not spare you. . . . Die at the right time ! " [2]

[1] " *Der Antichrist*," § 55.
[2] The quotations are from various chapters in the first part of " *Also sprach Zarathus ra.*"

The average man, said Nietzsche, is almost entirely lacking in this gorgeous, fatalistic courage and sublime egotism. He is ever reluctant to pit his private convictions and yearnings against those of the mass of men. He is either afraid to risk the consequences of originality or fearful that, since the majority of his fellows disagree with him, he must be wrong. Therefore, no matter how strongly an unconventional idea may possess a man, he commonly seeks to combat it and throttle it, and the ability to do this with the least possible expenditure of effort we call self-control. The average man, said Nietzsche, has the power of self-control well developed, and in consequence he seldom contributes anything positive to the thought of his age and almost never attempts to oppose it.

We have seen in the preceding chapter that if every man, without exception, were of this sort, all human progress would cease, because the ideas of one generation would be handed down unchanged to the next and there would be no effort whatever to improve the conditions of existence by the only possible method — constant experiment with new ideas. Therefore, it follows that the world must depend for its advancement upon those revolutionists who, instead of overcoming their impulse to go counter to convention, give it free rein. Of such is Nietzsche's " first caste " composed. It is plain that among the two lower castes, courage of this sort is regarded, not as an evidence of strength, but as a proof of weakness. The man who outrages conventions is a man who lacks self-control, and the majority, by a process we have examined in our consideration of slave-morality, has exalted self-control, which, at bottom, is the antithesis of courage, into a place of honor higher than that belonging, by right, to courage itself.

But Nietzsche pointed out that the act of denying or combating accepted ideas is a thing which always tends to inspire other acts of the same sort. It is true enough that a revolutionary idea, so soon as it replaces an old convention and obtains the sanction of the majority, ceases to be revolutionary and becomes itself conventional, but all the same the mere fact that it has succeeded gives courage to those who harbor other revolutionary ideas and inspires them to give these ideas voice. Thus, it happens that courage breeds itself, and that, in times of great conflict, of no matter what sort, the world produces more than an average output of originality, or, as we more commonly denominate it, genius. In this manner Nietzsche accounted for a fact that had been noticed by many men before him: that such tremendous struggles as the French Revolution and the American Civil War are invariably followed by eras of diligent inquiry, of bold overturning of existing institutions and of marked progress. People become accustomed to unrestrained combat and so the desirability of self-control becomes less insistent.

Nietzsche had a vast contempt for what he called " the green-grazing happiness of the herd." Its strong morality and its insistence upon the doctrine that whatever is, is right — that " God's in his heaven; all's well with the world " — revolted him. He held that the so-called rights of the masses had no justifiable existence, since everything they asserted as a right was an assertion, more or less disguised, of the doctrine that the unfit should survive. " There are," he said, " only three ways in which the masses appear to me to deserve a glance : first, as blurred copies of their betters, printed on bad paper and from worn out plates; secondly, as a necessary opposition to stimulate the master class, and thirdly, as instruments in the hands of the master class. Further than this I hand them over to statistics — and the devil." [1] Kant's proposal that the morality of every contemplated action be tested by the question, " Suppose everyone did as I propose to do ? " seemed utterly ridiculous to Nietzsche because he saw that " everyone " always opposed the very things which meant progress; and Kant's corollary that the sense of duty contemplated in this dictum was " the obligation to act in reverence for law," proved to Nietzsche merely that both duty and law were absurdities. " Contumely," he said, " always falls upon those who break through some custom or convention. Such men, in fact, are called criminals. Everyone who overthrows an existing law is, at the start, regarded as a wicked man. Long afterward, when it is found that this law was bad and so cannot be re-established, the epithet is changed. All history treats almost exclusively of wicked men who, in the course of time, have come to be looked upon as good men. All progress is the result of successful crimes." [2]

Dr. Turck,[3] Miss Paget, M. Nordau and other critics see in all this good evidence that Nietzsche was a criminal at heart. At the bottom of all philosophies, says Miss Paget,[4] there is always one supreme idea. Sometimes it

---

[1] " *Vom Nutzen und Nachtheil der Historie für das Leben.*"
[2] " *Morgenröte* ," § 20.
[3] " *Friedrich Nietzsche und seine philosophische Irrwege,*" Leipsic, 1891.
[4] *North American Review*, Dec., 1904.

is a conception of nature, sometimes it is a religious faith and sometimes it is a theory of truth. In Nietzsche's case it is "my taste." He is always irritated: "*I* dislike," "*I* hate," "*I* want to get rid of" appear on every page of his writings. He delights in ruthlessness, his fellow men disgust him, his physical senses are acute, he has a sick ego. For that reason he likes singularity, the lonely Alps, classic literature and Bizet's "clear yellow" music. Turck argues that Nietzsche was a criminal because he got pleasure out of things which outraged the majority of his fellow men, and Nordau, in supporting this idea, shows that it is possible for a man to experience and approve criminal impulses and still never act them: that there are criminals of the chair as well as of the dark lantern and sandbag. The answer to all of this, of course, is the fact that the same method of reasoning would convict every original thinker the world has ever known of black felony: that it would make Martin Luther a criminal as well as Jack Sheppard, John the Baptist as well as the Borgias, and Galileo as well as Judas Iscariot; that it would justify the execution of all the sublime company of heroes who have been done to death for their opinions, from Jesus Christ down the long line.

IX

WOMEN AND MARRIAGE

NIETZSCHE'S faithful sister, with almost comical and essentially feminine disgust, bewails the fact that, as a very young man, the philosopher became acquainted with the baleful truths set forth in Schopenhauer's immortal essay " On Women." That this daring work greatly influenced him is true, and that he subscribed to its chief arguments all the rest of his days is also true, but it is far from true to say that his view of the fair sex was borrowed bodily from Schopenhauer or that he would have written otherwise than as he did if Schopenhauer had never lived. Nietzsche's conclusions regarding women were the inevitable result, indeed, of his own philosophical system. It is impossible to conceive a man who held his opinions of morality and society laying down any other doctrines of femininity and matrimony than those he scattered through his books.

Nietzsche believed that there was a radical difference between the mind of man and the mind of woman and that the two sexes reacted in diametrically different ways to those stimuli which make up what might be called the clinical picture of human society. It is the function of man, he said, to wield a sword in humanity's battle with everything that makes life on earth painful or precarious.

It is the function of woman, not to fight herself, but to provide fresh warriors for the fray. Thus the exercise of the will to exist is divided between the two: the man seeking the welfare of the race as he actually sees it and the woman seeking the welfare of generations yet unborn. Of course, it is obvious that this division is by no means clearly marked, because the man, in struggling for power over his environment, necessarily improves the conditions under which his children live, and the woman, working for her children, often benefits herself. But all the same the distinction is a good one and empiric observation bears it out. As everyone who has given a moment's thought to the subject well knows, a man's first concern in the world is to provide food and shelter for himself and his family, while a woman's foremost duty is to bear and rear children. "Thus," said Nietzsche, "would I have man and woman: the one fit for warfare, the other fit for giving birth; and both fit for dancing with head and legs " [1] — that is to say: both capable of doing their share of the race's work, mental and physical, with conscious and superbundant efficiency.

Nietzsche points out that, in the racial economy, the place of woman may be compared to that of a slave-nation, while the position of man resembles that of a master-nation. We have seen how a weak nation, unable, on account of its weakness, to satisfy its will to survive and thirst for power by forcing its authority upon other nations, turns to the task of keeping these other nations, as much as possible, from enforcing their authority upon it. Realizing that it cannot rule, but must serve, it en-

" *Also sprach Zarathustra,*" III.

deavors to make the conditions of its servitude as **bearable** as possible. This effort is commonly made in two ways: first by ostensibly renouncing its desire to rule, and secondly, by attempts to inoculate its powerful neighbors with its ideas in subterranean and round-about ways, so as to avoid arousing their suspicion and opposition. It becomes, in brief, humble and cunning, and with its humility as a cloak, it seeks to pit its cunning against the sheer might of those it fears.

The position of women in the world is much the same. The business of bearing and rearing children is destructive to their physical strength, and in consequence makes it impossible for them to prevail by force when their ideas and those of men happen to differ. To take away the sting of this incapacity, they make a virtue of it, and it becomes modesty, humility, self-sacrifice and fidelity; to win in spite of it they cultivate cunning, which commonly takes the form of hypocrisy, cajolery, dissimulation and more or less masked appeals to the masculine sexual instinct. All of this is so often observed in every-day life that it has become commonplace. A woman is physically unable to force a man to do as she desires, but her very inability to do so becomes a sentimental weapon against him, and her blandishments do the rest. The spectacle of a strong man ruled by a weak woman is no rare one certainly, and Samson was neither the first nor last giant to fall before a Delilah. There is scarcely a household in all the world, in truth, in which the familiar drama is not being acted and reacted day after day.

Now, it is plain from the foregoing that, though **women's** business in the world is of such a character that it **inevi-**

tably leads to physical degeneration, her constant need to overcome the effects of this degeneration by cunning produces constant mental activity, which, by the law of exercise, should produce, in turn, great mental efficiency. This conclusion, in part, is perfectly correct, for women, as a sex, are shrewd, resourceful and acute; but the very fact that they are always concerned with imminent problems and that, in consequence, they are unaccustomed to dealing with the larger riddles of life, makes their mental attitude essentially petty. This explains the circumstance that despite their mental suppleness, they are not genuinely strong intellectually. Indeed, the very contrary is true. Women's constant thought is, not to lay down broad principles of right and wrong; not to place the whole world in harmony with some great scheme of justice; not to consider the future of nations; not to make two blades of grass grow where one grew before; but to deceive, influence, sway and please men. Normally, their weakness makes masculine protection necessary to their existence and to the exercise of their overpowering maternal instinct, and so their whole effort is to obtain this protection in the easiest way possible. The net result is that feminine morality is a morality of opportunism and imminent expediency, and that the normal woman has no respect for, and scarcely any conception of abstract truth. Thus is proved the fact noted by Schopenhauer and many other observers: that a woman seldom manifests any true sense of justice or of honor.

It is unnecessary to set forth this idea in greater detail, because everyone is familiar with it and proofs of its accuracy are supplied in infinite abundance by common

observation.   Nietzsche accepted it as demonstrated.
When he set out to pursue the subject further, he rejected
entirely the Schopenhauerean corollary that man should
ever regard woman as his enemy, and should seek, by all
means within his power, to escape her insidious influence.
Such a notion naturally outraged the philosopher of the
superman.   He was never an advocate of running away:
to all the facts of existence he said " yes."   His ideal was
not resignation or flight, but an intelligent defiance and
opposition.   Therefore, he argued that man should
accept woman as a natural opponent arrayed against him
for the benevolent purpose of stimulating him to constant
efficiency.   Opposition, he pointed out, was a necessary
forerunner of function, and in consequence the fact that
woman spent her entire effort in a ceaseless endeavor to
undermine and change the will of man, merely served to
make this will alert and strong, and so increased man's
capacity for meeting and overcoming the enemies of his
existence.

A man conscious of his strength, observes Nietzsche,
need have no fear of women.   It is only the man who finds
himself utterly helpless in the face of feminine cajolery
that must cry, " Get thee behind me, Satan ! " and flee.
" It is only the most sensual men," he says, " who have to
shun women and torture their bodies."   The normal,
healthy man, despite the strong appeal which women
make to him by their subtle putting forward of the sexual
idea — visually as dress, coquetry and what not — still
keeps a level head.   He is strong enough to weather the
sexual storm.   But the man who cannot do this, who
experiences no normal reaction in the direction of guarded-

ness and caution and reason, must either abandon himself utterly as a helpless slave to woman's instinct of race-
preservation, and so become a bestial voluptuary, or
avoid temptation altogether and so become a celibate.[1]

There is nothing essentially evil in woman's effort to
combat and control man's will by constantly suggesting
the sexual idea to him, because it is necessary, for the
permanence of the race, that this idea be presented frequently and powerfully. Therefore, the conflict between
masculine and feminine ideals is to be regarded, not as a
lamentable battle, in which one side is right and the other
wrong, but a convenient means of providing that stimula-
tion-by-opposition without which all function, and in
consequence all progress, would cease. "The man who
regards women as an enemy to be avoided," says Nietzsche,
"betrays an unbridled lust which loathes not only itself,
but also its means."[2]

There are, of course, occasions when the feminine
influence, by its very subtlety, works harm to the higher
sort of men. It is dangerous for a man to love too violently
and it is dangerous, too, for him to be loved too much.
"The natural inclination of women to a quiet, uniform
and peaceful existence" — that is to say, to a slave-

---

[1] Nietzsche saw, of course ("The Genealogy of Morals," III), that
temporary celibacy was frequently necessary to men with peculiarly
difficult and vitiating tasks ahead of them. The philosopher who
sought to solve world riddles, he said, had need to steer clear of women,
for reasons which appealed, with equal force, to the athlete who sought
to perform great feats of physical strength. It is obvious, however,
that this desire to escape distraction and drain differs vastly from ethical
celibacy.

[2] "*Morgenröte*," § 346.

morality — " operates adversely to the heroic impulse of the masculine free spirit. Without being aware of it, women act like a person who would remove stones from the path of a mineralogist, lest his feet should come in contact with them — forgetting entirely that he is faring forth for the very purpose of coming in contact with them. . . . The wives of men with lofty aspirations cannot resign themselves to seeing their husbands suffering, impoverished and slighted, even though it is apparent that this suffering proves, not only that its victim has chosen his attitude aright, but also that his aims — some day, at least — will be realized. Women always intrigue in secret against the higher souls of their husbands. They seek to cheat the future for the sake of a painless and agreeable present." [1]   In other words, the feminine vision is ever limited in range. Your typical woman cannot see far ahead; she cannot reason out the ultimate effect of a complicated series of causes; her eye is always upon the present or the very near future. Thus Nietzsche reaches, by a circuitous route, a conclusion supported by the almost unanimous verdict of the entire masculine sex, at all times and everywhere.

Nietzsche quite agrees with Schopenhauer (and with nearly everyone else who has given the matter thought) that the thing we call love is grounded upon physical desire, and that all of those arts of dress and manner in which women excel are mere devices for arousing this desire in man, but he points out, very justly, that a great many other considerations also enter into the matter. Love necessarily presupposes a yearning to mate, and

---

[1] *"Menschliches allzu Menschliches,"* § 431, 434.

mating is its logical consequence, but the human imagination has made it more than that. The man in love sees
in his charmer, not only an attractive instrument for
satisfying his comparatively rare and necessarily brief
impulses to dalliance, but also a worthy companion,
guide, counsellor and friend. The essence of love is confidence — confidence in the loved one's judgment, honesty
and fidelity and in the persistence of her charm. So large
do these considerations loom among the higher classes of
men that they frequently obscure the fundamental sexual
impulse entirely. It is a commonplace, indeed, that in
the ecstasies of amorous idealization, the notion of the
function itself becomes obnoxious. It may be impossible
to imagine a man loving a woman without having had, at
some time, conscious desire for her, but all the same it is
undoubtedly true that the wish for marriage is very often
a wish for close and constant association with the one
respected, admired and trusted rather than a yearning
for the satisfaction of desire.

All of this admiration, respect and trust, as we have
seen, may be interpreted as confidence, which, in turn, is
faith. Now, faith is essentially unreasonable, and in the
great majority of cases, is the very antithesis of reason.
Therefore, a man in love commonly endows the object of
his affection with merits which, to the eye of a disinterested
person, she obviously lacks. " Love . . . has a secret
craving to discover in the loved one as many beautiful
qualities as possible and to raise her as high as possible."
" Whoever idolizes a person tries to justify himself by
idealizing; and thus becomes an artist (or self-deceiver)
in order to have a clear conscience." Again there is a

tendency to illogical generalization. " Everything which pleases me once, or several times, is pleasing of and in itself." The result of this, of course, is quick and painful disillusion. The loved one is necessarily merely human and when the ideal gives way to the real, reaction necessarily follows. " Many a married man awakens one morning to the consciousness that his wife is far from attractive." [1] And it is only fair to note that the same awakening is probably the bitter portion of most married women, too.

In addition, it is plain that the purely physical desire which lies at the bottom of all human love, no matter how much sentimental considerations may obscure it, is merely a passion and so, in the very nature of things, is intermittent and evanescent. There are moments when it is overpowering, but there are hours, days, weeks and months when it is dormant. Therefore, we must conclude with Nietzsche, that the thing we call love, whether considered from its physical or psychical aspect, is fragile and short-lived.

Now, inasmuch as marriage, in the majority of cases, is a permanent institution (as it is, according to the theory of our moral code, in *all* cases), it follows that, in order to make the relation bearable, something must arise to take the place of love. This something, as we know, is ordinarily tolerance, respect, *camaraderie,* or a common interest in the well-being of the matrimonial firm or in the offspring of the marriage. In other words, the discovery that many of the ideal qualities seen in the life-companion through the rosy glasses of love do not exist

---

[1] All of these quotations are from " *Morgenröte.*"

is succeeded by a common-sense and unsentimental decision to make the best of those real ones which actually do exist.

From this it is apparent that a marriage is most apt to be successful when the qualities imagined in the beloved are all, or nearly all, real: that is to say, when the possibility of disillusion is at an irreducible minimum. This occurs sometimes by accident, but Nietzsche points out that such accidents are comparatively rare. A man in love, indeed, is the worst possible judge of his *inamorata's* possession of those traits which will make her a satisfactory wife, for, as we have noted, he observes her through an ideal haze and sees in her innumerable merits which, to the eye of an unprejudiced and accurate observer, she does not possess. Nietzsche, at different times, pointed out two remedies for this. His first plan proposed that marriages for love be discouraged, and that we endeavor to insure the permanence of the relation by putting the selection of mates into the hands of third persons likely to be dispassionate and far-seeing: a plan followed with great success, it may be recalled, by most ancient peoples and in vogue, in a more or less disguised form, in many European countries today. " It is impossible," he said, " to found a permanent institution upon an idiosyncrasy. Marriage, if it is to stand as the bulwark of civilization, cannot be founded upon the temporary and unreasonable thing called love. To fulfil its mission, it must be founded upon the impulse to reproduction, or race permanence; the impulse to possess property (women and children are property); and the impulse to rule, which constantly organizes for itself the smallest unit of sovereignty, the family, and which needs children and heirs to maintain, by physical force, whatever measure of power, riches and influence it attains."

Nietzsche's second proposal was nothing more or less than the institution of trial marriage, which, when it was proposed years later by an American sociologist,[1] caused all the uproar which invariably rises in the United States whenever an attempt is made to seek absolute truth. " Give us a term," said Zarathustra, " and a small marriage, that we may see whether we are fit for the great marriage."[2] The idea here, of course, is simply this: that, when a man and a woman find it utterly impossible to live in harmony, it is better for them to separate at once than to live on together, making a mock of the institution they profess to respect, and begetting children who, in Nietzsche's phrase, cannot be regarded other than as mere " scapegoats of matrimony." Nietzsche saw that this notion was so utterly opposed to all current ideals and hypocrisies that it would be useless to argue it, and so he veered toward his first proposal. The latter, despite its violation of one of the most sacred illusions of the Anglo-Saxon race, is by no means a mere fantasy of the chair. Marriages in which love is subordinated to mutual fitness and material considerations are the rule in many countries today, and have been so for thousands of years, and if it be urged that, in France, their fruit has been adultery, unfruitfulness and degeneration, it may be

---

[1] Elsie Clews Parsons: " The Family," New York, 1906. Mrs. Parsons is a doctor of philosophy, a Hartley house fellow and was for six years a lecturer on sociology at Barnard College.

[2] "*Also sprach Zarathustra*," III.

answered that, in Turkey, Japan and India, they have become the cornerstones of quite respectable civilizations.

Nietzsche believed that the ultimate mission and function of human marriage was the breeding of a race of supermen and he saw very clearly that fortuitous pairing would never bring this about. " Thou shalt not only propagate thyself," said Zarathustra, " but propagate thyself upward. Marriage should be the will of two to create that which is greater than either. But that which the many call marriage — alas! what call I that? Alas! that soul-poverty of two! Alas! that soul-filth of two! Alas! that miserable dalliance of two! Marriage they call it — and they say that marriages are made in heaven. I like them not: these animals caught in heavenly nets. . . Laugh not at such marriages! What child has not reason to weep over its parents? " It is the old argument against haphazard breeding. We select the sires and dams of our race-horses with most elaborate care, but the strains that mingle in our children's veins get there by chance. " Worthy and ripe for begetting the superman this man appeared to me, but when I saw his wife earth seemed a madhouse. Yea, I wish the earth would tremble in convulsions when such a saint and such a goose mate! This one fought for truth like a hero — and then took to heart a little dressed-up lie. He calls it his marriage. That one was reserved in intercourse and chose his associates fastidiously — and then spoiled his company forever. He calls it his marriage. A third sought for a servant with an angel's virtues. Now he is the servant of a woman. Even the most cunning buys his wife in a sack." [1]

[1] " *Also sprach Zarathustra*," I.

As has been noted, Nietzsche was by no means a declaimer against women. A bachelor himself and constitutionally suspicious of all who walked in skirts, he nevertheless avoided the error of damning the whole sex as a dangerous and malignant excrescence upon the face of humanity. He saw that woman's mind was the natural complement of man's mind; that womanly guile was as useful, in its place, as masculine truth; that man, to retain those faculties which made him master of the earth, needed a persistent and resourceful opponent to stimulate them and so preserve and develop them. So long as the institution of the family remained a premise in every sociological syllogism, so long as mere fruitfulness remained as much a merit among intelligent human beings as it was among peasants and cattle — so long, he saw, it would be necessary for the stronger sex to submit to the parasitic opportunism of the weaker.

But he was far from exalting mere women into goddesses, after the sentimental fashion of those virtuosi of illusion who pass for law-givers in the United States, and particularly in the southern part thereof. Chivalry, with its ridiculous denial of obvious facts, seemed to him unspeakable and the good old sub-Potomac doctrines that a woman who loses her virtue is, *ipso facto*, a victim and not a criminal or *particeps criminis*, and that a " lady," by virtue of being a " lady," is necessarily a reluctant and helpless quarry in the hunt of love — these ancient and venerable fallacies would have made him laugh. He admitted the great and noble part that woman had to play in the world-drama, but he saw clearly that her methods were essentially deceptive, insincere and pernicious, and so he held that she should be confined to her proper rôle and that any effort she made to take a hand in other matters should be regarded with suspicion, and when necessary, violently opposed. Thus Nietzsche detested the idea of women's suffrage almost as much as he detested the idea of chivalry. The participation of women in large affairs, he argued, could lead to but one result: the contamination of the masculine ideals of justice, honor and truth by the feminine ideals of dissimulation, equivocation and intrigue. In women, he believed, there was an entire absence of that instinctive liking for a square deal and a fair fight which one finds in all men — even the worst.

Hence, Nietzsche believed that, in his dealings with women, man should be wary and cautious. " Let men fear women when she loveth: for she sacrificeth all for love and nothing else hath value to her. . . . Man is for woman a means: the end is always the child. . . . Two things are wanted by the true man: danger and play. Therefore he seeketh woman as the most dangerous toy within his reach. . . . Thou goest to women? *Don't forget thy whip!* " [1] This last sentence has helped to make Nietzsche a stench in the nostrils of the orthodox, but the context makes his argument far more than a mere effort at sensational epigram. He is pointing out the utter unscrupulousness which lies at the foundation of the maternal instinct: an unscrupulousness familiar to every observer of humanity. [2] Indeed, it is so potent a

---

[1] " *Also sprach Zarathustra,*" I.

[2] Until quite recently it was considered indecent and indefensible to mention this fact, despite its obviousness. But it is now discussed

factor in the affairs of the world that we have, by our ancient device of labelling the inevitable the good, exalted it to the dignity and estate of a virtue. But all the same, we are instinctively conscious of its inherent opposition to truth and justice, and so our law books provide that a woman who commits a crime in her husband's presence is presumed to have been led to it by her desire to work what she regards as his good, which means her desire to retain his protection and good will. " Man's happiness is: ' I will.' Woman's happiness is: ' He will.' " [1]

Maternity, thought Nietzsche, was a thing even more sublime than paternity, because it produced a more keen sense of race responsibility. " Is there a state more blessed," he asked, " than that of a woman with child? . . . Even worldly justice does not allow the judge and hangman to lay hold on her." [2] He saw, too, that woman's insincere masochism [3] spurred man to heroic efforts and gave vigor and direction to his work by the very fact that it bore the outward aspect of helplessness. He saw that the resultant stimulation of the will to power was responsible for many of the world's great deeds, and that, if woman served no other purpose, she would still take an honorable place as the most splendid reward — greater

freely enough and in Henry Arthur Jones' play, " The Hypocrites," it is presented admirably in the character of the mother whose instinctive effort to protect her son makes her a scoundrel and the son a cad.

[1] " *Also sprach Zarathustra*," I.

[2] " *Morgenröte*," § 552

[3] Prof. Dr. R. von Krafft Ebing: " Masochism is . . . a peculiar perversion . . . consisting in this, that the individual seized with it is dominated by the idea that he is wholly and unconditionally subjected to the will of a person of the opposite sex, who treats him imperiously and humiliates and maltreats him."

than honors or treasures — that humanity could bestow upon its victors. The winning of a beautiful and much-sought woman, indeed, will remain as great an incentive to endeavor as the conquest of a principality so long as humanity remains substantially as it is today.

It is unfortunate that Nietzsche left us no record of his notions regarding the probable future of matrimony as an institution. We have reason to believe that he agreed with Schopenhauer's analysis of the " lady," *i. e.* the woman elevated to splendid, but complete parasitism. Schopenhauer showed that this pitiful creature was the product of the monogamous ideal, just as the prostitute was the product of the monogamous actuality. In the United States and England, unfortunately, it is impossible to discuss such matters with frankness, or to apply to them the standards of absolute truth, on account of the absurd axiom that monogamy is ordained of God, — with which maxim there appears the equally absurd corollary: that the civilization of a people is to be measured by the degree of dependence of its women. Luckily for posterity this last revolting doctrine is fast dying, though its decadence is scarcely noticed and wholly misunderstood. We see about us that women are becoming more and more independent and self-sufficient and that, as individuals, they have less and less need to seek and retain the good will and protection of individual men, but we overlook the fact that this tendency is fast undermining the ancient theory that the family is a necessary and impeccable institution and that without it progress would be impossible. As a matter of fact, the idea of the family, as it exists today, is based entirely upon the idea

of feminine helplessness. So soon as women are capable
of making a living for themselves and their children,
without the aid of the fathers of the latter, the old cornerstone of the family — the masculine defender and bread-
winner — will find his occupation gone, and it will
become ridiculous to force him, by law or custom, to
discharge duties for which there is no longer need. Wipe
out your masculine defender, and your feminine parasite-
haus-frau — and where is your family?

This tendency is exhibited empirically by the rising
revolt against those fetters which the family idea has
imposed upon humanity: by the growing feeling that
divorce should be a matter of individual expedience; by
the successful war of cosmopolitanism upon insularity
and clannishness and upon all other costly outgrowths
of the old idea that because men are of the same blood
they must necessarily love one another; and by the increasing reluctance among civilized human beings to become
parents without some reason more logical than the notion
that parenthood, in itself, is praiseworthy. It seems plain,
in a word, that so soon as any considerable portion of the
women of the world become capable of doing men's work
and of thus earning a living for themselves and their children without the aid of men, there will be in full progress
a dangerous, if unconscious, war upon the institution of
marriage.   It may be urged in reply that this will never
happen, because of the fact that women are physically unequal to men, and that in consequence of their duty of child-
bearing, they will ever remain so, but it may be answered
to this that use will probably vastly increase their physical
fitness; that science will rob child-bearing of most of its

terrors within a comparatively few years; and that the woman who seeks to go it alone will have only herself and her child to maintain, whereas, the man of today has not only himself and his child, but also the woman. Again, it is plain that the economic handicap of child-bearing is greatly overestimated. At most, the business of maternity makes a woman utterly helpless for no longer than three months, and in the case of a woman who has three children, this means nine months in a life time. It is entirely probable that alcohol alone, not to speak of other enemies of efficiency, robs the average man of quite that much productive activity during his three score years and ten.

X

GOVERNMENT

LIKE Spencer before him, Nietzsche believed, as we have seen, that the best possible system of government was that which least interfered with the desires and enterprises of the efficient and intelligent individual. That is to say, he held that it would be well to establish, among the members of his first caste of human beings, a sort of glorified anarchy. Each member of this caste should be at liberty to work out his own destiny for himself. There should be no laws regulating and circumscribing his relations to other members of his caste, except the easily-recognizable and often-changing laws of common interest, and above all, there should be no laws forcing him to submit to, or even to consider, the wishes and behests of the two lower castes. The higher man, in a word, should admit no responsibility whatever to the lower castes. The lowest of all he should look upon solely as a race of slaves bred to work his welfare in the most efficient and uncomplaining manner possible, and the military caste should seem to him a race designed only to carry out his orders and so prevent the slave caste marching against him.

It is plain from this that Nietzsche stood squarely

opposed to both of the two schemes of government which, on the surface, at least, seem to prevail in the western world to-day. For the monarchial ideal and for the democratic ideal he had the same words of contempt. Under an absolute monarchy, he believed, the military or law-enforcing caste was unduly exalted, and so its natural tendency to permanence was increased and its natural opposition to all experiment and progress was made well nigh irresistible. Under a communistic democracy, on the other hand, the mistake was made of putting power into the hands of the great, inert herd, which was necessarily and inevitably ignorant, credulous, superstitious, corrupt and wrong. The natural tendency of this herd, said Nietzsche, was to combat change and progress as bitterly and as ceaselessly as the military-judicial caste, and when, by some accident, it rose out of its rut and attempted experiments, it nearly always made mistakes, both in its premises and its conclusions and so got hopelessly bogged in error and imbecility. Its feeling for truth seemed to him to be almost *nil;* its mind could never see beneath misleading exteriors. " In the market place," said Zarathustra, " one convinces by gestures, but real reasons make the populace distrustful." [1]

That this natural incompetence of the masses is an actual fact was observed by a hundred philosophers before Nietzsche, and fresh proofs of it are spread copiously before the world every day. Wherever universal suffrage, or some close approach to it, is the primary axiom of government, the thing known in the United

---

[1] " *Also sprach Zarathustra,*" IV.

States as " freak legislation " is a constant evil. On the statute books of the great majority of American states there are laws so plainly opposed to all common-sense that they bear an air of almost pathetic humor. One state legislature,[1] in an effort to prevent the corrupt employment of insurance funds, passes laws so stringent that, in the face of them, it is utterly impossible for an insurance company to transact a profitable business. Another considers an act contravening rights guaranteed specifically by the state and national constitutions;[2] yet another[3] passes a law prohibiting divorce under any circumstances whatever. And the spectacle is by no means confined to the American states. In the Australian Commonwealth, mob-rule has burdened the statutes with regulations which make difficult, if not impossible, the natural development of the country's resources and trade. If, in England and Germany, the effect of universal suffrage has been less apparent, it is because in these countries the two upper castes have solved the problem of keeping the proletariat, despite its theoretical sovereignty, in proper leash and bounds.

The possibility of exercising this control seemed to Nietzsche to be the saving grace of all modern forms of government, just as their essential impossibility appeared as the saving grace alike of Christianity and of com-

[1] That of Wisconsin at the 1907 session.

[2] This has been done, time and again, by the legislature of every state in the Union, and the overturning of such legislation occupies part of the time of all the state courts of final judicature year after year.

[3] That of South Carolina.

munistic civilization. In England, as we have seen,[1] the military-judicial caste, despite the Reform Act of 1867, has retained its old dominance, and in Germany, despite the occasional success of the socialists, it is always possible for the military aristocracy, by appealing to the vanity of the *bourgeoisie*, to win in a stand-up fight. In America, the proletariat, when it is not engaged in functioning in its own extraordinary manner, is commonly the tool, either of the first of Nietzsche's castes or of the second. That is to say, the average legislature has its price, and this price is often paid by those who believe that old laws, no matter how imperfect they may be, are better than harum-scarum new ones. Naturally enough, the most intelligent and efficient of Americans — members of the first caste — do not often go to a state capital with corruption funds and openly buy legislation, but nevertheless their influence is frequently felt. President Roosevelt, for one, has more than once forced his views upon a reluctant proletariat and even enlisted it under his banner — as in his advocacy of centralization, a truly dionysian idea, for example — and in the southern states the educated white class — which there represents, though in a melancholy fashion, the Nietzschean first caste — has found it easy to take from the black masses their very right to vote, despite the fact that they are everywhere in a great majority numerically, and so, by the theory of democracy, represent whatever power lies in the state. Thus it is apparent that Nietzsche's argument against democracy, like his argument against brotherhood, is based upon the thesis that both are

[1] *Vide* the chapter on " Civilization."

rejected instinctively by all those men whose activity works for the progress of the human race. [1]

It is obvious, of course, that the sort of anarchy preached by Nietzsche differs vastly from the beery, collarless anarchy preached by Herr Most and his unwashed followers. The latter contemplates a suspension of all laws in order that the unfit may escape the natural and rightful exploitation of the fit, whereas the former reduces the unfit to *de facto* slavery and makes them subject to the laws of a master class, which, in so far as the relations of its own members, one to the other, are concerned, recognizes no law but that of natural selection. To the average American or Englishman the very name of anarchy causes a shudder, because it invariably conjures up a picture of a land terrorized by low-browed assassins with matted beards, carrying bombs in one hand and mugs of beer in the other. But as a matter of fact, there is no reason whatever to believe that, if all laws were abolished tomorrow, such swine would survive the day. They are incompetents under our present paternalism and they would be incompetents under dionysian anarchy.

[1] Said the Chicago *Tribune*, "the best all-round newspaper in the United States," in a leading article, June 10, 1907: "Jeremy Bentham speaks of 'an incoherent and undigested mass of law, shot down, as from a rubbish cart, upon the heads of the people.' This is a fairly accurate summary of the work of the average American legislature, from New York to Texas. . . . Bad, crude and unnecessary laws make up a large part of the output of every session. . . . Roughly speaking, the governor who vetoes the most bills is the best governor. When a governor vetoes none the legitimate presumption is, not that the work of the legislature was flawless, but that he was timid, not daring to oppose ignorant popular sentiment . . . or that he had not sense enough to recognize a bad measure when he saw it."

The only difference between the two states is that the former, by its laws, protects men of this sort, whereas the latter would work their speedy annihilation. In a word, the dionysian state would see the triumph, not of drunken loafers, but of the very men whose efforts are making for progress today: those strong, free, self-reliant, resourceful men whose capacities are so much greater than the mobs' that they are often able to force their ideas upon it, despite its theoretical right to rule them and its actual endeavor so to do. Nietzschean anarchy would create an aristocracy of efficiency. The strong man — which means the intelligent, ingenious and far-seeing man — would acknowledge no authority but his own will and no morality but his own advantage. As we have seen in previous chapters, this would re-establish the law of natural selection firmly upon its disputed throne, and so the strong would grow ever stronger and more efficient, and the weak would grow ever more obedient and tractile.

It may be well at this place to glance briefly at an objection that has been urged against Nietzsche's argument by many critics, and particularly by those in the socialistic camp. Led to it, no doubt, by their too literal acceptance of Marx's materialistic conception of history, they have assumed that Nietzsche's higher man must necessarily belong to the class denominated, by our after-dinner speakers and leader writers, "captains of industry," and to this class alone. That is to say, they have regarded the higher man as identical with the pushing, grasping buccaneer of finance, because this buccaneer has seemed to them to be the only man of today who is truly " strong, free, self-reliant and resourceful " and the only one who actually " acknowledges no authority but his own will." As a matter of fact, all of these assumptions are in error. For one thing, the " captain of industry " is not uncommonly the reverse of a dionysian, and without the artificial aid of our permanent laws, he might often perish in the struggle for existence. For another thing, it is an obvious fact that the men who go most violently counter to the view of the herd, and who battle most strenuously to prevail against it — our true criminals and transvaluers and breakers of the law — are not such men as Rockefeller, but men such as Pasteur; not such men as Morgan and Hooley, but sham-smashers and truth-tellers and mob-fighters after the type of Huxley, Lincoln, Bismarck, Darwin, Virchow, Haeckel, Hobbes, Macchiavelli, Harvey and Jenner, the father of vaccination.

Jenner, to choose one from the long list, was a real dionysian, because he boldly pitted his own opinion against the practically unanimous opinion of all the rest of the human race. Among those members of the ruling class in England who came after him — those men, that is, who made vaccination compulsory — the dionysian spirit was still more apparent. The masses themselves did not want to be vaccinated, because they were too ignorant to understand the theory of inoculation and too stupid to be much impressed by its unvisualized and — for years, at least — impalpable benefits. Yet their rulers forced them, against their will, to bare their arms. And why was this done? Was it because the ruling class was possessed by a boundless love for humanity and so yearned to lavish upon it a wealth of Christian devotion ?

Not at all. The real motive of the law makers was to be found in two considerations. In the first place, a proletariat which suffered from epidemics of small-pox was a crippled mob whose capacity for serving its betters, in the fields and factories of England, was sadly decreased. In the second place experience proved that when small-pox raged in the slums, it had an unhappy habit of stretching out its arms in the direction of mansion and castle, too. Therefore, the proletariat was vaccinated and small-pox was stamped out — not because the ruling class loved the workers, but because it wanted to make them work for it as continuously as possible and to remove or reduce their constant menace to its life and welfare. In so far as it took the initiative in these proceedings, the military ruling-class of England raised itself to the eminence of Nietzsche's first caste. That Jenner himself, when he put forward his idea and led the military caste to carry it into execution, was an ideal member of the first caste, is plain. The goal before him was fame everlasting — and he gained it.

I have made this rather long digression because the opponents of Nietzsche have voiced their error a thousand times and have well-nigh convinced a great many persons of its truth. It is apparent enough, of course, that a great many men whose energy is devoted to the accumulation of money are truly dionysian in their methods and aims, but it is apparent, too, that a great many others are not. Nietzsche himself was well aware of the dangers which beset a race enthralled by commercialism, and he sounded his warning against them. Trade, being grounded upon security, tends to work for permanence in laws and customs, even after the actual utility of these laws and customs is openly questioned. This is shown by the persistence of free trade in England and of protectionism in the United States, despite the fact that the conditions of existence, in both countries, have materially changed since the two systems were adopted, and there is now good ground, in each, for demanding reform. So it is plain that Nietzsche did not cast his higher man in the mold of a mere millionaire. It is conceivable that a careful analysis might prove Mr. Morgan to be a dionysian, but it is certain that his character as such would not be grounded upon his well-known and oft-repeated plea that existing institutions be permitted to remain as they are.

Yet again, a great many critics of Nietzsche mistake his criticism of existing governmental institutions for an argument in favor of their immediate and violent abolition. When he inveighs against monarchy or democracy, for instance, it is concluded that he wants to assassinate all the existing rulers of the world, overturn all existing governments and put chaos, carnage, rapine and anarchy in their place. Such a conclusion, of course, is a grievous error. Nietzsche by no means believed that reforms could be instituted in a moment or that the characters and habits of thought of human beings could be altered by a lightning stroke. His whole philosophy, in truth, was based upon the idea of slow evolution, through infinitely laborious and infinitely protracted stages. All he attempted to do was to indicate the errors that were being made in his own time and to point out the probable character of the truths that would be accepted in the future. He believed that it was only by constant skepticism, criticism and opposition that progress could be made, and that the greatest of all dangers was inanition. Therefore, when he condemned all existing schemes of government, it meant no more than that he regarded them as based upon fundamental errors, and that he hoped and believed that, in the course of time, these errors would be observed, admitted and swept away, to make room for other errors measurably less dangerous, and in the end for truths. Such was his mission, as he conceived it: to attack error wherever he saw it and to proclaim truth whenever he found it. It is only by such iconoclasm and proselyting that humanity can be helped. It is only after a mistake is perceived and admitted that it can be rectified.

Nietzsche's argument for the " free spirit " by no means denies the efficacy of co-operation in the struggle upward, but neither does it support that blind fetishism which sees in co-operation the sole instrument of human progress. In one of his characteristic thumb-nail notes upon evolution he says: " The most important result of progress in the past is the fact that we no longer live in constant fear of wild beasts, barbarians, gods and our own dreams." [1] It may be argued, in reference to this, that organized government is to be thanked for our deliverance, but a moment's thought will show the error of the notion. Humanity's war upon wild beasts was fought and won by individualists, who had in mind no end but their personal safety and that of their children, and the subsequent war upon barbarians would have been impossible, or at

[1] " *Morgenröte*," § 5.

least unsuccessful, had it not been for the weapons invented and employed during the older fight against beasts.
Again, it is apparent that our emancipation from the
race's old superstitions regarding gods and omens has been
achieved, not by communal effort, but by individual effort.
Knowledge and not government brought us the truth that
made us free. Government, in its very essence, is opposed
to all increase of knowledge. Its tendency is always toward
permanence and against change. It is unthinkable without
some accepted scheme of law or morality, and such
schemes, as we have seen, stand in direct antithesis to
every effort to find the absolute truth. Therefore, it is
plain that the progress of humanity, far from being the
result of government, has been made entirely without its
aid and in the face of its constant and bitter opposition.
The code of Hammurabi, the laws of the Medes and
Persians, the Code Napoleon and the English common
law have retarded the search for the ultimate verities
almost as much, indeed, as the Ten Commandments.

Nietzsche denies absolutely that there is inherent in
mankind a yearning to gather into communities. There
is, he says, but one primal instinct in human beings (as
there is in all other animals), and that is the desire to
remain alive. All those systems of thought which assume
the existence of a " natural morality " are wrong. Even
the tendency to tell the truth, which seems to be inborn
in every civilized white man, is not " natural," for there
have been — and are today — races in which it is, to all
intents and purposes, entirely absent. [1] And so it is with

---

[1] "The word ' honesty ' is not to be found in the code of either the
Socratic or the Christian virtues. It represents a new virtue, not quite

the so-called social instinct. Man, say the communists, is a gregarious animal and can be happy only in company with his fellows, and in proof of it they cite the fact that loneliness is everywhere regarded as painful and that, even among the lower animals, there is an impulse toward association. The facts set forth in the last sentence are indisputable, but they by no means prove the existence of an elemental social feeling sufficiently strong to make its satisfaction an end in itself. In other words, while it is plain that men flock together, just as birds flock together, it is going too far to say that the mere joy of flocking — the mere desire to be with others — is at the bottom of the tendency. On the contrary, it is quite possible to show that men gather in communities for the same reason that deer gather in herds: because each individual realizes (unconsciously, perhaps) that such a combination materially aids him in the business of self-protection. One deer is no match for a lion, but fifty deer make him impotent. [1]

Nietzsche shows that, even after communities are

ripened, frequently misunderstood and hardly conscious of itself. It is yet something in embryo, which we are at liberty either to foster or to check." — "*Morgenröte*," § 456.

[1] An excellent discussion of this subject, by Prof. Warner Fite, of Indiana University, appeared in *The Journal of Philosophy, Psychology and Scientific Methods* of July 18, 1907. Prof. Fite's article is called " The Exaggeration of the Social," and is a keen and sound criticism of " the now popular tendency to regard the individual as the product of society." As he points out, " any consciousness of belonging to one group rather than another must involve some sense of individuality." In other words, gregariousness is nothing more than an instinctive yearning to profit personally by the possibility of putting others, to some measurable ex-tent, in the attitude of slaves.

formed, the strong desire of every individual to look out
for himself, regardless of the desires of others, persists,
and that, in every herd there are strong members and
weak members. The former, whenever the occasion
arises, sacrifice the latter: by forcing the heavy, killing
drudgery of the community upon them or by putting
them, in time of war, into the forefront of the fray.
The result is that the weakest are being constantly
weeded out and the strongest are always becoming
stronger and stronger. "Hence," says Nietzsche, "the
first 'state' made its appearance in the form of a terrible
tyranny, a violent and unpitying machine, which kept
grinding away until the primary raw material, the
man-ape, was kneaded and fashioned into alert, efficient
man."

Now, when a given state becomes appreciably more
efficient than the states about it, it invariably sets about
enslaving them. Thus larger and larger states are formed,
but always there is a ruling master-class and a serving
slave-class. "This," says Nietzsche, "is the origin of the
state on earth, despite the fantastic theory which would
found it upon some general agreement among its members.
He who can command, he who is a master by nature, he
who, in deed and gesture, behaves violently — what need
has he for agreements? Such beings come as fate comes,
without reason or pretext. . . . Their work is the instinctive creation of forms: they are the most unconscious
of all artists; wherever they appear, something new is at
once created — a governmental organism which lives; in
which the individual parts and functions are differentiated
and brought into correlation, and in which nothing at all

is tolerable unless some utility with respect to the whole
is implanted in it. They are innocent of guilt, of responsibility, of charity — these born rulers. They are ruled by
that terrible art-egotism which knows itself to be justified
by its work, as the mother knows herself to be justified by
her child."

Nietzsche points out that, even after nations have
attained some degree of permanence and have introduced
ethical concepts into their relations with one another, they
still give evidence of that same primary will to power
which is responsible, at bottom, for every act of the
individual man. " The masses, in any nation," he says,
" are ready to sacrifice their lives, their goods and chattels,
their consciences and their virtue, to obtain that highest
of pleasures: the feeling that they rule, either in reality or
in imagination, over others. On these occasions they
make virtues of their instinctive yearnings, and so they
enable an ambitious or wisely provident prince to rush
into a war with the good conscience of his people as
his excuse. The great conquerors have always had the
language of virtue on their lips: they have always had
crowds of people around them who felt exalted and
would not listen to any but the most exalted sentiments.
. . . When man feels the sense of power, he feels and
calls himself good, and at the same time those who have
to endure the weight of his power call him evil. Such is
the curious mutability of moral judgments ! . . . Hesiod,
in his fable of the world's ages, twice pictured the
age of the Homeric heroes and made two out of one.
To those whose ancestors were under the iron heel of
the Homeric despots, it appeared evil; while to the

grandchildren of these despots it appeared good.   Hence
the poet had no alternative but to do as he did: his
audience was composed of the descendants of both
classes." [1]

Nietzsche saw naught but decadence and illusion in
humanitarianism and nationalism. To profess a love for
the masses seemed to him to be ridiculous and to profess
a love for one race or tribe of men, in preference to all
others, seemed to him no less so.   Thus he denied the
validity of two ideals which lie at the base of all civilized
systems of government, and constitute, in fact, the very
conception of the state.   He called himself, not a German,
but " a good European."

" We good Europeans," he said, " are not French
enough to ' love mankind.'   A man must be afflicted by
an excess of Gallic eroticism to approach mankind with
ardour.   Mankind!   Was there ever a more hideous old
woman among all the old women?   No, we do not love
mankind! . . . On the other hand, we are not German
enough to advocate nationalism and race-hatred, or to
take delight in that national blood-poisoning which sets
up quarantines between the nations of Europe.   We are
too unprejudiced for that — too perverse, too fastidious,
too well-informed, too much travelled.   We prefer to live
on mountains — apart, unseasonable. . . . We are too
diverse and mixed in race to be patriots.   We are, in a
word, good Europeans — the rich heirs of millenniums of
European thought. . . .

" We rejoice in everything, which like ourselves, loves
danger, war and adventure — which does not make

[1] " *Morgenröte*," § 189.

compromises, nor let itself be captured, conciliated or faced. . . . We ponder over the need of a new order of things — even of a new slavery, for the strengthening and elevation of the human race always involves the existence of slaves. . . ." [1]

" The horizen is unobstructed. . . . Our ships can start on their voyage once more in the face of danger. . . . The sea — our sea ! — lies before us ! " [2]

---

[1] " *Die fröhliche Wissenschaft,* " § 377.
[2] " *Die fröhliche Wissenschaft,*" § 343.

XI

CRIME AND PUNISHMENT

NIETZSCHE says that the thing which best differentiates man from the other animals is his capacity for making and keeping a promise. That is to say, man has a trained and efficient memory and it enables him to project an impression of today into the future. Of the millions of impressions which impinge upon his consciousness every day, he is able to save a chosen number from the oblivion of forgetfulness. An animal lacks this capacity almost entirely. The things that it remembers are far from numerous and it is devoid of any means of reinforcing its memory. But man has such a means and it is commonly called conscience. At bottom it is based upon the principle that pain is always more enduring than pleasure. Therefore, " in order to make an idea stay it must be burned into the memory; only that which never ceases to hurt remains fixed." [1] Hence all the world's store of tortures and sacrifices. At one time they were nothing more than devices to make man remember his pledges to his gods. Today they survive in the form of legal punishments, which are nothing more, at bottom, than devices to make a man remember his pledges to his fellow men.

[1] " *Zur Geneologie der Moral,*" II, § 3.

From all this Nietzsche argues that our modern law is the outgrowth of the primitive idea of barter — of the idea that everything has an equivalent and can be paid for — that when a man forgets or fails to discharge an obligation in one way he may wipe out his sin by discharging it in some other way. " The earliest relationship that ever existed," he says, " was the relationship between buyer and seller, creditor and debtor. On this ground man first stood face to face with man. No stage of civilization, however inferior, is without the institution of bartering. To fix prices, to adjust values, to invent equivalents, to exchange things — all this has to such an extent preoccupied the first and earliest thought of man, that it may be said to constitute thinking itself. Out of it sagacity arose, and out of it, again, arose man's first pride — his first feeling of superiority over the animal world. Perhaps, our very word man (*manus*) expresses something of this. [1] Man calls himself the being who weighs and measures." [2]

Now besides the contract between man and man, there is also a contract between man and the community. The community agrees to give the individual protection and the individual promises to pay for it in labor and obedience. Whenever he fails to do so, he violates his promise, and the community regards the contract as broken. Then " the anger of the outraged creditor — or community — withdraws its protection from the debtor — or law-breaker — and he is laid open to all the

---

[1] In the ancient Sanskrit the word from which " man " comes meant " to think, to weigh, to value, to reckon, to estimate."

[2] " *Zur Geneologie der Moral*," II, § 8.

dangers and disadvantages of life in a state of barbarism. Punishment, at this stage of civilization, is simply the image of a man's normal conduct toward a hated, disarmed and cast-down enemy, who has forfeited not only all claims to protection, but also all claims to mercy. This accounts for the fact that war (including the sacrificial cult of war) has furnished all the forms in which punishment appears in history." [1]

It will be observed that this theory grounds all ideas of justice and punishment upon ideas of expedience. The primeval creditor forced his debtor to pay because he knew that if the latter didn't pay he (the creditor) would suffer. In itself, the debtor's effort to get something for nothing was not wrong, because, as we have seen in previous chapters, this is the ceaseless and unconscious endeavor of every living being, and is, in fact, the most familiar of all manifestations of the primary will to live, or more understandably, of the will to acquire power over environment. But when the machinery of justice was placed in the hands of the state, there came a transvaluation of values. Things that were manifestly costly to the state were called wrong, and the old individualistic standards of good and bad — i. e. beneficial and harmful — became the standards of good and evil — i. e. right and wrong.

In this way, says Nietzsche, the original purpose of punishment has become obscured and forgotten. Starting out as a mere means of adjusting debts, it has become a machine for enforcing moral concepts. Moral ideas came into the world comparatively late, and it was not

[1] "*Zur Geneologie der Moral*," II, § 9.

until man had begun to be a speculative being that he invented gods, commandments and beatitudes. But the institution of punishment was in existence from a much earlier day. Therefore, it is apparent that the moral idea, — the notion that there is such a thing as good and such a thing as evil, — far from being the inspiration of punishment, was engrafted upon it at a comparatively late period. Nietzsche says that man, in considering things as they are today, is very apt to make this mistake about their origins. He is apt to conclude, because the human eye is used for seeing, that it was created for that purpose, whereas it is obvious that it may have been created for some other purpose and that the function of seeing may have arisen later on. In the same way, man believes that punishment was invented for the purpose of enforcing moral ideas, whereas, as a matter of fact, it was originally an instrument of expediency only, and did not become a moral machine until a code of moral laws was evolved. [1]

To show that the institution of punishment itself is older than the ideas which now seem to lie at the base of it, Nietzsche cites the fact that these ideas themselves are constantly varying. That is to say, the aim and purpose of punishment are conceived differently by different races and individuals. One authority calls it a means of rendering the criminal helpless and harmless and so preventing further mischief in future. Another says that

[1] A familiar example of this superimposition of morality is afforded by the history of costume. It is commonly assumed that garments were originally designed to hide nakedness as much as to afford warmth and adorn the person, whereas, as a matter of fact, the idea of modesty probably did not appear until man had been clothed for ages.

it is a means of inspiring others with fear of the law and its agents. Another says that it is a device for destroying the unfit. Another holds it to be a fee exacted by society from the evil-doer for protecting him against the excesses of private revenge. Still another looks upon it as society's declaration of war against its enemies. Yet another says that it is a scheme for making the criminal realize his guilt and repent. Nietzsche shows that all of these ideas, while true, perhaps, in some part, are fallacies at bottom. It is ridiculous, for instance, to believe that punishment makes the law-breaker acquire a feeling of guilt and sinfulness. He sees that he was indiscreet in committing his crime, but he sees, too, that society's method of punishing his indiscretion consists in committing a crime of the same sort against *him*. In other words, he cannot hold his own crime a sin without also holding his punishment a sin — which leads to an obvious absurdity. As a matter of fact, says Nietzsche, punishment really does nothing more than " augment fear, intensify prudence and subjugate the passions." And in so doing it *tames* man, but does not make him better. If he refrains from crime in future, it is because he has become more prudent and not because he has become more moral. If he regrets his crimes of the past, it is because his punishment, and not his so-called conscience, hurts him.

But what, then, is conscience? That there is such a thing every reasonable man knows. But what is its nature and what is its origin? If it is not the regret which follows punishment, what is it? Nietzsche answers that it is nothing more than the old will to power, turned inward.   In the days of the cave men, a man gave his will to power free exercise.   Any act which increased his power over his environment, no matter how much it damaged other men, seemed to him good.   He knew nothing of morality.   Things appeared to him, not as good or evil, but as good or bad — beneficial or harmful. But when civilization was born, there arose a necessity for controlling and regulating this will power.   The individual had to submit to the desire of the majority and to conform to nascent codes of morality.   The result was that his will to power, which once spent itself in battles with other individuals, had to be turned upon himself. Instead of torturing others, he began to torture his own body and mind.   His ancient delight in cruelty and persecution (a characteristic of all healthy animals) remained, but he could not longer satisfy it upon his fellow men and so he turned it upon himself, and straightway became a prey to the feeling of guilt, of sinfulness, of wrong-doing — with all its attendant horrors.

Now, one of the first forms that this self-torture took was primitive man's accusation against himself that he was not properly grateful for the favors of his god.   He saw that many natural phenomena benefited him, and he thought that these phenomena occurred in direct obedience to the deity's command.   Therefore, he regarded himself as the debtor of the deity, and constantly accused himself of neglecting to discharge this debt, because he felt that, by so accusing, he would be most apt to discharge it in full, and thus escape the righteous consequences of insufficient payment.   This led him to make sacrifices — to place food and drink upon his god's altar, and in the end; to sacrifice much more valuable things, such, for instance, as his first born child. The more vivid the idea of the deity became and the more terrible he appeared, the more man tried to satisfy and appease him. In the early days, it was sufficient to sacrifice a square meal or a baby. But when Christianity — with its elaborate and certain theology — arose, it became necessary for a man to sacrifice himself.

Thus arose the Christian idea of sin. Man began to feel that he was in debt to his creator hopelessly and irretrievably, and that, like a true bankrupt, he should offer all he had in partial payment. So he renounced everything that made life on earth bearable and desirable and built up an ideal of poverty and suffering. Sometimes he hid himself in a cave and lived like an outcast dog — and then he was called a saint. Sometimes he tortured himself with whips and poured vinegar into his wounds — and then he was a flagellant of the middle ages. Sometimes, he killed his sexual instinct and his inborn desire for property and power — and then he became a penniless celibate in a cloister.

Nietzsche shows that this idea of sin, which lies at the bottom of all religions, was and is an absurdity; that nothing, in itself, is sinful, and that no man is, or can be a sinner. If we could rid ourselves of the notion that here is a God in Heaven, to whom we owe a debt, we would rid ourselves of the idea of sin. Therefore, argues Nietzsche, it is evident that skepticism, while it makes no actual change in man, always makes him feel better. It makes him lose his fear of hell and his consciousness of sin. It rids him of that most horrible instrument of useless, senseless and costly torture — his conscience. " Atheism," says Nietzsche, " will make a man innocent."

XII

EDUCATION

EDUCATION, as everyone knows, has two main objects: to impart knowledge and to implant culture. It is the object of a teacher, first of all, to bring before his pupil as many concrete facts about the universe — the fruit of long ages of inquiry and experience — as the latter may be capable of absorbing in the time available. After that, it is the teacher's aim to make his pupil's habits of mind sane, healthy and manly, and his whole outlook upon life that of a being conscious of his efficiency and eager and able to solve new problems as they arise. The educated man, in a word, is one who knows a great deal more than the average man and is constantly increasing his area of knowledge, in a sensible, orderly logical fashion; one who is wary of sophistry and leans automatically and almost instinctively toward clear thinking.

Such is the purpose of education, in its ideal aspect. As we observe the science of teaching in actual practice, we find that it often fails utterly to attain this end. The concrete facts that a student learns at the average school are few and unconnected, and instead of being led into habits of independent thinking he is trained to accept authority. When he takes his degree it is usually no more than a sign that he has joined the herd. His opinion of Napoleon is merely a reflection of the opinion expressed in the books he has studied; his philosophy of life is simply the philosophy of his teacher — tinctured a bit, perhaps, by that of his particular youthful idols. He knows how to spell a great many long words and he is familiar with the table of logarithms, but in the readiness and accuracy of his mental processes he has made comparatively little progress. If he was illogical and credulous and a respecter of authority as a freshman he remains much the same as a graduate. In consequence, his usefulness to humanity has been increased but little, if at all, for, as we have seen in previous chapters, the only man whose life is appreciably more valuable than that of a good cow is the man who thinks for himself, clearly and logically, and lends some sort of hand, during his lifetime, in the eternal search for the ultimate verities.

The cause for all this lies, no doubt, in the fact that school teachers, taking them by and large, are probably the most ignorant and stupid class of men in the whole group of mental workers. Imitativeness being the dominant impulse in youth, their pupils acquire some measure of their stupidity, and the result is that the influence of the whole teaching tribe is against everything included in genuine education and culture.

That this is true is evident on the surface and a moment's analysis furnishes a multitude of additional proofs. For one thing, a teacher, before he may begin work, must sacrifice whatever independence may survive within him upon the altar of authority. He becomes a cog in the school wheel and must teach only the things countenanced and approved by the powers above him, whether those powers be visible in the minister of education, as in Germany; in the traditions of the school, as in England, or in the private convictions of the millionaire who provides the cash, as in the United States. As Nietzsche points out, the schoolman's thirst for the truth is always conditioned by his yearning for food and drink and a comfortable bed. His archetype is the university philosopher, who accepts the state's pay[1] and so surrenders that liberty to inquire freely which alone makes philosophy worth while.

"No state," says Nietzsche, "would ever dare to patronize such men as Plato and Schopenhauer. And why? Simply because the state is always afraid of them. They tell the truth. . . . Consequently, the man who submits to be a philosopher in the pay of the state must also submit to being looked upon by the state as one who has waived his claim to pursue the truth into all its fastnesses. So long as he holds his place, he must acknowledge something still higher than the truth — and that is the state. . . .

"The sole criticism of a philosophy which is possible and the only one which proves anything — namely, an attempt to live according to it — is never put forward in the universities. There the only thing one hears of is a wordy criticism of words. And so the youthful mind, without much experience in life, is confronted by fifty

---

[1] Nietzsche is considering, of course, the condition of affairs in Germany, where all teaching is controlled by the state. But his arguments apply to other countries as well and to teachers of other things besides philosophy.

verbal systems and fifty criticisms of them, thrown together and hopelessly jumbled. What demoralization!
What a mockery of education! It is openly acknowledged,
in fact, that the object of education is not the acquire-
ment of learning, but the successful meeting of examinations. No wonder then, that the examined student says
to himself ' Thank God, I am not a philosopher, but a
Christian and a citizen! . . .'

"Therefore, I regard it as necessary to progress that
we withdraw from philosophy all governmental and
academic recognition and support. . . . Let philosophers
spring up naturally, deny them every prospect of appointment, tickle them no longer with salaries — yea, persecute
them! Then you will see marvels! They will then
flee afar and seek a roof anywhere. Here a parsonage
will open its doors; there a schoolhouse. One will
appear upon the staff of a newspaper, another will write
manuals for young ladies' schools. The most rational of
them will put his hand to the plough and the vainest will
seek favor at court. Thus we shall get rid of bad philosophers." [1]

The argument here is plain enough. The professional
teacher must keep to his rut. The moment he combats
the existing order of things he loses his place. Therefore
he is wary, and his chief effort is to transmit the words of
authority to his pupils unchanged. Whether he be a
philosopher, properly so-called, or something else matters
not. In a medical school wherein Chauveau's theory of
immunity was still maintained it would be hazardous for
a professor of pathology to teach the theory of Ehrlich.

[1] "*Schopenhauer als Erzieher*," § 8.

In a Methodist college in Indiana it would be foolhardy
to dally with the doctrine of apostolic succession. Everywhere the teacher must fashion his teachings according
to the creed and regulations of his school and he must
even submit to authority in such matters as text books
and pedagogic methods. Again, his very work itself
makes him an unconscious partisan of authority, as
against free inquiry. During the majority of his waking
hours he is in close association with his pupils, who are
admittedly his inferiors, and so he rapidly acquires the
familiar, self-satisfied professorial attitude of mind.
Other forces tend to push him in the same direction and
the net result is that all his mental processes are based
upon ideas of authority. He believes and teaches a thing,
not because he is convinced by free reasoning that it is
true, but because it is laid down as an axiom in some
book or was laid down at some past time, by himself.

In all this, of course, I am speaking of the teacher
properly so-called — of the teacher, that is, whose sole
aim and function is teaching. The university professor
whose main purpose in life is original research and whose
pupils are confined to graduate students engaged in much
the same work, is scarcely a professional teacher, in the
customary meaning of the word. The man I have been
discussing is he who spends all or the greater part of
his time in actual instruction. Whether his work be
done in a primary school, a secondary school or in the
undergraduate department of a college or university does
not matter. In all that relates to it, he is essentially
and almost invariably a mere perpetuator of doctrines.
In some cases, naturally enough, these doctrines are

truths, but in a great many other cases they are errors. An examination of the physiology, history and " English " books used in the public schools of America will convince anyone that the latter proposition is amply true.

Nietzsche's familiarity with these facts is demonstrated by numerous passages in his writings. " Never," he says, " is either real proficiency or genuine ability the result of toilsome years at school." The study of the classics, he says, can never lead to more than a superficial acquaintance with them, because the very modes of thought of the ancients, in many cases, are unintelligible to men of today. But the student who has acquired what is looked upon in our colleges as a mastery of the humanities is acutely conscious of his knowledge, and so the things that he cannot understand are ascribed by him to the dulness, ignorance or imbecility of the ancient authors. As a result he harbors a sort of subconscious contempt for the learning they represent and concludes that learning cannot make real men happy, but is only fit for the futile enthusiasm of " honest, poor and foolish old book-worms."

Nietzsche's own notion of an ideal curriculum is substantially that of Spencer. He holds that before anything is put forward as a thing worth teaching it should be tested by two questions: Is it a fact? and, Is the presentation of it likely to make the pupil measurably more capable of discovering other facts? In consequences, he holds the old so-called " liberal " education in abomination, and argues in favor of a system of instruction based upon the inculcation of facts of imminent value and designed to instill into the pupil orderly and logical habits of mind and a clear and accurate view of the universe. The educated man, as he understands the term, is one who is above the mass, both in his thirst for knowledge and in his capacity for differentiating between truth and its reverse. It is obvious that a man who has studied biology and physics, with their insistent dwelling upon demonstrable facts, has proceeded further in this direction than the man who has studied Greek mythology and metaphysics, with their constant trend toward unsupported and gratuitous assumption and their essential foundation upon undebatable authority.

Nietzsche points out, in his early essay upon the study of history, that humanity is much too prone to consider itself historically. That is to say, there is too much tendency to consider man as he has seemed rather than man as he has been — to dwell upon creeds and manifestoes rather than upon individual and racial motives, characters and instincts.[1] The result is that history piles up misleading and useless records and draws erroneous conclusions from them. As a science in itself, it bears but three useful aspects — the monumental, the antiquarian and the critical. Its true monuments are not the constitutions and creeds of the past — for these, as we have seen, are always artificial and unnatural — but the great men of the past — those fearless free spirits who achieved immortality by their courage and success in pitting their own instincts against the morality of the majority. Such men, he says, are the only human beings

---

[1] An excellent discussion of this error will be found in Dr. Alex. Tille's introduction to William Haussmann's translation of "*Zur Genealogie der Moral*," pp. xi *et seq.*; London, 1907.

whose existence is of interest to posterity. " They live together as timeless contemporaries: " they are the landmarks along the weary road the human race has traversed. In its antiquarian aspect, history affords us proof that the world is progressing, and so gives the men of the present a definite purpose and justifiable enthusiasm. In its critical aspect, history enables us to avoid the delusions of the past, and indicates to us the broad lines of evolution. Unless we have in mind some definite program of advancement, he says, all learning is useless. History, which merely accumulates records, without " an ideal of humanistic culture " always in mind, is mere pedantry and scholasticism.

All education, says Nietzsche, may be regarded as a continuation of the process of breeding. [1] The two have the same object: that of producing beings capable of surviving in the struggle for existence. A great many critics of Nietzsche have insisted that since the struggle for existence means a purely physical contest, he is in error, for education does not visibly increase a man's chest expansion or his capacity for lifting heavy weights. But it is obvious none the less that a man who sees things as they are, and properly estimates the world about him, is far better fitted to achieve some measure of mastery over his environment than the man who is a slave to delusions. Of two men, one of whom believes that the moon is made of green cheese and that it is possible to cure smallpox by merely denying that it exists, and the other of whom harbors no such superstitions, it is plain that the latter is more apt to live long and acquire power.

[1] *Morgenröte,*" § 397.

A further purpose of education is that of affording individuals a means of lifting themselves out of the slave class and into the master class. That this purpose is accomplished — except accidently — by the brand of education ladled out in the colleges of today is far from true. To transform a slave into a master we must make him intelligent, self-reliant, resourceful, independent and courageous. It is evident enough, I take it, that a college directed by an ecclesiastic and manned by a faculty of asses — a very fair, and even charitable, picture of the average small college in the United States — is not apt to accomplish this transformation very often. Indeed, it is a commonplace observation that a truly intelligent youth is aided but little by the average college education, and that a truly stupid one is made, not less, but more stupid. The fact that many graduates of such institutions exhibit dionysian qualities in later life merely proves that they are strong enough to weather the blight they have suffered. Every sane man knows that, after a youth leaves college, he must devote most of his energies during three or four years, to ridding himself of the fallacies, delusions and imbecilities inflicted upon him by messieurs, his professors.

The intelligent man, in the course of his life, nearly always acquires a vast store of learning, because his mind is constantly active and receptive, but intelligence and mere learning are by no means synonymous, despite the popular notion that they are. Disregarding the element of sheer good luck — which is necessarily a small factor — it is evident that the man who, in the struggle for wealth and power, seizes a million dollars for himself, is appreciably more intelligent than the man who starves. That this achievement, which is admittedly difficult, requires more intelligence again, than the achievement of mastering the Latin language, which presents so few difficulties that it is possible to any healthy human being with sufficient leisure and patience, is also evident. In a word, the illiterate contractor, who says, " I seen " and " I done " and yet manages to build great bridges and to acquire a great fortune, is immeasurably more vigorous intellectually, and immeasurably more efficient and respectable, as a man, than the college professor who laughs at him and presumes to look down upon him. A man's mental powers are to be judged, not by his ability to accomplish things that are possible to every man foolish enough to attempt them, but by his capacity for doing things beyond the power of other men. Education, as we commonly observe it today, works toward the former, rather than toward the latter end.

XIII

SUNDRY IDEAS

Death. — It is Schopenhauer's argument in his essay "On Suicide," that the possibility of easy and painless self-destruction is the only thing that constantly and considerably ameliorates the horror of human life. Suicide is a means of escape from the world and its tortures — and therefore it is good. It is an ever-present refuge for the weak, the weary and the hopeless. It is, in Pliny's phrase, "the greatest of all blessings which Nature gives to man," and one which even God himself lacks, for "he could not compass his own death, if he willed to die." In all of this exaltation of surrender, of course, there is nothing whatever in common with the dionysian philosophy of defiance. Nietzsche's teaching is all in the other direction. He urges, not surrender, but battle; not flight, but war to the end. His curse falls upon those "preachers of death" who counsel "an abandonment of life " — whether this abandonment be partial, as in asceticism, or actual, as in suicide. And yet Zarathustra sings the song of "free death " and says that the higher man must learn "to die at the right time." Herein an inconsistency appears, but it is on the surface only. Schopenhauer regards suicide as a means of escape,

Nietzsche sees in it as a means of good riddance. It is time to die, says Zarathustra, when the purpose of life ceases to be attainable — when the fighter breaks his sword arm or falls into his enemy's hands. And it is time to die, too, when the purpose of life is attained — when the fighter triumphs and sees before him no more worlds to conquer. "He who hath a goal and an heir wisheth death to come at the right time for goal and heir." One who has "waxed too old for victories," one who is "yellow and wrinkled," one with a "toothless mouth" — for such an one a certain and speedy death. The earth has no room for cumberers and pensioners. For them the highest of duties is the payment of nature's debt, that there may be more room for those still able to wield a sword and bear a burden in the heat of the day. The best death is that which comes in battle "at the moment of victory;" the second best is death in battle in the hour of defeat. "Would that a storm came," sings Zarathustra, "to shake from the tree of life all those apples that are putrid and gnawed by worms. It is cowardice that maketh them stick to their branches" — cowardice which makes them afraid to die. But there is another cowardice which makes men afraid to live, and this is the cowardice of the Schopenhauerean pessimist. Nietzsche has no patience with it. To him a too early death seems as abominable as a death postponed too long. "Too early died that Jew whom the preachers of slow death revere. Would that he had remained in the desert and far away from the good and just! Perhaps he would have learned how to live and how to love the earth — and even how to laugh. He died too early. He himself would have revoked his doctrine, had he reached mine age ! " [1] Therefore Nietzsche pleads for an intelligent regulation of death. One must not die too soon and one must not die too late. " Natural death," he says, " is destitute of rationality. It is really *ir*rational death, for the pitiable substance of the shell determines how long the kernel shall exist. The pining, sottish prison-warder decides the hour at which his noble prisoner is to die. . . . The enlightened regulation and control of death belongs to the morality of the future. At present religion makes it seem immoral, for religion presupposes that when the time for death comes, God gives the command." [2]

The Attitude at Death. — Nietzsche rejects entirely that pious belief in signs and portents which sees a significance in death-bed confessions and " dying words." The average man, he says, dies pretty much as he has lived, and in this Dr. Osler [3] and other unusually competent and accurate observers agree with him. When the dying man exhibits unusual emotions or expresses ideas out of tune with his known creed, the explanation is to be found in the fact that, toward the time of death the mind commonly gives way and the customary processes of thought are disordered. " The way in which a man thinks of death, in the full bloom of his life and strength, is certainly a good index of his general character and habits of mind, but at the hour of death itself his attitude is of little importance or significance. The exhaustion of the last hours — especially when an old

[1] " *Also sprach Zarathustra*," I.
[2] " *Menschliches allzu Menschliches*," III, § 185.
[3] " Science and Immortality," New York, 1904.

man is dying — the irregular or insufficient nourishment of the brain, the occasional spasms of severe physical pain, the horror and novelty of the whole situation, the atavistic return of early impressions and superstitions, and the feeling that death is a thing unutterably vast and important and that bridges of an awful kind are about to be crossed — all of these things make it irrational to accept a man's attitude at death as an indication of his character during life. Moreover, it is not true that a dying man is more honest than a man in full vigor. On the contrary, almost every dying man is led, by the solemnity of those at his bedside, and by their restrained or flowing torrents of tears, to conscious or unconscious conceit and make-believe. He becomes, in brief, an actor in a comedy. . . . No doubt the seriousness with which every dying man is treated has given many a poor devil his only moment of real triumph and enjoyment. He is, *ipso facto*, the star of the play, and so he is indemnified for a life of privation and subservience." [1]

The Origin of Philosophy. — Nietzsche believed that introspection and self-analysis, as they were ordinarily manifested, were signs of disease, and that the higher man and superman would waste little time upon them. The first thinkers, he said, were necessarily sufferers, for it was only suffering that made a man think and only disability that gave him leisure to do so. " Under primitive conditions," he said, " the individual, fully conscious of his power, is ever intent upon transforming it into action. Sometimes this action takes the form of hunting, robbery, ambuscade, maltreatment or murder, and at

[1] " *Menschliches allzu Menschliches*," II, § 88.

other times it appears as those feebler imitations of these things which alone are countenanced by the community. But when the individual's power declines — when he feels fatigued, ill, melancholy or satiated, and in consequence, temporarily lacks the yearning to function — he is a comparatively better and less dangerous man. That is to say, he contents himself with thinking instead of doing, and so puts into thought and words " his impressions and feelings regarding his companions, his wife or his gods." Naturally enough, since his efficiency is lowered and his mood is gloomy his judgments are evil ones. He finds fault and ponders revenges. He gloats over enemies or envies his friends. "In such a state of mind he turns prophet and so adds to his store of superstitions or devises new acts of devotion or prophesies the downfall of his enemies. Whatever he thinks, his thoughts reflect his state of mind: his fear and weariness are more than normal; his tendency to action and enjoyment are less than normal. Herein we see the genesis of the poetic, thoughtful, priestly mood. Evil thoughts must rule supreme therein. . . . In later stages of culture, there arose a caste of poets, thinkers, priests and medicine men who all acted the same as, in earlier years, individuals used to act in their comparatively rare hours of illness and depression. These persons led sad, inactive lives and judged maliciously. . . . The masses, perhaps, yearned to turn them out of the community, because they were parasites, but in this enterprise there was great risk, because these men were on terms of familiarity with the gods and so possessed vast and mysterious power. Thus the most ancient philosophers were viewed. The masses hearkened unto them in proportion to the amount of dread they inspired. In such a way contemplation made its appearance in the world, with an evil heart and a troubled head. It was both weak and terrible, and both secretly abhorred and openly worshipped. . . . *Pudenda origo!* " [1]

Priestcraft. — So long as man feels capable of taking care of himself he has no need of priests to intercede for him with the deity. Efficiency is proverbially identified with impiety: it is only when the devil is sick that the devil a monk would be. Therefore " the priest must be regarded as the saviour, shepherd and advocate of the sick. . . . It is his providence to rule over the sufferers. . . . " In order that he may understand them and appeal to them he must be sick himself, and to attain this end there is the device of asceticism. The purpose of asceticism, as we have seen, is to make a man voluntarily destroy his own efficiency. But the priest must have a certain strength, nevertheless, for he must inspire both confidence and dread in his charges, and must be able to defend them — against whom? " Undoubtedly against the sound and strong. . . . He must be the natural adversary and despiser of all barbarous, impetuous, unbridled, fierce, violent, beast-of-prey healthiness and power." Thus he must fashion himself into a new sort of fighter — " a new zoological terror, in which the polar bear, the nimble and cool tiger and the fox are blended into a unity as attractive as it is awe-inspiring." He appears in the midst of the strong as " the herald and mouth·

---

[1] " *Morgenröte,*" § 42.
[2] " *Zur Genealogie der Moral,*" III, 11 to 17.

piece of mysterious powers, with the determination to sow upon the soil, whenever and wherever possible, the seeds of suffering, dissension and contradiction. . . . Undoubtedly he brings balms and balsams with him, but he must first inflict the wound, before he may act as physician. . . . It is only the unpleasantness of disease that is combated by him — not the cause, not the disease itself!" He dispenses, not specifics, but narcotics. He brings surcease from sorrow, not by showing men how to attain the happiness of efficiency, but by teaching them that their sufferings have been laid upon them by a god who will one day repay them with bliss illimitable.

God. — " A god who is omniscient and omnipotent and yet neglects to make his wishes and intentions certainly known to his creatures — certainly this is not a god of goodness. One who for thousands of years has allowed the countless scruples and doubts of men to afflict them and yet holds out terrible consequences for involuntary errors — certainly this is not a god of justice. Is he not a cruel god if he knows the truth and yet looks down upon millions miserably searching for it? Perhaps he is good, but is unable to communicate with his creatures more intelligibly. Perhaps he is wanting in intelligence — or in eloquence. So much the worse! For, in that case, he may be mistaken in what he calls the truth. He may, indeed, be a brother to the ' poor, duped devils ' below him. If so, must he not suffer agonies on seeing his creatures, in their struggle for knowledge of him, submit to tortures for all eternity? Must it not strike him with grief to realize that he cannot advise them or help them, except by uncertain and ambiguous signs? . . . All

religions bear traces of the fact that they arose during the
intellectual immaturity of the human race — before it
had learned the obligation to speak the truth. Not one
of them makes it the duty of its god to be truthful and
understandable in his communications with man." [1]

Self-Control. — Self-control, says Nietzsche, consists
merely in combating a given desire with a stronger one.
Thus the yearning to commit a murder may be combated
and overcome by the yearning to escape the gallows and
to retain the name and dignity of a law-abiding citizen.
The second yearning is as much unconscious and instinctive as the first, and in the battle between them the
intellect plays but a small part. In general there are but
six ways in which a given craving may be overcome.
First, we may avoid opportunities for its gratification and
so, by a long disuse, weaken and destroy it. Secondly,
we may regulate its gratification, and by thus encom-
passing its flux and reflux within fixed limits, gain
intervals during which it is faint. Thirdly, we may
intentionally give ourselves over to it and so wear it out
by excess — provided we do not act like the rider who
lets a runaway horse gallop itself to death and, in so doing,
breaks his own neck, — which unluckily is the rule in
this method. Fourthly, by an intellectual trick, we may
associate gratification with an unpleasant idea, as we
have associated sexual gratification, for example, with
the idea of indecency. Fifthly, we may find a substitute
in some other craving that is measurably less dangerous.
Sixthly, we may find safety in a general war upon all
cravings, good and bad alike, after the manner of the

[1] " *Morgenröte,*" § 91.

ascetic, who, in seeking to destroy his sensuality, at the same time destroys his physical strength, his reason and, not infrequently, his life.

The Beautiful. — Man's notion of beauty is the fruit of his delight in his own continued existence. Whatever makes this existence easy, or is associated, in any manner, with life or vigor, seems to him to be beautiful. " Man mirrors himself in things. He counts everything beautiful which reflects his likeness. The word ' beautiful ' represents the conceit of his species. . . . Nothing is truly ugly except the degenerating man. But other things are called ugly, too, when they happen to weaken or trouble man. They remind him of impotence, deterioration and danger: in their presence he actually suffers a loss of power. Therefore he calls them ugly. Whenever man is at all depressed he has an intuition of the proximity of something ' ugly.' His sense of power, his will to power, his feeling of pride and efficiency — all sink with the ugly and rise with the beautiful. The ugly is instinctively understood to be a sign and symptom of degeneration. That which reminds one, in the remotest degree, of degeneracy seems ugly. Every indication of exhaustion, heaviness, age, or lassitude, every constraint — such as cramp or paralysis — and above all, every odor, color or counterfeit of decomposition — though it may be no more than a far-fetched symbol — calls forth the idea of ugliness. Aversion is thereby excited — man's aversion to the decline of his type."[1] The phrase " art for art's sake " voices a protest against subordinating art to morality — that is, against

1 " *Götzendämmerung,*" IX, § 19.

making it a device for preaching sermons — but as a matter of fact, all art must praise and glorify and so must lay down values. It is the function of the artist, indeed, to select, to choose, to bring into prominence. The very fact that he is able to do this makes us call him an artist. And when do we approve his choice? Only when it agrees with our fundamental instinct — only when it exhibits " the desirableness of life." " Therefore art is the great stimulus to life. We cannot conceive it as being purposeless or aimless. ' Art for art's sake ' is a phrase without meaning." [1]

Liberty. — The worth of a thing often lies, not in what one attains by it, but in the difficulty one experiences in getting it. The struggle for political liberty, for example, has done more than any other one thing to develop strength, courage and resourcefulness in the human race, and yet liberty itself, as we know it today, is nothing more or less than organized morality, and as such, is necessarily degrading and degenerating. " It undermines the will to power, it levels the racial mountains and valleys, it makes man small, cowardly and voluptuous. Under political liberty the herd-animal always triumphs." But the very fight to attain this burdensome equality develops the self-reliance and unconformity which stand opposed to it, and these qualities often persist. Warfare, in brief, makes men fit for real, as opposed to political freedom. " And what is freedom? The will to be responsible for one's self. The will to keep that distance which separates man from man. The will to become indifferent to hardship, severity, privation and even to

[1] " *Götzendämmerung*," IX, § 24.

life. The will to sacrifice men to one's cause and to sacrifice one's self, too. . . . The man who is truly free tramples under foot the contemptible species of well-being dreamt of by shop-keepers, Christians, cows, women, Englishmen and other democrats. The free man is a warrior. . . . How is freedom to be measured? By the resistance it has to overcome — by the effort required to maintain it. We must seek the highest type of freemen where the highest resistance must be constantly overcome: five paces from tyranny, close to the threshold of thraldom . . . . Those peoples who were worth something, who became worth something, never acquired their greatness under political liberty. Great danger made something of them — danger of that sort which first teaches us to know our resources, our virtues, our shields and swords, our genius — which compels us to be strong." [1]

Science — The object of all science is to keep us from drawing wrong inferences — from jumping to conclusions. Thus it stands utterly opposed to all faith and is essentially iconoclastic and skeptical. " The wonderful in science is the reverse of the wonderful in juggling. The juggler tries to make us see a very simple relation between things which, in point of fact, have no relation at all. The scientist, on the contrary, compels us to abandon our belief in simple casualities and to see the enormous complexity of phenomena. The simplest things, indeed, are extremely complex — a fact which will never cease to make us wonder." The effect of science is to show the absurdity of attempting to reach perfect happiness and

[1] *"Götzendämmerung."* IX, § 38

the impossibility of experiencing utter woe. "The gulf between the highest pitch of happiness and the lowest depth of misery has been created by imaginary things."[1] That is to say, the heights of religious exaltation and the depths of religious fear and trembling are alike creatures of our own myth-making. There is no such thing as perfect and infinite bliss in heaven and there is no such thing as eternal damnation in hell. Hereafter our highest happiness must be less than that of the martyrs who saw the heavenly gates opening for them, and our worst woe must be less than that of those medieval sinners who died shrieking and trembling and with the scent of brimstone in their noses. "This space is being reduced further and further by science, just as through science we have learned to make the earth occupy less and less space in the universe, until it now seems infinitely small and our whole solar system appears as a mere point."[2]

The Jews. — For the Jewish slave-morality which prevails in the western world today, under the label of Christianity, Nietzsche had, as we know, the most violent aversion and contempt, but he saw very clearly that this same morality admirably served and fitted the Jews themselves; that it had preserved them through long ages and against powerful enemies, and that its very persistence proved alike its own ingenuity and the vitality of its inventors as a race. "The Jews," said Nietzsche, " will either become the masters of Europe or lose Europe, as they once lost Egypt. And it seems to be improbable that they will lose again. In Europe, for eighteen centuries,

[1] "*Morgenröte*," § 6. [2] "*Morgenröte*," § 7.

they have passed through a school more terrible than
that known to any other nation, and the experiences of
this time of stress and storm have benefited the individual
even more than the community. In consequence, the
resourcefulness and alertness of the modern Jew are
extraordinary. . . . In times of extremity, the people
of Israel less often sought refuge in drink or suicide than
any other race of Europe. Today, every Jew finds in the
history of his forebears a voluminous record of coolness
and perseverance in terrible predicaments — of artful
cunning and clever fencing with chance and misfortune.
The Jews have hid their bravery under the cloak of
submissiveness; their heroism in facing contempt sur-
passes that of the saints. People tried to make them
contemptible for twenty centuries by refusing them all
honors and dignities and by pushing them down into
the mean trades. The process did not make them cleaner,
alas! but neither did it make them contemptible. They
have never ceased to believe themselves qualified for the
highest of activities. They have never failed to show the
virtues of all suffering peoples. Their manner of honor-
ing their parents and their children and the reasonable-
ness of their marriage customs make them conspicuous
among Europeans. Besides, they have learned how to de-
rive a sense of power from the very trades forced upon
them. We cannot help observing, in excuse for their
usury, that without this pleasant means of inflicting
torture upon their oppressors, they might have lost
their self-respect ages ago, for self-respect depends
upon being able to make reprisals. Moreover, their
vengeance has never carried them too far, for they

have that liberality which comes from frequent changes of place, climate, customs and neighbors. They have more experience of men than any other race and even in their passions there appears a caution born of this experience. They are so sure of themselves that, even in their bitterest straits, they never earn their bread by manual labor as common workmen, porters or peasants. . . . Their manners, it may be admitted, teach us that they have never been inspired by chivalrous, noble feelings, nor their bodies girt with beautiful arms: a certain vulgarity always alternates with their submissiveness. But now they are intermarrying with the gentlest blood of Europe, and in another hundred years they will have enough good manners to save them from making themselves ridiculous, as masters, in the sight of those they have subdued." It was Nietzsche's belief that the Jews would take the lead before long, in the intellectual progress of the world. He thought that their training, as a race, fitted them for this leadership. " Where," he asked, " shall the accumulated wealth of great impressions which forms the history of every Jewish family — that great wealth of passions, virtues, resolutions, resignations, struggles and victories of all sorts — where shall it find an outlet, if not in great intellectual functioning? " The Jews, he thought, would be safe guides for mankind, once they were set free from their slave-morality and all need of it. " Then again," he said, " the old God of the Jews may rejoice in Himself, in His creation and in His chosen people — and all of us will rejoice with Him." [1]

---

[1] " *Morgenröte*," § 205.

The Gentleman. — A million sages and diagnosticians, in all ages of the world, have sought to define the gentleman, and their definitions have been as varied as their own minds. Nietzsche's definition is based upon the obvious fact that the gentleman is ever a man of more than average influence and power, and the further fact that this superiority is admitted by all. The vulgarian may boast of his bluff honesty, but at heart he looks up to the gentleman, who goes through life serene and imperturbable. There is in the latter, in truth, an unmistakable air of fitness and efficiency, and it is this which makes it possible for him to be gentle and to regard those below him with tolerance. "The demeanor of high-born persons," says Nietzsche, "shows plainly that in their minds the consciousness of power is ever-present. Above all things, they strive to avoid a show of weakness, whether it takes the form of inefficiency or of a too-easy yielding to passion or emotion. They never sink exhausted into a chair. On the train, when the vulgar try to make themselves comfortable, these higher folk avoid reclining. They do not seem to get tired after hours of standing at court. They do not furnish their houses in a comfortable, but in a spacious and dignified manner, as if they were the abodes of a greater and taller race of beings. To a provoking speech, they reply with politeness and self-possession — and not as if horrified, crushed, abashed, enraged or out of breath, after the manner of plebeians. The aristocrat knows how to preserve the appearance of ever-present physical strength, and he knows, too, how to convey the impression that his soul and intellect are a match to all dangers and surprises, by keeping up an unchanging serenity and civility, even under the most trying circumstances." [1]

Dreams. — Dreams are symptoms of the eternal law of compensation. In our waking hours we develop a countless horde of yearnings, cravings and desires, and by the very nature of things, the majority of them must go ungratified. The feeling that something is wanting, thus left within us, is met and satisfied by our imaginary functionings during sleep. That is to say, dreams represent the reaction of our yearnings upon the phenomena actually encountered during sleep — the motions of our blood and intestines, the pressure of the bedclothes, the sounds of church-bells, domestic animals, etc., and the state of the atmosphere. These phenomena are fairly constant, but our dreams vary widely on successive nights. Therefore, the variable factor is represented by the yearnings we harbor as we go to bed. Thus, the man who loves music and must go without it all day, hears celestial harmonies in his sleep. Thus the slave dreams of soaring like an eagle. Thus the prisoner dreams that he is free and the sailor that he is safely at home. Inasmuch as the number of our conscious and unconscious desires, each day, is infinite, there is an infinite variety in dreams. But always the relation set forth may be predicated.

[1] "*Morgenröte,*" § 201.

XIV

NIETZSCHE believed in heroes and, in his youth, was a hero worshipper. First Arthur Schopenhauer's bespectacled visage stared from his shrine and after that the place of sacredness and honor was held by Richard Wagner. When the Wagner of the philosopher's dreams turned into a Wagner of very prosaic flesh and blood, there came a time of doubt and stress and suffering for poor Nietzsche. But he had courage as well as loyalty, and in the end he dashed his idol to pieces and crunched the bits underfoot. Faith, doubt, anguish, disillusion — it is not a rare sequence in this pitiless and weary old world.

Those sapient critics who hold that Nietzsche discredited his own philosophy by constantly writing against himself, find their chief ammunition in his attitude toward the composer of " *Tristan und Isolde.*" In the decade from 1869 to 1878 the philosopher was the king of German Wagnerians. In the decade from 1879 to 1889, he was the most bitter, the most violent, the most resourceful and the most effective of Wagner's enemies. On their face these things seem to indicate a complete change of front and a careful examination bears out the thought. But the same careful examination reveals another fact: that the change of front was made, not by Nietzsche, but by Wagner.

As we have seen, the philosopher was an ardent musician from boyhood and so it was not unnatural that he should be among the first to recognize Wagner's genius. The sheer musicianship of the man overwhelmed him and he tells us that from the moment the piano transcription of "*Tristan und Isolde*" was printed he was a Wagnerian. The music was bold and daring: it struck out into regions that the *süsslich* sentimentality of Donizetti and Bellini and the pallid classicism of Beethoven and Bach had never even approached. In Wagner Nietzsche saw a man of colossal originality and sublime courage, who thought for himself and had skill at making his ideas comprehensible to others. The opera of the past had been a mere *potpourri* of songs, strung together upon a filament of banal recitative. The opera of Wagner was a symmetrical and homogeneous whole, in which the music was unthinkable without the poetry and the poetry impossible without the music.

Nietzsche, at the time, was saturated with Schopenhauer's brand of individualism, and intensely eager to apply it to realities. In Wagner he saw a living, breathing individualist — a man who scorned the laws and customs of his craft and dared to work out his own salvation in his own way. And when fate made it possible for him to meet Wagner, he found the composer preaching as well as practising individualism. In a word, Wagner was well nigh as enthusiastic a Schopenhauerean as Nietzsche himself. His individualism almost touched

the boundary of anarchy. He had invented a new **art**
of music and he was engaged in the exciting task **of**
smashing the old one to make room **for it.**

Nietzsche met Wagner in Leipsic and was invited to
visit the composer at his home near Tribschen, a suburb
of Lucerne. He accepted, and on May 15, 1869, got his
first glimpse of that queer household in which the erratic
Richard, the ingenious Cosima and little Siegfried lived
and had their being. When he moved to Basel, he was
not far from Tribschen and so he fell into the habit of
going there often and staying long. He came, indeed, to
occupy the position of an adopted son, and spent the
Christmas of 1869 and that of 1870 under the Wagner
rooftree. This last fact alone is sufficient to show the
intimate footing upon which he stood. Christmas,
among the Germans, is essentially a family festival and
mere friends are seldom asked to share its joys.

Nietzsche and Wagner had long and riotous disputations at Tribschen, but in all things fundamental they
agreed. Together they accepted Schopenhauer's **data**
and together they began to diverge from his **conclusions.**
Nietzsche saw in Wagner that old dionysian spirit which
had saved Greek art. The music of the day was colorless
and coldblooded. A too rigid formalism stood in the
way of all expression of actual life. Wagner proposed to
batter this formalism to pieces and Nietzsche **was his**
prophet and *claque.*

It was this enthusiasm, indeed, which determined the
plan of " *Die Geburt der Tragödie.*" Nietzsche had
conceived it as a mere treatise upon the philosophy of
the Greek drama. His ardor as an apostle, **his yearning**

to convert the stolid Germans, his wild desire to do something practical and effective for Wagner, made him turn it into a gospel of the new art. To him Wagner was Dionysus, and the whole of his argument against Apollo was nothing more than an argument against classicism and for the Wagnerian romanticism. It was a bomb-shell and its explosion made Germany stare, but another — perhaps many more — were needed to shake the foundations of philistinism. Nietzsche loaded the next one carefully and hurled it at him who stood at the very head of that self-satisfied conservatism which lay upon all Germany. This man was David Strauss. Strauss was the prophet of the good-enough. He taught that German art was sound, that German culture was perfect. Nietzsche saw in him the foe of Dionysus and made an example of him. In every word of that scintillating philippic there was a plea for the independence and individualism and outlawry that the philosopher saw in Wagner. [1]

Unluckily the disciple here ran ahead of the master and before long Nietzsche began to realize that he and Wagner were drifting apart. So long as they met upon

---

[1] That Wagner gave Nietzsche good reason to credit him with these qualities is amply proved. " I have never read anything better than your book," wrote the composer in 1872. " It is masterly." And Frau Cosima and Liszt, who were certainly familiar with Wagner's ideas, supported Nietzsche's assumption, too. " Oh, how fine is your book," wrote the former, " how fine and how deep — how deep and how keen ! " Liszt sent from Prague (Feb. 29, 1872) a pompous, patronizing letter. " I have read your book twice," he said. In all of this correspondence there is no hint that Nietzsche had misunderstood Wagner's position or had laid down any propositions from which the composer dissented.

the safe ground of Schopenhauer's data, the two agreed,
but after Nietzsche began to work out his inevitable
conclusions, Wagner abandoned him. To put it plainly,
Wagner was the artist before he was the philosopher, and
when philosophy began to grow ugly he turned from it
without regret or qualm of conscience. Theoretically,
he saw things as Nietzsche saw them, but as an artist he
could not afford to be too literal. It was true enough,
perhaps, that self-sacrifice was a medieval superstition,
but all the same it made effective heroes on the stage.

Nietzsche was utterly unable, throughout his life, to
acknowledge anything but hypocrisy or ignorance in
those who descended to such compromises. When he
wrote " *Richard Wagner in Bayreuth* " he was already
the prey of doubts, but it is probable that he still saw the
" ifs " and " buts " in Wagner's individualism but
dimly. He could not realize, in brief, that a composer
who fought beneath the banner of truth, against custom
and convention, could ever turn aside from the battle.
Wagner agreed with Nietzsche, perhaps, that European
civilization and its child, the European art of the day,
were founded upon lies, but he was artist enough to see
that, without these lies, it would be impossible to make
art understandable to the public. So in his librettos he
employed all of the old fallacies — that love has the
supernatural power of making a bad man good, that one
man may save the soul of another, that humility is a
virtue. [1]

It is obvious from this, that the apostate was not Niet-

---

[1] There is an interesting discussion of this in James Huneker's book,
"Mezzotints in Modern Music," page 285 *et. seq.*, New York, 1899.

zsche, but Wagner. Nietzsche started out in life as a
seeker after truth, and he sought the truth his whole life
long, without regarding for an instant the risks and
dangers and consequences of the quest. Wagner, so long
as it remained a mere matter of philosophical disputation, was equally radical and courageous, but he saw very
clearly that it was necessary to compromise with tradition
in his operas. He was an atheist and a mocker of the
gods, but the mystery and beauty of the Roman Catholic
ritual appealed to his artistic sense, and so, instead of
penning an opera in which the hero spouted aphorisms
by Huxley, he wrote " *Parsifal.*" And in the same way,
in his other music dramas, he made artistic use of all the
ancient fallacies and devices in the lumber room of
chivalry. He was, indeed, a philosopher in his hours of
leisure only. When he was at work over his music paper,
he saw that St. Ignatius was a far more effective and
appealing figure than Herbert Spencer and that the conventional notion that marriage was a union of two immortal
souls was far more picturesque than the Schopenhauer-
Nietzschean idea that it was a mere symptom of the
primary will to live.

In 1876 Nietzsche began to realize that he had left
Wagner far behind and that thereafter he could expect no
support from the composer. They had not met since
1874, but Nietzsche went to Bayreuth for the first opera
season. A single conversation convinced him that his
doubts were well-founded — that Wagner was a mere
dionysian of the chair and had no intention of pushing
the ideas they had discussed to their bitter and revolutionary conclusion. Most other men would have seen in this

nothing more than an evidence of a common-sense decision to sacrifice the whole truth for half the truth, but Nietzsche was a rabid hater of compromise. To make terms with the philistines seemed to him to be even worse than joining their ranks. He saw in Wagner only a traitor who knew the truth and yet denied it.

Nietzsche was so much disgusted that he left Bayreuth and set out upon a walking tour, but before the end of the season he returned and heard some of the operas. But he was no longer a Wagnerian and the music of the " Ring " did not delight him. It was impossible, indeed, for him to separate the music from the philosophy set forth in the librettos. He believed, with Wagner, that the two were indissolubly welded, and so, after awhile, he came to condemn the whole fabric — harmonies and melodies as well as heroes and dramatic situations.

When Wagner passed out of his life Nietzsche sought to cure his loneliness by hard work and " *Menschliches allzu Menschliches* " was the result. He sent a copy of the first volume to Wagner and on the way it crossed a copy of " *Parsifal.*" In this circumstance is well exhibited the width of the breach between the two men. To Wagner " *Menschliches allzu Menschliches* " seemed impossibly and insanely radical; to Nietzsche " *Parsifal,*" with all its exaltation of ritualism, was unspeakable. Neither deigned to write to the other, but we have it from reliable testimony that Wagner was disgusted and Nietzsche's sister tells us how much the music-drama of the grail enraged him.

A German, when indignation seizes him, rises straight-way to make a loud and vociferous protest. And so,

although Nietzsche retained, to the end of his life, a
pleasant memory of the happy days he spent at Tribschen
and almost his last words voiced his loyal love for Wagner
the man, he conceived it to be his sacred duty to combat
what he regarded as the treason of Wagner the philosopher.
This notion was doubtlessly strengthened by his belief
that he himself had done much to launch Wagner's bark.
He had praised, and now it was his duty to blame. He
had been enthusiastic at the first task, and he determined
to be pitiless at the second.

But he hesitated for ten years, because, as has been
said, he could not kill his affection for Wagner, the man.
It takes courage to wound one's nearest and dearest, and
Nietzsche, for all his lack of sentiment, was still no more
than human. In the end, however, he brought himself
to the heroic surgery that confronted him, and the result was " *Der Fall Wagner.*" In this book all friendship and pleasant memories were put aside. Wagner
was his friend of old? Very well: that was a reason
for him to be all the more exact and all the more
unpitying.

" What does a philosopher firstly and lastly require of
himself?" he asks. " To overcome his age in himself;
to become timeless! With what, then, has he to fight his
hardest fight? With those characteristics and ideas
which most plainly stamp him as the child of his age."
Herein we perceive Nietzsche's fundamental error.
Deceived by Wagner's enthusiasm for Schopenhauer and
his early, amateurish dabbling in philosophy, he regarded
the composer as a philosopher. But Wagner, of course,
was first of all an artist, and it is the function of an artist,

not to reform humanity, but to depict it as he sees it, or as his age sees it — fallacies, delusions and all. George Bernard Shaw, in his famous criticism of Shakespeare, shows us how the Bard of Avon made just such a compromise with the prevailing opinion of his time. Shakespeare, he says, was too intelligent a man to regard Rosalind as a plausible woman, but the theatre-goers of his day so regarded her and he drew her to their taste.[1] An artist who failed to make such a concession to convention would be an artist without an audience. Wagner was no Christian, but he knew that the quest of the holy grail was an idea which made a powerful appeal to nine-tenths of civilized humanity, and so he turned it into a drama. This was not conscious lack of sincerity, but merely a manifestation of the sub-conscious artistic feeling for effectiveness. [2]

Therefore, it is plain that Nietzsche's whole case against Wagner is based upon a fallacy and that, in consequence, it is not to be taken too seriously. It is true enough that his book contains some remarkably acute and searching observations upon art, and that, granting his premises, his general conclusions would be correct, but we are by no means granting his premises. Wagner may have been a traitor to his philosophy, but if he had remained loyal to it, his art would have been impossible. And in view of the sublime beauty of that art we may well pardon him for not keeping the faith.

[1] See " George Bernard Shaw: His Plays; " page 102 *et seq.*, Boston, 1905.

[2] " Wagner's creative instinct gave the lie to his theoretical system: " R. A. Streatfield, " Modern Music and Musicians," p 272; New York, 1906.

" *Der Fall Wagner* " caused a horde of stupid critics to maintain that Nietzsche, and not Wagner, was the apostate, and that the mad philosopher had begun to argue against himself. As an answer to this ridiculous charge, Nietzsche published a little book called " *Nietzsche contra Wagner.*" It was made up entirely of passages from his earlier books and these proved conclusively that, ever since his initial divergence from Schopenhauer's conclusions, he had hoed a straight row. He was a dionysian in " *Die Geburt der Tragödie* " and he was a dionysian still in " *Also Sprach Zarathustra.*"

NIETZSCHE THE PROPHET

I

NIETZSCHE'S ORIGINS

THE construction of philosophical family trees for
Nietzsche has ever been one of the favorite pastimes of
his critics and interpreters. Thus Dr. Oscar Levy, editor
of the English translation of his works, makes him the
heir of Goethe and Stendhal, and the culminating figure
of the " Second Renaissance " launched by the latter,
who was " the first man to cry halt to the Kantian philosophy which had flooded all Europe.[1]   Dr. M. A.
Mügge agrees with this genealogy so far as it goes, but
points out that Nietzsche was also the intellectual de-
scendant of certain pre-Socratic Greeks, particularly
Heracleitus, and of Spinoza and Stirner.[2]   Alfred Fouillée, the Frenchman, is another who gives him Greek
blood, but in seeking his later forebears Fouillée passes
over the four named by Levy and Mügge and puts
Hobbes, Schopenhauer, Darwin, Rousseau and Diderot
in place of them.[3]   Again, Thomas Common says that
" perhaps Nietzsche is most indebted to Chamfort and
Schopenhauer," but also allows a considerable influence
to Hobbes, and endeavors to show how Nietzsche car-

[1] " The Revival of Aristocracy," London, 1906, pp. 14-59.
[2] " Friedrich Nietzsche: His Life and Work," New York, 1909, pp.
315-320.
[3] " *Nietzsche et l'Immoralisme*," Paris, 1902, p. 294.

ried on, consciously and unconsciously, certain ideas
originating with Darwin and developed by Huxley,
Spencer and the other evolutionists.[1]   Dr. Alexander
Tille has written a whole volume upon this latter relationship.[2]   Finally, Paul Elmer More, the American,
taking the cue from Fouillée, finds the germs of many
of Nietzsche's doctrines in Hobbes, and then proceeds
to a somewhat elaborate discussion of the mutations of
ethical theory during the past two centuries, showing
how Hume superimposed the idea of sympathy as a
motive upon Hobbes' idea of self-interest, and how this
sympathy theory prevailed over that of self-interest,
and degenerated into sentimentalism, and so opened the
way for Socialism and other such delusions, and how
Nietzsche instituted a sort of Hobbesian revival.[3]   Many
more speculations of that sort, some of them very ingenious and some merely ingenuous, might be rehearsed.
By one critic or another Nietzsche has been accused of
more or less frank borrowings from Xenophanes, De-
mocritus, Pythagoras, Callicles, Parmenides, Arcelaus,
Empedocles, Pyrrho, Hegesippus, the Eleatic Zeno,
Machiavelli, Comte, Montaigne, Mandeville, La Bruyère, Fontenelle, Voltaire, Kant, La Rochefoucauld,
Helvétius, Adam Smith, Malthus, Butler, Blake, Prou-
dhon, Paul Rée, Flaubert, Taine, Gobineau, Renan, and
even from Karl Marx! — a long catalogue of meaningless names, an exhaustive roster of pathfinders and pro-

---

[1] " Nietzsche as Critic, Philosopher, Poet and Prophet," London,
1901, pp. xi–xxiii.

[2] " *Von Darwin bis Nietzsche*," Leipsic, 1895.

[3] " Nietzsche," Boston, 1912, pp. 18-45.

testants. A Frenchman, Jules de Gaultier, has devoted a whole book to the fascinating subject.[1]

But if we turn from this laborious and often irrelevant search for common ideas and parallel passages to the actual facts of Nietzsche's intellectual development, we shall find, perhaps, that his ancestry ran in two streams, the one coming down from the Greeks whom he studied as school-boy and undergraduate, and the other having its source in Schopenhauer, the great discovery of his early manhood and the most powerful single influence of his life. No need to argue the essentially Greek color of Nietzsche's apprentice thinking. It was, indeed, his interest in Greek literature and life that made him a philologist by profession, and the same interest that converted him from a philologist into a philosopher. The foundation of his system was laid when he arrived at his conception of the conflict between the Greek gods Apollo and Dionysus, and all that followed belonged naturally to the working out of that idea. But what he got from the Greeks of his early adoration was more than a single idea and more than the body of miscellaneous ideas listed by the commentators: it was the Greek outlook, the Greek spirit, the Greek attitude toward God and man. In brief, he ceased to be a German pastor's son, brought up in the fear of the Lord, and became a citizen of those gorgeous and enchanted isles, much as Shelley had before him. The sentimentality of Christianity dropped from him like an old garment; he stood forth, as it were, bare and unashamed, a pagan in the springtime of the world, a *ja-*

[1] " *De Kant à Nietzsche,*" Paris, 1900.

sager. More than the reading of books, of course, was needed to work that transformation — the blood that leaped had to be blood capable of leaping — but it was out of books that the stimulus came, and the feeling of surety, and the beginnings of a workable philosophy of life. It is not a German that speaks in " The Antichrist," nor even the Polish noble that Nietzsche liked to think himself, but a Greek of the brave days before Socrates, a spokesman of Hellenic innocence and youth.

No doubt it was the unmistakably Greek note in Schopenhauer — the delivery of instinct, so long condemned to the ethical dungeons — that engendered Nietzsche's first wild enthusiasm for the Frankfort sage. The atmosphere of Leipsic in 1865 was heavy with moral vapors, and the daring dissent of Schopenhauer must have seemed to blow through it like a sharp wind from the sea. And Nietzsche, being young and passionate, was carried away by the ecstasy of discovery, and so accepted the whole Schopenhauerean philosophy without examining it too critically — the bitter with the sweet, its pessimism no less than its rebellion. He, too, had to go through the green-sickness of youth, particularly of German youth. The Greek was yet but half way from Naumburg to Attica, and he now stopped a moment to look backward. " Every line," he tells us somewhere, " cried out renunciation, denial, resignation. . . . Evidences of this sudden change are still to be found in the restless melancholy of the leaves of my diary at that period, with all their useless self-reproach and their desperate gazing upward for recovery and for the transformation of the whole spirit of mankind. By drawing all my qualities and my aspirations before the forum of gloomy self-contempt I became bitter, unjust and unbridled in my hatred of myself. I even practised bodily penance. For instance, I forced myself for a fortnight at a stretch to go to bed at two o'clock in the morning and to rise punctually at six." But not for long. The fortnight of self-accusing and hair-shirts was soon over. The green-sickness vanished.[1] The Greek emerged anew, more Hellenic than ever. And so, almost from the start, Nietzsche rejected quite as much of Schopenhauer as he accepted. The Schopenhauerean premise entered into his system — the will to live was destined to become the father, in a few years, of the will to power — but the Schopenhauerean conclusion held him no longer than it took him to inspect it calmly. Thus he gained doubly — first, by the acquisition of a definite theory of human conduct, one giving clarity to his own vague feelings, and secondly, by the reaction against an abject theory of human destiny, the very antithesis of that which rose within him.

And yet, for all his dissent, for all his instinctive revolt against the resignationism which overwhelmed him for an hour, Nietzsche nevertheless carried away with him, and kept throughout his life, some touch of Schopenhauer's distrust of the search for happiness. Nine years after his great discovery we find him quoting and approving his teacher's words: " A happy life is impossible; the highest thing that man can aspire to is a

---

[1] Nietzsche himself, in after years, viewed this attack humorously, and was wont to say that it was caused, not by Schopenhauer alone, but also (and chiefly) by the bad cooking of Leipsic. See " *Ecce Homo*," II, i.

heroic life." And still later we find him thundering
against "the green-grazing happiness of the herd."
What is more, he gave his assent later on, though always
more by fascination than by conviction, to the doctrine
of eternal recurrence, the most hopeless idea, perhaps,
ever formulated by man. But in all this a certain distinction is to be noted: Schopenhauer, despairing of the
happy life, renounced even the heroic life, but Nietzsche never did anything of the sort. On the contrary,
his whole philosophy is a protest against that very despair. The heroic life may not bring happiness, and it
may even fail to bring good, but at all events it will
shine gloriously in the light of its own heroism. In
brief, high endeavor is an end in itself — nay, the noblest of all ends. The higher man does not work for a
wage, not even for the wage of bliss: his reward is in the
struggle, the danger, the aspiration. As for the happiness
born of peace and love, of prosperity and tranquillity,
that is for "shopkeepers, women, Englishmen and
cows." The man who seeks it thereby confesses his incapacity for the loftier joys and hazards of the free
spirit, and the man who wails because he cannot find it
thereby confesses his unfitness to live in the world.
"My formula for greatness," said Nietzsche toward the
end of his life, "is *amor fati* . . . not only to bear up
under necessity, but to *love* it." Thus, borrowing Schopenhauer's pessimism, he turned it, in the end, into a
defiant and irreconcilable optimism — not the slave
optimism of hope, with its vain courting of gods, but the
master optimism of courage.

So much for the larger of the direct influences upon

Nietzsche's thinking. Scarcely less was the influence of that great revolution in man's view of man, that genuine " transvaluation of all values," set in motion by the publication of Charles Darwin's " The Origin of Species," in 1859. In the chapter on Christianity I have sketched briefly the part that Nietzsche played in the matter, and have shown how it rested squarely upon the parts played by those who went before him. He himself was fond of attacking Darwin, whom he disliked as he disliked all Englishmen, and of denying that he had gotten anything of value out of Darwin's work, but it is not well to take such denunciations and denials too seriously. Like Ibsen, Nietzsche was often an unreliable witness as to his own intellectual obligations. So long as he dealt with ideas his thinking was frank and clear, but when he turned to the human beings behind them, and particularly when he discussed those who had presumed to approach the problems he undertook to solve himself, his incredible intolerance, jealousy, spitefulness and egomania, and his savage lust for bitter, useless and unmerciful strife, combined to make his statements dubious, and sometimes even absurd. Thus with his sneers at Darwin and the other evolutionists, especially Spencer. If he did not actually follow them, then he at least walked side by side with them, and every time they cleared another bit of the path he profited by it too. One thing, at all events, they gave to the world that entered into Nietzsche's final philosophy, and without which it would have stopped short of its ultimate development, and that was the conception of man as a mammal. Their great service to human knowledge was precisely this. They found man a loiterer at the gates of heaven, a courtier in the ante-chambers of gods. They brought him back to earth and bade him help himself.

Meanwhile, the reader who cares to go into the matter further will find Nietzsche elbowing other sages in a multitude of places. He himself has testified to his debt to Stendhal (Marie Henri Beyle), that great apologist for Napoleon Bonaparte and exponent of the Napoleonic philosophy. "Stendhal," he says, "was one of the happiest accidents of my life. . . . He is quite priceless, with his penetrating psychologist's eye and his grip upon facts, recalling that of the greatest of all masters of facts (*ex ungue Napoleon* —); and last, but not least, as an *honest* atheist — one of a species rare and hard to find in France. . . . Maybe I myself am jealous of Stendhal? He took from me the best of atheistic jokes, that I might best have made: ' the only excuse for God is that He doesn't exist.' "[1] Of his debt to Max Stirner the evidence is less clear, but it has been frequently alleged, and, as Dr. Mügge says, "quite a literature has grown up around the question." Stirner's chief work, "*Der Einzige und sein Eigentum*,"[2] was first published in 1844, the year of Nietzsche's birth, and in its strong plea for the emancipation of the individual there are many ideas and even phrases that were later voiced by Nietzsche. Dr. Mügge quotes a few of them: " What is good and what is evil? I myself am my own

---

[1] "*Ecce Homo*," II, 3.

[2] Eng. tr. by Steven T. Byington, " The Ego and His Own," New York, 1907.

rule, and I am neither good nor evil. Neither word means anything to me. . . . Between the two vicissitudes of victory and defeat swings the fate of the struggle — master or slave! . . . Egoism, not love, must decide." Others will greet the reader of Stirner's book: " As long as you believe in the truth, you do not believe in yourself; you are a servant, a religious man. You alone are the truth. . . . Whether what I think and do is Christian, what do I care? Whether it is human, liberal, humane, whether unhuman, illiberal, unhumane, what do I ask about that? If only it accomplishes what I want, if only I satisfy myself in it, then overlay it with predicates if you will: it is all one to me. . . ." But, as Dr. J. L. Walker well says, in his introduction to Mr. Byington's English translation, there is a considerable gulf between Stirner and Nietzsche, even here. The former's plea is for absolute liberty for all men, great and small. The latter is for liberty only in the higher castes: the chandala he would keep in chains. Therefore, if Nietzsche actually got anything from Stirner, it certainly did not enter unchanged into the ultimate structure of his system.

The other attempts to convict him of appropriating ideas come to little more. Dr. Mügge, for example, quotes these pre-Nietzschean passages from Heracleitus: " War is universal and right, and by strife all things arise and are made use of . . . God and evil are the same. . . . To me, one is worth ten thousand, if he be the best." And Mr. More quotes this from Hobbes: " In the first place, I put forth, for a general inclination of all mankind, a perpetual and restless desire of power after power, that ceaseth only with death " — to which the reader may add, " Whatsoever is the object of any man's appetite or desire, that is it which he for his part calleth good . . . for these words of good, evil and contemptible are ever used with relation to the person that useth them; there being nothing simply and absolutely so; nor any common rule of good and evil, to be taken for the nature of objects themselves." [1] But all these passages prove no more than that men of past ages saw the mutability of criteria, and their origin in human aspiration and striving. Not only Heracleitus, but many other Greeks, voiced that ethical scepticism. It was for many years, indeed, one of the dominant influences in Greek philosophy, and so, if Nietzsche is accused of borrowing it, that is no more than saying what I have already said: that he ate Greek grapes in his youth and became, to all intellectual intents and purposes, a Greek himself. A man must needs have a point of view, a manner of approach to life, and that point of view is no less authentic when he reaches it through his reading and by the exercise of a certain degree of free choice than when he accepts it unthinkingly from the folk about him. The service of Heracleitus and the other Greeks to Nietzsche was not that they gave him his philosophy, but that they made him a philosopher. It was the questions they asked rather than the answers they made that interested and stimulated him, and if, at times, he answered much as they had done, that was only proof of his genuine kinship with them.

On the artistic, as opposed to the analytical side,

[1] The Leviathan, I, vi; London, 1651.

Nietzsche's most influential teacher, perhaps, was
Goethe, the noblest intellectual figure of modern Germany, the common *stammvater* of all the warring schools
of today — in Nietzsche's own phrase, " not only a good
and great man, but a culture itself." His writings are
full of praises of his hero, whom he began to read as a
boy of eight or ten years. His grandmother, Frau Erd-
muthe Nietzsche, was a sister to Dr. Krause, professor
of divinity at Weimar in Goethe's day, and she lived
in the town while the poet held his court there, and undoubtedly came into contact with him. Her mother,
Frau Pastor Krause, was probably the Muthgen of
Goethe's diary. But despite all this, she thought that
" Faust " and " Elective Affinities " were " not fit for
little boys " and so it remained for Judge Pindar, the
father of one of young Nietzsche's Naumburg playmates,
to conduct the initiation. Thirty years afterward,
Nietzsche gratefully acknowledged his debt to Herr
Pindar, and his vastly greater debt to Goethe — " a
thoroughgoing realist in the midst of an unreal age. . . .
He did not sever himself from life, but entered into it.
Undaunted, he took as much as possible to himself. . . .
What he sought was *totality*." [2]

Nietzsche was also an extravagant admirer of Hein-
rich Heine, and tried to imitate that poet's " sweet and
passionate music." " People will say some day," he
declared, " that Heine and I were the greatest artists,
by far, that ever wrote in German, and that we left the

[1] Frau Förster-Nietzsche: " The Life of Nietzsche " (Eng. tr.), Vol. I,
p. 31.
[2] " *Götzendämmerung*," IX, 49.

best any mere German [1] could do an incalculable distance behind us." [2]   Another poet he greatly revered
was Friedrich Hölderlin, a South German rhapsodist of
the Goethe-Schiller period, who wrote odes in free
rhythms and philosophical novels in gorgeous prose,
and died the year before Nietzsche was born, after forty
years of insanity.   Karl Joel,[3] Dr. Mügge and other
critics have sought to connect Nietzsche, through Hölderlin, with the romantic movement in Germany, but
the truth is that both Nietzsche and Hölderlin, if they
were romantics at all, were of the Greek school rather
than the German.   Certainly, nothing could be further
from genuine German romanticism, with its sentimentality, its begging of questions and its booming patriotism, than the gospel of the superman.   What Nietzsche
undoubtedly got from the romantics was a feeling of
ease in the German language, a disregard for the artificial bonds of the schools, a sense of hospitality to the
gipsy phrase.   In brief, they taught him how to write.
But they certainly did not teach him what to write.

Even so, it is probable that he was as much influenced
by certain Frenchmen as he ever was by Germans —
particularly by Montaigne, La Bruyère, La Rochefoucauld, Fontenelle, Vauvenarges and Chamfort, his constant companions on his wanderings.   He borrowed
from them, not only the somewhat obvious device of
putting his argument into the form of apothegms and

---

[1] Heine was a Jew — and Nietzsche, as we know, liked to think himself a Pole.

[2] " *Ecce Homo,*" II, 4.

[3] " *Nietzsche und die Romantik,*" Jena, 1905.

epigrams, but also their conception of the dialectic as one of the fine arts — in other words, their striving after style. " It is to a small number of French authors," he once said, " that I return again and again. I believe only in French culture, and regard all that is called culture elsewhere in Europe, especially in Germany, as mere misunderstanding. . . . The few persons of higher culture that I have met in Germany have had French training — above all, Frau Cosima Wagner, by long odds the best authority on questions of taste I ever heard of." [1] This preference carried him so far, indeed, that he usually wrote more like a Frenchman than like a German, toying with words, experimenting with their combinations, matching them as carefully as pearls for a necklace. " Nietzsche," says one critic,[2] " whether for good or evil, introduced Romance (not romantic!) qualities of terseness and clearness into German prose; it was his endeavor to free it from those elements which he described as *deutsch und schwer*." (German and heavy.)

For the rest, he denounced Klopstock, Herder, Wieland, Lessing and Schiller, the remaining gods in Germany's literary valhalla, even more bitterly than he denounced Kant and Hegel, the giants of orthodox German philosophy.

[1] " *Ecce Homo*," II, 3.
[2] J. G. Robertson: " A History of German Literature," Edinburgh, 1902, pp. 611–615.

II

NIETZSCHE AND HIS CRITICS

LET us set aside at the start that great host of critics whose chief objection to Nietzsche is that he is blasphemous, that his philosophy and his manner outrage the piety and prudery of the world. Of such sort are the pale parsons who arise in suburban pulpits to dispose of him in the half hour between the first and second lessons, as their predecessors of the 70's and 80's disposed of Darwin, Huxley and Spencer. Let them read their indictments and bring in their verdicts and pronounce their bitter sentences! The student of Nietzsche must perceive at once the irrelevance of that sort of criticism. It was the deliberate effort of the philosopher, from the very start of what he calls his tunnelling period, to provoke and deserve the accusation of sacrilege. In framing his accusations against Christian morality he tried to make them, not only persuasive and just, but also as offensive as possible. No man ever had more belief in the propagandist value of a *succes de scandale*. He tried his best to shock the guardians of the sacred vessels, to force upon them the burdens of an active defense, to bring them out into the open, to attract attention to the combat by accentuating its mere fuming and fury. If he succeeded in the effort, if he really outraged Christendom, then it is certainly absurd to bring forward that deliberate achievement as an exhibit against itself.

The more pertinent and plausible criticisms of Nietzsche, launched against him in Europe and America by many industrious foes, may be reduced for convenience to five fundamental propositions, to wit:

(a) He was a decadent and a lunatic, and in consequence his philosophy is not worthy of attention.

(b) His writings are chaotic and contradictory and it is impossible to find in them any connected philosophical system.

(c) His argument that self-sacrifice costs more than it yields, and that it thus reduces the average fitness of a race practising it, is contradicted by human experience.

(d) The scheme of things proposed by him is opposed by ideas inherent in all civilized men.

(e) Even admitting that his criticism of Christian morality is well-founded, he offers nothing in place of it that would work as well.

It is scarcely worth while to linger over the first and second of these propositions. The first has been defended most speciously by Max Nordau, in " Degeneration," a book which made as much noise, when it was first published in 1893, as any of Nietzsche's own. Nordau's argument is based upon a theory of degeneration borrowed quite frankly from Cesare Lombroso, an Italian quasi-scientist whose modest contributions to psychiatry were offset by many volumes of rubbish about spooks, table-tapping, mental telepathy, spirit photography and the alleged stigmata of criminals and men of genius. Degeneracy and decadence were terms that filled the public imagination in the 80's and 90's, and even Nietzsche himself seemed to think, at times, that they had definite meanings and that his own type of mind was degenerate. As Nordau defines degeneracy it is " a morbid deviation from the original type " — i. e., from the physical and mental norm of the species — and he lays stress upon the fact that by " morbid " he means " infirm " or " incapable of fulfilling normal functions." But straightway he begins to regard *any* deviation as morbid and degenerate, despite the obvious fact that it may be quite the reverse. He says, for example, that a man with web toes is a degenerate, and then proceeds to argue elaborately from that premise, entirely overlooking the fact that web toes, under easily imaginable circumstances, might be an advantage instead of a handicap, and that, under the ordinary conditions of life, we are unable to determine with any accuracy whether they are the one thing or the other. So with the symptoms of degeneracy that he discovers in Nietzsche. He shows that Nietzsche differed vastly from the average, everyday German of his time, and even from the average German of superior culture — that he thought differently, wrote differently, admired different heroes and believed in different gods — but he by no means proves thereby that Nietzsche's processes of thought were morbid or infirm, or that the conclusions he reached were invalid *a priori*. Since Nordau startled the world with his book, the Lombrosan theory of degeneracy has lost ground among psychologists and pathologists, but it is still launched against Nietzsche by an occasional critic, and so it deserves to be noticed.

Nordau s discussion of Nietzsche's insanity is rather more intelligent than his discussion of the philosopher's alleged degeneracy, if only because his facts are less open to dispute, but here, too, he forgets that the proof of an idea is not to be sought in the soundness of the man fathering it, but in the soundness of the idea itself. One asks of a pudding, not if the cook who offers it is a good woman, but if the pudding itself is good. Nordau, in attempting to dispose of Nietzsche's philosophy on the ground that the author died a madman, succeeds only in piling up a mass of uncontroverted but irrelevant accusations. He shows that Nietzsche was an utter believer in his own wisdom, that he had a fondness for repeating certain favorite arguments *ad nauseam*, that he was violently impatient of criticism, that he chronically underestimated the man opposed to him, that he sometimes indulged in blasphemy for the sheer joy of shocking folks, and that he was often hypnotized by the exuberance of his own verbosity, but it must be plain that this indictment has its effective answer in the fact that it might be found with equal justice against almost any revolutionary enthusiast one selected at random — for example, Savonarola, Tolstoi, Luther, Ibsen, Garrison, Phillips, Wilkes, Bakúnin, Marx, or Nordau himself. That Nietzsche died insane is undoubted, and that his insanity was not sudden in its onset is also plain, and one may even admit frankly that it is visible, here and there, in his writings, particularly those of his last year or two; but that his principal doctrines, the ideas upon

which his fame are based, are the fantasies of a maniac
is certainly wholly false. Had he sought to prove that
cows had wings, it might be fair today to dismiss him as
Nordau attempts to dismiss him. But when he essayed
to prove that Christianity impeded progress, he laid
down a proposition that, whatever its novelty and
daring, was obviously not irrational, and neither was
there anything irrational in the reasoning whereby he
supported it. One need go no further for proof of this
than the fact that multitudes of sane men, while he lived
and since his death, have debated that proposition in all
seriousness and found a plentiful food for sober thought
in Nietzsche's statement and defense of it. Ibsen also
passed out of life in mental darkness, and so did Schumann, but no reasonable critic would seek thereby to
deny all intelligibility to " Peer Gynt " or to the piano
quintet in E flat.

Again, it is Nordau who chiefly voices the second of
the objections noted at the beginning of this chapter,
though here many another self-confessed serpent of
wisdom follows him. Nietzsche, he says, tore down
without building up, and died without having formulated
any workable substitute for the Christian morality he
denounced. Even to the reader who has got no further
into Nietzsche than the preceding chapters of this book,
the absurdity of such a charge must be manifest without
argument. No man, indeed, ever left a more comprehensive system of ethics, not even Comte or Herbert
Spencer, and if it be true that he scattered it through a
dozen books and that he occasionally modified it in some
of its details, it is equally true that his fundamental

principles were always stated with perfect clearness and that they remained substantially unchanged from first to last. But even supposing that he had died before he had arranged his ideas in a connected and coherent form, and that it had remained for his disciples to deduce and group his final conclusions, and to rid the whole of inconsistency — even then it would have been possible to study those conclusions seriously and to accept them for what they were worth. Nordau lays it down as an axiom that a man cannot be a reformer unless he proposes some ready-made and perfectly symmetrical scheme of things to take the place of the notions he seeks to overturn, that if he does not do this he is a mere hurler of bricks and shouter of blasphemies. But all of us know that this is not true. Nearly every considerable reform the world knows has been accomplished, not by one man, but by many men working in series. It seldom happens, indeed, that the man who first points out the necessity for change lives long enough to see that change accomplished, or even to define its precise manner and terms. Nietzsche himself was not the first critic of Christian morality, nor did he so far dispose of the question that he left no room for successors. But he made a larger contribution to it than any man had ever made before him, and the ideas he contributed were so acute and so convincing that they must needs be taken into account by every critic who comes after him.

So much for the first two arguments against the prophet of the superman. Both raise immaterial objections and the second makes an allegation that is grotesquely untrue. The other three are founded upon

sounder logic, and, when maintained skillfully, afford
more reasonable ground for objecting to the Nietzschean
system, either as a whole or in part. It would be interesting, perhaps, to attempt a complete review of the
literature embodying them, but that would take a great
deal more space than is here available, and so we must be
content with a glance at a few typical efforts at refutation. One of the most familiar of these appears in the
argument that the messianic obligation of self-sacrifice,
whatever its cost, has yet yielded the race a large profit
— that we are the better for our Christian charity and
that we owe it entirely to Christianity. This argument
has been best put forward, perhaps, by Bennett Hume,
an Englishman. If it were not for Christian charity,
says Mr. Hume, there would be no hospitals and asylums
for the sick and insane, and in consequence, no concerted
and effective effort to make man more healthy and efficient. Therefore, he maintains, it must be admitted
that the influence of Christianity, as a moral system,
has been for the good of the race. But this argument,
in inspection, quickly goes to pieces, and for two reasons.
In the first place, it must be obvious that the advantages of preserving the unfit, few of whom ever become
wholly fit again, are more than dubious; and in the
second place, it must be plain that modern humanitarianism, in so far as it is scientific and unsentimental
and hence profitable, is so little a purely Christian idea
that the Christian church, even down to our own time,
has actually opposed it. No man, indeed, can read Dr.
Andrew D. White's great history of the warfare between
science and the church without carrying away the con-

viction that such great boons as the conquest of small-pox and malaria, the development of surgery, the im-proved treatment of the insane, and the general lowering of the death rate have been brought about, not by the maudlin alms-giving of Christian priests, but by the intelligent meliorism of rebels against a blind faith, ruthless in their ways and means but stupendously suc-cessful in their achievement.

Another critic, this time a Frenchman, Alfred Fouil-lée by name,[1] chooses as his point of attack the Niet-zschean doctrine that a struggle is welcome and benefi-cial to the strong, that intelligent self-seeking, accom-panied by a certain willingness to take risks, is the road of progress. A struggle, argues M. Fouillée, always means an expenditure of strength, and strength, when so expended, is further weakened by the opposing strength it arouses and stimulates. Darwin is summoned from his tomb to substantiate this argument, but its expo-nent seems to forget (while actually stating it!) the fa-miliar physiological axiom, so often turned to by Dar-win, that strength is one of the effects of use, and the Darwinian corollary that disuse, whether produced by organized protection or in some other way, leads in-evitably to weakness and atrophy. In other words, the ideal strong man of M. Fouillée's dream is one who seeks, with great enthusiasm, the readiest possible way of rid-ding himself of his strength.

Nordau, Violet Paget and various other critics attack

---

[1] Author of " *Nietzsche et l'Immoralisme* " and other books. The argument discussed appears in an article in the *International Monthly* for March, 1901, pp. 134-165.

Nietzsche from much the same side. That is to say, they
endeavor to controvert his criticism of humility and self-
sacrifice and to show that the law of natural selection,
with its insistence that only the fittest shall survive, is
insufficient to insure human progress. Miss Paget, for
example,[1] argues that if there were no belief in every
man's duty to yield something to his weaker brother the
race would soon become a herd of mere wild beasts. She
sees humility as a sort of brake or governor, placed upon
humanity to keep it from running amuck. A human
being is so constituted, she says, that he necessarily
looms in his own view as large as all the rest of the world
put together. This distortion of values is met with in
the consciousness of every individual, and if there were
nothing to oppose it, it would lead to a hopeless conflict
between exaggerated egos. Humility, says Miss Paget,
tempers the conflict, without wholly ending it. A m n's
inherent tendency to magnify his own importance and
to invite death by trying to force that view upon others
is held in check by the idea that it is his duty to consider
the welfare of those others. The objection to all this is
that the picture of humility Miss Paget draws is not at
all a picture of self-sacrifice, of something founded upon
an unselfish idea of duty, but a picture of highly intelligent egoism. Whatever his pharisaical account of his
motives, it must be obvious that her Christian gentleman is merely a man who throws bones to the dogs about
him. Between such wise prudence and the immolation
of the Beatitudes a wide gulf is fixed. As a matter of
fact, that prudence is certainly not opposed by Niet-

[1] In the *North American Review* for Dec., 1904.

zsche. The higher man of his visions is far from a mere
brawler. He is not afraid of an open fight, and he is
never held back by fear of hurting his antagonist, but
he also understands that there are times for truce and
guile. In brief, his self-seeking is conducted, not alone
by his fists, but also by his head. He knows when to
pounce upon his foes and rivals, but he also knows when
to keep them from pouncing upon him. Thus Miss
Paget's somewhat elaborate refutation, though it leads
to an undoubtedly sound conclusion, by no means dis-
poses of Nietzsche.

The other branches of the argument that self-sacrifice
is beneficial open an endless field of debate, in which the
same set of facts is often susceptible of diametrically
opposite interpretations. We have already glanced at
the alleged effects of Christian charity upon progress,
and observed the enormous difference between sentimental efforts to preserve the unfit and intelligent efforts to make them fit, and we have seen how practical
Christianity, whatever its theoretical effects, has had
the actual effect of furthering the former and hindering
the latter. It is often argued that there is unfairness in
thus burdening the creed with the crimes of the church,
but how the two are to be separated is never explained.
What sounder test of a creed's essential value can we
imagine than that of its visible influence upon the men
who subscribe to it? And what sounder test of its terms
than the statement of its ordained teachers and interpreters, supported by the unanimous approval of all
who profess it? We are here dealing, let it be remembered, not with esoteric doctrines, but with practical

doctrines — that is to say, with working policies. If the Christian ideal of charity is to be defended as a working policy, then it is certainly fair to examine it at work. And when that is done the reflective observer is almost certain to conclude that it is opposed to true progress, that it acts as a sentimental shield to the unfit without helping them in the slightest to shake off their unfitness. What is more, it stands contrary to that wise forethought which sacrifices one man today that ten may be saved tomorrow. Nothing could be more patent, indeed, than the high cost to humanity of the Christian teaching that it is immoral to seek the truth outside the Word of God, or to take thought of an earthly tomorrow, or to draw distinctions in value between beings who all possess souls of infinite, and therefore of exactly equal preciousness.

But setting aside the doctrine that self-sacrifice is a religious duty, there remains the doctrine that it is a measure of expediency, that when the strong help the weak they also help themselves. Let it be said at once that this second doctrine, provided only it be applied intelligently and without any admixture of sentimentality, is not in opposition to anything in Nietzsche's philosophy. On the contrary, he is at pains to point out the value of exploiting the inefficient masses, and obviously that exploitation is impossible without some concession to their habits and desires, some offer, however fraudulent, of a *quid pro quo* — and unprofitable unless they can be made to yield more than they absorb. For one thing, there is the business of keeping the lower castes in health. They themselves are too ignorant and lazy to manage it, and therefore it must be managed by their betters. When we appropriate money from the public funds to pay for vaccinating a horde of negroes, we do not do it because we have any sympathy for them or because we crave their blessings, but simply because we don't want them to be falling ill of smallpox in our kitchens and stables, to the peril of our own health and the neglect of our necessary drudgery.[1] In so far as the negroes have any voice in the matter at all, they protest against vaccination, for they can't understand its theory and so they see only its tyranny, but we vaccinate them nevertheless, and thus increase their mass efficiency in spite of them. It costs something to do the work, but we see a profit in it. Here we have a good example of self-sacrifice based frankly upon expediency, and Nietzsche has nothing to say against it.

But what he does insist upon is that we must beware of mixing sentimentality with the business, that we must keep the idea of expediency clear of any idea of altruism. The trouble with the world, as he describes it, is that such a corruption almost always takes place. That is to say, we too often practise charity, not because it is worth while, but merely because it is pleasant. The Christian ideal, he says, "knows how to enrapture." Starting out from the safe premise, approved by human experience, that it is sometimes a virtue — *i. e.*, a measure of intelligent prudence — to help the weak, we proceed to the illogical conclusion that it is *always* a

---

[1] A more extended treatment of this point will be found in "Men *vs.* the Man," by Robert Rives La Monte and the present author: New York, 1910.

virtue. Hence our wholesale coddling of the unfit, our
enormous expenditure upon vain schemes of ameliora-
tion, our vain efforts to combat the laws of nature. We
nurse the defective children of the lower classes into some
appearance of health, and then turn them out to beget
their kind. We parole the pickpocket, launch him upon
society with a tract in his hand — and lose our pocket-
books next day. We send missionaries to the heathen,
build hospitals for them, civilize and educate them —
and later on have to fight them. We save a pauper con-
sumptive today, on the ostensible theory that he is
more valuable saved than dead — and so open the way
for saving his innumerable grandchildren in the future.
In brief, our self-sacrifice of expediency seldom remains
undefiled. Nine times out of ten a sentimental color
quickly overcomes it, and soon or late there is apt to be
more sentimentality in it than expediency.

What is worse, this sentimentalism results in attach-
ing a sort of romantic glamour to its objects. Just as
the Sunday-school teaching virgin, beginning by trying
to save the Chinese laundryman's soul, commonly ends
by falling in love with him, so the virtuoso of any other
sort of charity commonly ends by endowing its bene-
ficiary with a variety of imaginary virtues. Sympathy,
by some subtle alchemy, is converted into a sneaking
admiration. " Blessed are the poor in spirit " becomes
" Blessed are the poor." This exaltation of inefficiency,
it must be manifest, is a dangerous error. There is, in
fact, nothing at all honorable about unfitness, considered
in the mass. On the contrary, it is invariably a symptom of actual dishonor — of neglect, laziness, **ignorance**

and depravity — if not primarily in the individual him-self, then at least in his forebears, whose weakness he carries on. It is highly important that this fact should be kept in mind by the human race, that the essential inferiority of the inefficient should be insisted upon, that the penalties of deliberate slackness should be swift and merciless. But as it is, those penalties are too often re-duced to nothing by charity, while the offense they should punish is elevated to a fictitious martyrdom. Thus we have charity converted into an instrument of debauch-ery. Thus we have it playing the part of an active agent of decay, and so increasing the hazards of life on earth. "We may compare civilized man," says Sir Ray Lan-kester,[1] "to a successful rebel against nature, who by every step forward renders himself liable to greater and greater penalties." No need to offer cases in point. Every one of us knows what the Poor Laws of England have accomplished in a hundred years — how they have multiplied misery enormously and created a caste of professional paupers — how they have seduced that caste downward into depths of degradation untouched by any other civilized race in history — and how, by hanging the crushing burden of that caste about the necks of the English people, they have helped to weaken and sicken the whole stock and to imperil the future of the nation.

So much for the utility of self-sacrifice — undeniable, perhaps, so long as a wise and ruthless foresight rules, but immediately questionable when sentimentality enters into the matter. There remains the answer in rebuttal

[1] In "The Kingdom of Man," London, 1907.

that sentimentality, after all, is native to the soul of man, that we couldn't get rid of it if we tried. Herein, if we look closely, we will observe tracks of an idea that has colored the whole stream of human thought since the dawn of Western philosophy, and is accepted today, as irrefutably true, by all who pound pulpits and wave their arms and call upon their fellow men to repent. It has clogged all ethical inquiry for two thousand years, it has been a premise in a million moral syllogisms, it has survived the assaults of all the iconoclasts that ever lived. It is taught in all our schools today and lies at the bottom of all our laws, prophecies and revelations. It is the foundation and cornerstone, not only of Christianity, but also of every other compound of theology and morality known in the world. And what is this king of all axioms and emperor of all fallacies? Simply the idea that there are rules of " natural morality " engraven indelibly upon the hearts of man — that all men, at all times and everywhere, have ever agreed, do now agree and will agree forevermore, unanimously and without reservation, that certain things are right and certain other things are wrong, that certain things are nice and certain other things are not nice, that certain things are pleasing to God and certain other things are offensive to God.

In every treatise upon Christian ethics and " natural theology," so called, you will find these rules of " natural morality " in the first chapter. Thomas Aquinas called them " the eternal law." Even the Greeks and Romans, for all their skepticism in morals, had a sneaking belief in them. Aristotle tried to formulate them and the Latin lawyers constantly assumed their existence. Most of them are held in firm faith today by all save a small minority of the folk of Christendom. The most familiar of them, perhaps, is the rule against murder — the sixth commandment. Another is the rule against the violation of property in goods, wives and cattle — the eighth and tenth commandments. A third is the rule upon which the solidity of the family is based, and with it the solidity of the tribe — the fifth commandment. The theory behind these rules is, not only that they are wise, but that they are innate and sempiternal, that every truly enlightened man recognizes their validity intuitively, and is conscious of sin when he breaks them. To them Christianity added an eleventh commandment, a sort of infinite extension of the fifth, " that ye love one another " [1] — and in two thousand years it has been converted from a novelty into a universality. That is to say, its point of definite origin has been lost sight of, and it has been moved over into the group of " natural virtues," of " eternal laws." When Christ first voiced it, in his discourse at the Last Supper, it was so far from general acceptance that he named a belief in it as one of the distinguishing marks of his disciples, but now our moralists tell us that it is in the blood of all of us, and that we couldn't repudiate it if we would. Brotherhood, indeed, is the very soul of Christianity, and the only effort of the pious today is to raise it from a universal theory to a universal fact.

But the truth is, of course, that it is not universal at all, and that nothing in the so-called soul of man prompts

[1] John XIII, 34.

him to subscribe to it. We cling to it today, not because it is inherent in us, but simply because it is the moral fashion of our age. When the disciples first heard it put into terms, it probably struck them as a revolutionary novelty, and on some dim tomorrow our descendants may regard it as an archaic absurdity. In brief, rules of morality are wholly temporal and temporary, for the good and sufficient reason that there is no " natural morality " in man — and the sentimental rule that the strong shall give of their strength to the weak is no exception. There have been times in the history of the race when few, if any intelligent men subscribed to it, and there are thousands of intelligent men who refuse to subscribe to it today, and no doubt there will come a time when those who are against it will once more greatly outnumber those who are in favor of it. So with all other "eternal laws." Their eternality exists only in the imagination of those who seek to glorify them. Nietzsche himself spent his best years demonstrating this, and we have seen how he set about the task — how he showed that the " good " of one race and age was the " bad " of some other race and age — how the " natural morality " of the Periclean Greeks, for example, differed diametrically from the " natural morality " of the captive Jews. All history bears him out. Mankind is ever revising and abandoning its " inherent " ideas. We say today that the human mind instinctively revolts against cruel punishments, and yet a moment's reflection recalls the fact that the world is, and always has been peopled by millions to whom cruelty, not only to enemies but to the weak in general, seems and has seemed wholly natural and agreeable. We say that man has an " innate " impulse to be fair and just, and yet it is a commonplace observation that multitudes of men, in the midst of our most civilized societies, have little more sense of justice than so many jackals. Therefore, we may safely set aside the argument that a " natural " instinct for sentimental self-sacrifice stands as an impassable barrier to Nietzsche's dionysian philosophy. There is no such barrier. There is no such instinct. It is an idea merely — an idea powerful and persistent, but still mutable and mortal. Certainly, it is absurd to plead it in proof against the one man who did most to establish its mutability.

We come now to the final argument against Nietzsche — the argument, to wit, that, even admitting his criticism of Christian morality to be well-founded, he offers nothing in place of it that would serve the world as well. The principal spokesman of this objection, perhaps, is Paul Elmer More, who sets it forth at some length in his hostile but very ingenious little study of Nietzsche.[1] Mr. More goes back to Locke to show the growth of the two ideas which stand opposed as Socialism and individualism, Christianity and Nietzscheism today. So long, he says, as man believed in revelation, there was no genuine effort to get at the springs of human action, for every impulse that was ratified by the Scriptures was believed to be natural and moral, and every impulse that went counter to the Scriptures was believed to be sinful, even by those who yielded to it

[1] " Nietzsche," Boston, 1912. Reprinted in " The Drift of Romanticism," pp. 147-190, Boston, 1913.

habitually. But when that idea was cleared away, there arose a need for something to take its place, and Locke came forward with his theory that the notion of good was founded upon sensations of pleasure and that of bad upon sensations of pain. There followed Hume, with his elaborate effort to prove that sympathy was a source of pleasure, by reason of its grateful tickling of the sense of virtue, and so the new conception of good finally stood erect, with one foot on frank self-interest and the other on sympathy. Mr. More shows how, during the century following, the importance of the second of these factors began to be accentuated, under the influence of Rousseau and his followers, and how, in the end, the first was forgotten almost entirely and there arose a non-Christian sentimentality which was worse, if anything, than the sentimentality of the Beatitudes. In England, France and Germany it colored almost the whole of philosophy, literature and politics. Stray men, true enough, raised their voices against it, but its sweep was irresistible. Its fruits were diverse and memorable — the romantic movement in Germany, humanitarianism in England, the Kantian note in ethics, and, most important of all, Socialism.

That this exaltation of sympathy was imprudent, and that its effects, in our own time, are far from satisfactory, Mr. More is disposed to grant freely. It is perfectly true, as Nietzsche argues, that humanitarianism has been guilty of gross excesses, that there is a " danger that threatens true progress in any system of education and government which makes the advantage of the average rather than the distinguished man its chief object." But Mr. More holds that the danger thus inherent in sympathy is matched by a danger inherent in selfishness, that we are no worse off on one horn of Hume's dual ethic than we should be on the other. Sympathy unbalanced by self-seeking leads us into maudlin futilities and crimes against efficiency; self-seeking unchecked by sympathy would lead us into sheer savagery. If there is any choice between the two, that choice is probably in favor of sympathy, for the reason that it is happily impossible of realization. The most lachrymose of the romantics, in the midst of their sentimentalizing, were yet careful of their own welfare. Many of them, indeed, displayed a quite extraordinary egoism, and there was some justice in Byron's sneer that Sterne, for one, preferred weeping over a dead ass to relieving the want (at cost to himself) of a living mother.

But in urging all this against Nietzsche, Mr. More and the other destructive critics of the superman make a serious error, and that is the error of assuming that Nietzsche hoped to abolish Christian morality completely, that he proposed a unanimous desertion of the idea of sympathy for the idea of intelligent self-seeking. As a matter of fact, he had no such hope and made no such proposal. Nothing was more firmly fixed in his mind, indeed, than the notion that the vast majority of men would cling indefinitely, and perhaps for all time, to some system of morality more or less resembling the Christian morality of today. Not only did he have no expectation of winning that majority from its idols, but he bitterly resented any suggestion that such a result might follow from his work. The whole of his preaching was addressed, not to men in the mass, but to the small minority of exceptional men — not to those who live by obeying, but to those who live by commanding — not to the race as a race, but only to its masters. It would seem to be impossible that any reader of Nietzsche should overlook this important fact, and yet it is constantly overlooked by most of his critics. They proceed to prove, elaborately and, it must be said, quite convincingly, that if his transvaluation of values were made by all men, the world would be no better off than it is today, and perhaps a good deal worse, but all they accomplish thereby is to demolish a hobgoblin of straw. Nietzsche himself sensed the essential value of Hume's dualism. What he sought to do was not to destroy it, but to restore it, and, restoring it, to raise it to a state of active conflict — to dignify self-interest as sympathy has been dignified, and so to put the two in perpetual opposition. He believed that the former was by long odds the safer impulse for the higher castes of men to follow, if only because of its obviously closer kinship to the natural laws which make for progress upward, but by the same token he saw that these higher castes could gain nothing by disturbing the narcotic contentment of the castes lower down. Therefore, he was, to that extent, an actual apologist for the thing he elsewhere so bitterly attacked. Sympathy, self-sacrifice, charity — these ideas lulled and satisfied the chandala, and so he was content to have the chandala hold to them. " Whom do I hate most among the rabble of today? The Socialist who undermines the workingman's instincts, who destroys his satisfaction with his insignificant existence,

who makes him envious and teaches him revenge." [1]
In brief, Nietzsche dreamed no dream of all mankind
converted into a race of supermen: the only vision he
saw was one of supermen at the top.

To make an end, his philosophy was wholly aristocratic, in aim as well as in terms. He believed that
superior men, by which he meant alert and restless men,
were held in chains by the illusions and inertia of the
mass — that their impulse to move forward and upward,
at whatever cost to those below, was restrained by false
notions of duty and responsibility. It was his effort to
break down those false notions, to show that the progress of the race was more important than the comfort
of the herd, to combat and destroy the lingering spectre
of sin — in his own phrase, to make man innocent. But
when he said man he always meant the higher man,
the man of tomorrow, and not mere men. For the latter
he had only contempt: he sneered at their heroes, at
their ideals, at their definitions of good and evil. " There
are only three ways," he said, " in which the masses
appear to me to deserve a glance: first, as blurred copies
of their betters, printed on bad paper and from worn-
out plates; secondly, as a necessary opposition; and
thirdly, as tools. Further than that I hand them over
to statistics — and the devil.[2] . . . I am writing for a
race of men which does not yet exist. I am writing for
the lords of the earth." [3]

[1] " Der Antichrist," 57.
[2] " Vom Nutzen und Nachtheil der Historie für das Leben," IX.
[3] " Der Wille zur Macht," 958.

HOW TO STUDY NIETZSCHE

THROUGH the diligence and enthusiasm of Dr. Oscar Levy, author of " The Revival of Aristocracy," a German by birth but for some time a resident of London, the whole canon of Nietzsche's writings is now to be had in English translation. So long ago as 1896 a complete edition in eleven volumes was projected, and Dr. Alexander Tille, lecturer on German in the University of Glasgow, and author of " *Von Darwin bis Nietzsche*," was engaged to edit it. But though it started fairly with a volume including " The Case of Wagner " and " The Antichrist," and four more volumes followed after a year or so, it got no further than that. Ten years later came Dr. Levy. He met with little encouragement when he began, but by dint of unfailing perseverance he finally gathered about him a corps of competent translators, made arrangements with publishers in Great Britain and the United States, and got the work under way. His eighteenth and last volume was published early in 1913.

These translations, in the main, are excellent, and explanatory prefaces and notes are added wherever needed. The contents of the various volumes are as follows:

I. " The Birth of Tragedy," translated by Wm. A. Haussmann, Ph. D., with a biographical introduction by Frau

Förster-Nietzsche, a portrait of Nietzsche, and a facsimile of his manuscript.

II. "Early Greek Philosophy and Other Essays," translated by Maximilian A. Mügge, Ph. D., author of "Friedrich Nietzsche: His Life and Work." Contents: "The Greek Woman," "On Music and Words," "Homer's Contest," "The Relation of Schopenhauer's Philosophy to a German Culture," "Philosophy During the Tragic Age of the Greeks," and "On Truth and Falsity in Their Ultramoral Sense."

III. "On the Future of Our Educational Institutions" and "Homer and Classical Philology," translated by J. M. Kennedy, author of "The Quintessence of Nietzsche," with an introduction by the translator.

IV. "Thoughts Out of Season," I ("David Strauss, the Confessor and the Writer" and "Richard Wagner in Bayreuth"), translated by Anthony M. Ludovici, author of "Nietzsche: His Life and Works," "Nietzsche and Art," and "Who is to be Master of the World?" with an introduction by Dr. Levy and a preface by the translator.

V. "Thoughts Out of Season," II ("The Use and Abuse of History" and "Schopenhauer as Educator"), translated by Adrian Collins, M. A., with an introduction by the translator.

VI. "Human All-Too Human," I, translated by Helen Zimmern, with an introduction by J. M. Kennedy.

VII. "Human All-Too Human," II, translated by Paul V. Cohn, B. A., with an introduction by the translator.

VIII. "The Case of Wagner" (including "Nietzsche contra Wagner" and selected aphorisms), translated by A. M. Ludovici, and "We Philologists," translated by J. M. Kennedy, with prefaces by the translators.

IX. " The Dawn of Day," translated by J. M. Kennedy, with an introduction by the translator.

X. ¸" The Joyful Wisdom," translated by Thomas Common, author of " Nietzsche as Critic, Philosopher, Poet and Prophet " (including " Songs of Prince Free-as-a-Bird," translated by Paul V. Cohn and Maude D. Petre).

XI. " Thus Spake Zarathustra," translated by Thomas Common, with an introduction by Frau Förster-Nietzsche and explanatory notes by A. M. Ludovici.

XII. " Beyond Good and Evil," translated by Helen Zimmern, with an introduction by Thomas Common.

XIII. " The Genealogy of Morals," translated by Horace B. Samuel, M. A., and " People and Countries," translated by J. M. Kennedy, with an editor's note by Dr. Levy.

XIV. " The Will to Power," I, translated by A. M. Ludovici, with a preface by the translator.

XV. " The Will to Power," II, translated by A. M. Ludovici, with a preface by the translator.

XVI. " The Twilight of the Idols " (including " The Antichrist," " Eternal Recurrence " and explanatory notes to " Thus Spake Zarathustra "), translated by A. M. Ludovici, with a preface by the translator.

XVII. " Ecce Homo," translated by A. M. Ludovici; various songs, epigrams and dithyrambs, translated by Paul V. Cohn, Herman Scheffauer, Francis Bickley and Dr. G. T. Wrench; and the music of Nietzsche's " Hymn to Life " (words by Lou Salomé), with an introduction by Mr. Ludovici, a note to the poetry by Dr. Levy, and a reproduction of Karl Donndorf's bust of Nietzsche.

XVIII. Index.

The student who would read Nietzsche had better begin with one of the aphoristic books, preferably " The

Dawn of Day." From that let him proceed to " Beyond Good and Evil," " The Genealogy of Morals " and " The Antichrist." He will then be ready to understand " Thus Spake Zarathustra." Later on he may read " Ecce Homo " and dip into " The Joyful Wisdom," " Human All-Too Human " and " The Will to Power," as his fancy suggests. The Wagner pamphlets are of more importance to Wagnerians than to students of Nietzsche's ideas, and the early philological and critical essays have lost much of their interest by the passage of time. Nietzsche's poetry had better be avoided by all who cannot read it in the original German. The English translations are mostly very free and seldom satisfactory.

Of the larger Nietzschean commentaries in English the best is " Friedrich Nietzsche: His Life and Work," by M. A. Mügge. Appended to it is a bibliography of 850 titles — striking evidence of the attention that Nietzsche's ideas have gained in the world. Other books that will be found useful are " The Quintessence of Nietzsche," by J. M. Kennedy; " Nietzsche: His Life and Works," by Anthony M. Ludovici; " The Gospel of Superman," by Henri Lichtenberger, translated from the French by J. M. Kennedy; " The Philosophy of Nietzsche," by Georges Chatterton-Hill, and " The Philosophy of Friedrich Nietzsche," by Grace Neal Dolson, Ph. D., this last a pioneer work of permanent value. Lesser studies are to be found in " Friedrich Nietzsche," by A. R. Orage; " Nietzsche as Critic, Philosopher, Poet and Prophet," by Thomas Common; " Friedrich Nietzsche and His New Gospel," by Emily

S. Hamblen, and "Nietzsche," by Paul Elmer More. Interesting discussions of various Nietzschean ideas are in "The Revival of Aristocracy," by Dr. Oscar Levy; "Who is to be Master of the World?" by A. M. Ludovici; "On the Tracks of Life," by Leo G. Sera, translated from the Italian by J. M. Kennedy; "Nietzsche and Art," by A. M. Ludovici, and "The Mastery of Life," by G. T. Wrench. Selections from Nietzsche's writings are put together under subject headings in "Nietzsche in Outline and Aphorism," by A. R. Orage; "Nietzsche: His Maxims," by J. M. Kennedy, and "The Gist of Nietzsche," by H. L. Mencken. An elaborate and invaluable summary of all Nietzsche's writings, book by book, is to be found in "What Nietzsche Taught," by Willard H. Wright. This volume, the fruit of very diligent labor, is admirably concise and well-ordered.

The standard biography of Nietzsche is "*Das Leben Friedrich Nietzsches*," by Frau Förster-Nietzsche, a large work in three volumes. In 1911 Frau Förster-Nietzsche prepared a shorter version and this has since been done into English by A. M. Ludovici, and published in two volumes, under the title of "The Life of Nietzsche." Unluckily, so devoted a sister was not the best person to deal with certain episodes in the life of her brother and hero. The gaps she left and the ameliorations she attempted are filled and corrected in "The Life of Friedrich Nietzsche," by Daniel Halévy, translated from the French by J. M. Hone, with an extraordinarily brilliant introduction by T. M. Kettle, M. P.

Small but suggestive studies of Nietzsche and his

ideas are to be found in " Egoists," " Mezzotints in Modern Music," and " The Pathos of Distance," by James Huneker; " Degeneration," by Max Nordau; " Affirmations," by Havelock Ellis; " Aristocracy and Evolution," by W. H. Mallock; " Heretics " and " Orthodoxy," by G. K. Chesterton; " Lectures and Essays on Natural Theology," by William Wallace; " Heralds of Revolt," by William Barry, D. D.; " Essays in Sociology," by J. M. Robertson; " The Larger Aspects of Socialism," by William English Walling; " Three Modern Seers," by Mrs. Havelock Ellis; " Slaves to Duty," by J. Badcock; " In Peril of Change," by C. F. G. Masterman; " Man's Place in the Cosmos," by A. Seth Pringle Pattison; and " Gospels of Anarchy," by Vernon Lee (Violet Paget). George Bernard Shaw's variations upon Nietzschean themes are in " The Revolutionist's Handbook," appended to " Man and Superman." Of magazine articles dealing with the prophet of the superman there has been no end of late. Most of them are worthless, but any bearing the name of Grace Neal Dolson, Thomas Common, Thomas Stockham Baker or Maude D. Petre may be read with profit. One of the best discussions of Nietzsche I have ever encountered was contributed to the *Catholic World* during December, 1905, and January, February, March, May and June, 1906, by Miss Petre. It is to be regretted that these excellent papers, which sought to rescue Nietzsche from the misunderstandings of Christian critics, have not been re-printed in book-form.

INDEX